MW01289356

THE BRAZILIAN
JIU JITSU
GLOBETROTTER

The true story about a frantic, 140 day long,
around-the-world trip to train Brazilian Jiu Jitsu

Christian Graugart

To everyone who was part of this trip.

"So many people live within unhappy circumstances and yet will not take the initiative to change their situation because they are conditioned to a life of security, conformity and conservationism, all of which may appear to give one peace of mind, but in reality nothing is more damaging to the adventurous spirit within a man than a secure future. The very basic core of a man's living spirit is his passion for adventure. The joy of life comes from our encounters with new experiences, and hence there is no greater joy than to have an endless, changing horizon, for each day to have a new and different sun."

-Christopher McCandless

CONTENTS

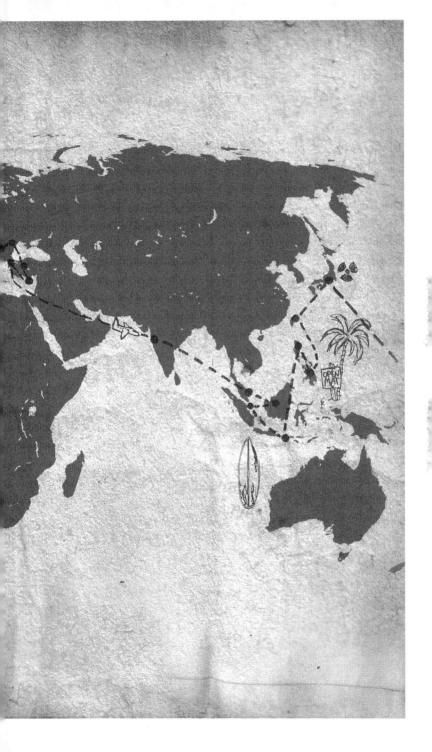

CHAPTER ONE

Introduction

My father used to stop time.

Or at least that's what I believed, when I was a kid.

He became a black belt in both Karate and Taekwondo all the way back in the 1970s, when martial arts was first introduced in Denmark. He always told me a lot of stories about training, and one of them stuck with me throughout my childhood. When he was at his peak, competing in full contact tournaments in his twenties, he could sometimes slow down time.

I remember he said that every second seemed to last for two or three seconds; how his opponents looked like they were moving in slow motion when they attacked, giving him time to block and counter.

I was training with him in the living room now and then and was still waiting for the day when I was old enough to start in a real gym. I often wondered if I would ever reach that same magical moment that he talked about, where time slowed down.

Fast forward twenty something years. I had been on the road for three months and traveled east, half way around the globe. It was my second match in middleweight brown belt division at the 2011 Brazilian Jiu Jitsu World Championships. I had won by advantages against a big guy from Mongolia in the first round, but now I was behind 5-0. My opponent was strong and in good shape. His bicep was pressing firmly down on my chin, pinning me in the side control position. The perfume in the detergent he had used to wash his gi caught my nose. I could feel every detail of the rough texture of the fabric on his sleeve that was tightly wrapped around my chin and neck.

I noticed the skin on my forearm that was framing on his neck to keep the pressure of his weight off me. I had a golden brown tan from surfing in Hawaii, sailing in the Caribbean, and swimming in Bali. The little hairs were completely white, bleached by the sun and salt water. I looked up at the ceiling and wondered what the architect had thought when designing it. It was constructed as a metal framework of thousands of triangles.

I was completely relaxed. The shouts from my coach Robson, my friend Søren, and my fellow traveler Jonathan on the sideline faded away. The buzz of the thousands of people in the audience was merely a deep humming noise. Like the sound of a deep bass, drowning under water. Everything had stopped. It felt like I was in a movie and someone just pressed pause.

"How did I get here?"

I was lying on some puzzle mats in California. Every single decision I had made in my whole life, had lead me to that place, that moment. The room was enormous and I was on the floor in the middle of it. Thousands of eyes were focused on me. I could have been anywhere in the world. I was losing, on the bottom and couldn't escape, but I was exactly where I wanted to be. I smiled to myself, almost laughed. Time stood still.

I didn't care about what would happen. He might win the match, but he could never beat me. I was living my dream, traveling the world unhindered, completely free. Nothing could put me down.

The play button was pressed again. My opponent took my back and I tapped out to a bow and arrow choke. I laughed and shook his hand as I stood back up. I was out of the competition. Everything was perfect.

Life couldn't be better.

CHAPTER TWO

A Flash of White Light

In 2008, I felt for the first time how it was to lose someone close to me.

Frank was around my age and one of my best friends from the gym. He had been training with us for several years and was quite a character. Whenever we went out, held gym parties or social events, he was always the center of attention. His extreme intelligence and unique sense of humor was hard not to be fascinated by.

For years, Frank and I took the same bus home from training. It was about half an hour, three times a week, where we spent the time discussing training and the meaning of life before we both jumped off at the same stop. He lived right around the corner from me, however, I never went to see his apartment. He studied philosophy and had a burning interest in deadlift, heavy metal music, and Jiu Jitsu. His observations on people and the world around him captivated me, and I sucked in as much of his ideas as I could. He even created a political party, based on Nihilism, as a provocation towards the established system's view on life. The party still exists today and had collected enough signatures to be included in the Danish national election in 2011.

However, Frank also had a darker side to him. Depression. In a way, he was two people. One who was the most athletic and outgoing, social person you could imagine, and one who would lock himself inside his own apartment for six months or more and disappear into a world of online poker.

He could be away from the gym for long periods at a time, but was that type of guy who always came back one day. He would be standing there in the doorway, laughing, a backpack slung over his shoulder, making some joke about how little I had progressed in deadlift while he had been gone.

"I was just one hand away from winning a luxury cruise in a poker tournament last night! Then I realized that it was probably time to turn off the computer and get back to training," he said with a grin as he put on his gi.

One day, he stopped coming back.

He had just gotten his blue belt after almost three years of on and off training. Of all the guys promoted, he got the undoubtedly biggest applause. Everyone knew how big an accomplishment it was for him. After that, I didn't see him for half a year or so, and was expecting him to drop by the gym any day for a roll. Then I got the message.

It was in the middle of a beautiful, warm summer. One Sunday, at five in the morning, he had somehow broken into a dormitory in the city center and kicked the door in to one of the rooms on the fourth floor. The girl who slept there described him as being in complete panic, crying and screaming about a war. She had managed to calm him down and tried to find out who he was so she could call someone. He had been sitting on her bed, crying, as she turned around for a moment to find her phone.

Then he jumped out the window.

Two police officers were on the spot just minutes later, and he died in the arms of one of them.

To this day, still no one knows why it happened. He was out with a few friends but left them at two a.m. without looking particularly drunk. He liked to drink—especially Fernet Branca that he always made us take shots of, only to enjoy the disgusted look on our faces—but he would never touch drugs. What he had done in those three hours between leaving his friends and breaking into the dormitory, no one will ever know. The autopsy showed nothing.

It hit me like a bullet train. I was devastated.

I put a note on the door of the gym saying that all classes were canceled, jumped on my bike, and drove towards home, tears running down my cheeks. Waiting at a red light by the edge of the city center, my arms felt like jelly. The light turned green, but I couldn't move. I had to drag my bike to a nearby bench. I sat there for an hour—at least—and stared at nothing, focusing on an empty space of air in front of me. The world just passed by. I wanted to call my girlfriend and tell her what had happened, but I couldn't say anything. I felt so empty inside, like someone had torn out everything and only left me as a shell of a human being.

A woman was running past me on the little trail going around the lake, where I was sitting. She asked if I was ok. I nodded slightly and dried my eyes. No words could come out of my mouth.

The usual thirty-minute bike ride home took me hours to complete that day. I drove by the place where he jumped. It was just twenty meters from the main tourist street in the city center. People from around the world were still walking there, like nothing had ever happened. I observed the spot from far away. I couldn't get myself to go any closer.

I could count the number of times I had cried as an adult on one hand, but when I heard the news about Frank, I couldn't stop for days. It just poured out of me.

Up until that point, I had felt invincible. It had never even crossed my mind that I or any of my friends were going to die one day. That life had an end.

Suddenly, I became very aware of just that. Frank only lived for 31 years. He often joked about how he was stuck in his little apartment in the suburbs and never won enough money in poker to break away from the life he seemed destined to live.

I felt horrible for him. The depression had been so obvious, and I blamed myself for not talking to him about it. I had thought about it many times, when I felt he was having a down period. Could I have saved him? Should I have acted?

When his family cleaned out his apartment, they found a note he had written more than ten years earlier. It's accuracy in describing the event was scary and made chills run down my spine when I read it. The demons of his depression had been permeating in his mind for a long time.

"It is an accident that I lie here
It happened so violently, so stupidly

If only I had known it was today – could be today
I admire the terminally ill, who wait and wait, and wait.
Wish I had time like them.
Have had time, time to live life, prepare for death.
Learned to love in the summer, and in the night.
Meaning, as I had created,
disappeared when I was forced to pick up death.
A flash of white light,
and my trained body was annihilated.
It was never essential,
so I can still enjoy life, as I see it.
I laugh at my worst nightmare, my destruction.

I do not care.

Frank Lindvig, 1998"

Like most people, I too have always had a dream of doing something great with my life. That dream, however, had never been concrete as to what it was I wanted to do or accomplish, but nevertheless, it had been there since childhood. I had to figure out a master plan to get the most out of my time.

If it wasn't for the kick in the ass I got when Frank died, reminding me that everybody has an expiration date and it could be any day around the corner, I might have left it at that. As some blurry fantasy in the back of my head that would get less and less realistic as my life got more and more settled along the fixed railroad tracks it was about to follow.

I was determined to do something. Frank never had the chance, so the least I could do for him would be to get something out of my own life before it was too late.

Things had to happen.

A year and a half later, I was still trying to figure out the master plan that would be my life.

My girlfriend had dragged her rootless soul on an eight-month long trip backpacking around Asia, Australia, and the islands of Polynesia. She was doing voluntary work in a school in Fiji, and I was going to visit her there for three weeks.

I was impressed by her courage to travel for so long on her own. The longest I had ever been on the road was five weeks, and that had seemed like it was enough for me. Since I met her, she always talked about going on long travels, and now she had finally made it happen. It inspired me, and as we walked around the city of Sydney—kicking brown leaves on the sidewalk of an old, stone bridge, dirty cameras hanging over our shoulders—I started to realize what I had been searching for in my mind. I could do something similar.

I had traveled a lot for Jiu Jitsu training, but always shorter trips. Seeing how my girlfriend effortlessly moved around a vast area, between countries, across oceans and cultures, made my own idea come to life. My obligations at home were already minimal, so the time was right.

I should go on a Jiu Jitsu trip. A really long one.

Lying in the bunk bed of the hostel in Sydney that night, I couldn't sleep. My thoughts were racing around my head. I was on a three-week long trip around Australia and Fiji, and all I could think about was another travel project. The mother of all travels in my life.

We were sat in the common room and had breakfast with a hundred other backpackers when I told her about it. She thought it was the best idea ever.

Back home in Denmark, the first thing I did was start writing down ideas for my trip. I had already traveled extensively for training in the United States and a bit in Asia. My list of dream Jiu Jitsu destinations was still long as I wanted to visit places like Japan, Hawaii, a few islands around the Caribbean and of course, Brazil. What would a life of Jiu Jitsu be, without a visit to Brazil?

As I looked at pins I had set on Google Earth on my computer, trying to decide where to go, the right thing to do became very obvious to me.

I could go all the way around the globe.

My gym had been running for seven years at that point, and it was doing fairly well. I wasn't making a lot of money but enough to put a little aside. More importantly, I had the freedom and flexibility to leave, with lots of skilled guys being able to take over my classes for me while I was gone.

I had put myself in a unique situation, and it had taken me a lot of work to get there. So many other people were trapped in lives with very little freedom to realize ideas like that, so it would almost be disrespectful to them if I didn't do it. I could not think of a single reason not to.

With a financially cautious lifestyle, I had already saved up a fair amount of money, and trying to set a vague budget for the project, I realized that I just needed to save up a bit more to be able to finance everything. There would be little money for paying for accommodation, so I would have to rely on the hospitality of people in the Jiu Jitsu community instead. I had been sleeping on Jiu Jitsu people's couches on all my prior travels anyways so it was the obvious solution to do that again, just on a grander scale. My already strong network within the sport would have to be expanded to allow me to go even more places. A blog would be my tool for that.

Two of my Canadian friends, a couple I had visited and trained with back in 2005, had sold everything and started living on a boat instead. I admired their adventurous spirit and with my own idea taking shape, their home on the water was an obvious destination for me on my route.

I wrote them an email and pitched the idea. They were on their way down towards the Caribbean from Canada and with my rough idea of my schedule, it looked like I could just catch them somewhere around the Virgin Islands. With nothing else to do on the boat that day, waiting for a storm to pass, we spent several hours chatting about ideas for names for my blog. With English being my second language, my vocabulary is a bit limited, and Mike helped me coin the right one.

BJJ Globetrotter.

It sounded good when I said it out loud.

Having worked as a programmer, I had built so many websites in my life that they became the foundation of every project and idea I started. In my world, if there was a website for something, then it was real. Everything before that only existed in my mind. It had to be written down and put online.

I spent most of the night setting up the blog. The sooner I would have it ready, the sooner other people could hear about the project and invite me to come visit them on the way.

"Will teach BJJ for food and shelter," I wrote on a photo of a cardboard, put it in the header, and imagined myself standing at the side of a road somewhere in the middle of nowhere, holding a sign like that.

I started to realize that if everything fell into place financially and my plan succeeded, I would be able to travel anywhere I wanted. Literally, *anywhere* in the world. As long as someone there would invite me to come stay with them, there were no limits to my list of destinations.

Initially, I had thought of a classic round-the-world itinerary with cities like London, Bangkok, Tokyo, Los Angeles, New York, and Rio de Janeiro. I already knew people there, could stay a month each place, and it would be the fastest and easiest way around the globe, both travel and training wise.

That idea quickly sounded trivial as I realized the actual potential of my project. There were basically no limits for it. I could go where ever I wanted, so nothing else made sense than to put everything into making the craziest itinerary I possibly could.

I had plenty of time to plan the most extreme, amazing Jiu Jitsu trip I could come up with, to figure out just how far the sport could actually take me.

My blog had started to take shape and I was sending out the link to every Jiu Jitsu forum I could find. I got lots of emails back, mostly from the United States. I knew that place would be easy traveling, but I was more interested in finding training in some seriously faraway places. A few companies heard about my idea as well and offered to sponsor my clothes and training gear for the trip. One guy even suggested that I should write a book about my experiences, but I quickly turned down that idea as being too crazy.

While my girlfriend was still traveling around Asia and Australia on her own, I was sitting every night in front of my computer, setting little pins on the map. I was looking for Jiu Jitsu in places I had never heard about before.

Could I travel around Africa by foot? What is the most remote island in the world where someone is training? Could I wrestle with the Mongolians in the mountains, or maybe train Sambo somewhere deep inside Russia? Was anyone training in the Arctic?

I couldn't allow myself to do it the easy way. It would be the trip of my life and maybe even the only one I could ever do, so I'd better get the best out of it.

My mind was consumed with the thoughts about planning my project. As the months passed, I added more and more potential destinations to my list. It started to look ambitious. My initial idea of staying a month each place quickly went out the window. I would have to cut that down to just a few days if I wanted to make it to all the places I had written down.

Saving up money for the trip became almost a sport for me. When I got home from visiting my girlfriend in Fiji, the only thing on my mind was to prepare for my own adventure. I wasn't earning a lot of money from the gym, so I knew it would take a serious effort to save up enough to make my travel dream come true.

When I shopped for food, I tried always to find cheaper alternatives to what I was looking to buy. If I saved five kroner on apples, I would go right home and transfer those to my savings account. If someone asked me if I wanted to go out on the weekend and I decided not to go, I took the money I would have expected to use that night and put it aside.

In Denmark, we have coins equivalent to around four dollars, and everything above that is bills. When I had to pay for something, I always paid in cash and only in bills. All the coins I got back in change, I put in my little pink piggy bank so I made sure I wouldn't use them on anything else.

I knew that my heating and electricity bills would be a big expense, coming in January right before I was taking off. Cutting those down to a minimum became one of my dearest projects. Living on the top floor of my apartment building with a badly insulated roof, keeping the place warm in the cold, Scandinavian winter was a bit difficult. I made sure to wear extra clothes indoors during the day, and at night, I turned off the heaters and slept with two or three duvets to keep me warm. I got my hands on an electricity meter and measured every device in the house. I calculated that buying a new energy efficient fridge I had seen on sale would save me money in the long run and all my light bulbs were changed into low energy ones. Every time I left the apartment, I turned everything off, and for a full year leading up to the trip, no device was ever in standby mode when not used.

Needless to say, when the electricity and heating bill came, it was an all time record low. The money I had saved there was more than enough to buy two or three extra plane tickets.

All the small amounts I had transferred to my savings account over the year had added up, and together with the coins in the piggy bank, I had managed to collect a fair bit.

The sport of saving and making every little coin count was extremely satisfying to me. Knowing that each krone I was saving while being home would be worth tenfold while on the road kept me going. I didn't need to spend that money at home, but I needed it for the trip.

The next challenge would be to make the money I had last as long as possible.

I was wondering a lot about what an ambitious trip like this would look like in reality. From sharing the link to the blog around the Internet, I already had more than a hundred invitations in my inbox, even before I'd left home. Which ones should I pick? What should the route be? Would I have to plan the whole itinerary from home, or should I figure it out along the way?

My mind was set on Brazil and going around the world. I would have to either begin or end my trip there. With the tough training I expected to run into in the birthplace of Jiu Jitsu, I concluded that it would probably be best to pick up some skills first before I got there. The direction was set. I would be heading east.

In between getting vaccinations, finding the right backpack, planning what to bring and, more importantly, what not to bring, I tried to settle my mind on a route. I would buy as many tickets from home as possible. When they ran out, I would hopefully have upped my travel skills to a level where I could easily make out the rest of the schedule on the road.

I emailed back and forth with people, and it felt like every time I had settled on something, I got a new, interesting invitation from another place that screwed up my route and I had to re-think everything. I was juggling everything in my head, trying to solve the great puzzle. At one point, I almost gave up and thought I'd just buy the first ticket and wing it from there. On the other hand, there was a lot of money to save by buying tickets ahead of time, and saving money was going to be a very important thing for me if I was not to run out of it halfway around the globe.

As I was only a few months away from my set departure date, I had the first part of a very, very ambitious schedule planned out.

Starting in Paris, I was going down to Montpelier in Southern France, then on to Romania, a few places in Moldova, Turkey, Northern Cyprus, back to Turkey, on to India, then Borneo, Singapore, Bali, and the Philippines. I ditched the Sambo training in Russia after some guy told me that there was a pretty much one hundred percent chance of getting dumped on my neck and injured if I wasn't very comfortable with falling techniques. I definitely wasn't, and with an east-bound trip, I couldn't afford a high risk of injury so early on the route.

After the Philippines, I would have to figure out the rest along the way, counting on the right connections to be made through the blog and people I would meet. With all the destinations in the first part of my journey already set, I was going to give myself a serious kick in the ass, get out the door and up into travel gear.

The music filled the room of our newly built CrossFit gym. We were near the end of the road for my little competition team that season. The European Championships. It was a motley crowd of guys—made up of talent from Denmark, Iceland,

Belarus and Estonia—that had all signed up for the project six months earlier.

We had been training together almost daily since going to competitions in Sweden, The Netherlands, England, and of course, Denmark. It was all part of the preparations for the big one in Portugal, where our goal was to get the first medal for our small gym.

The song "Not an addict" by K's Choice, was playing on the stereo. I definitely was. My drug was training and had been so since I was a kid. An endless amount of hours spent in gyms since my childhood had shaped me into the person I had become. Training had been a lifelong friend. A sanctuary, a temple, where I could relieve myself from the thoughts and stress that otherwise would build up in my head.

My legs and lower back hurt. It was our bi-weekly workout for the team. Every Monday and Wednesday evening, we would push each other through a grinding workout, conditioning our bodies for the challenges on the mats of Europe that we faced together. It was our fourth month of preparations and we were almost at the end.

I was worried about the herniated disc in my back that I had gotten five years earlier but worked through the pain. Kasper's face was twisting in exhaustion as he was pulling a thick rope across the floor with a sixty kilogram kettlebell tied to the end. I was ignoring my own logical sense telling me that I couldn't possibly do more box jumps. The projector in the ceiling behind me cast my shadow onto the wrestling video that was playing on the wall in front of me. My shadow wasn't sweating, breathing heavily, or grinding it's face. It was just getting the job done—no complaints. The sweat was pouring down my face. My mind empty. I was completely in the zone.

Martin and Erik were rhythmically beating the tractor tire with heavy sledgehammers, while Jan was sprinting up and down the stairs right outside the door. Everyone around me was pushed to their individual limit, but we were in it together. We were going to get that medal at the Europeans.

I wasn't particularly nervous when I stepped on the mat in the Lisbon sports hall. Three of our guys had already taken medals, winning one in each color for the team. My mission as a coach was accomplished, and I felt no pressure on my own shoulders to win. I was still an inexperienced competitor in the brown belt division and didn't have any big expectations for my own performance. In fact, there was nothing inside of me that believed I could reach the podium.

The opponent was from Spain, and was considerably bigger than me. He looked intimidating. I was sure he had trained and competed way more and way harder than myself. My team mates were biting their nails as I stepped onto the mat. My heart was beating a bit faster than usual, but as we clapped hands, I was calm and pulled guard right away. He had a heavy pressure game, constantly working to pass my guard. It almost succeeded a few times until I caught him with a bicep sweep and got on top.

My training partner Kári shouted to me that I was ahead by two points. Throughout the years, I had developed an ear for picking out his voice in even the loudest of crowds.

Then I made the mistake. As I stood up to open my opponent's closed guard, he jumped off and immediately took me down with a double leg. Constantly fighting his grips from there, my energy started to run out and eventually, he passed my guard, beating me 5-2.

It was my debut on the big competition scene, and I was pleased with my performance. There were lots of things to improve, and I would have plenty of different people to do that with on the road.

Everyone else on the team performed fantastically, and I was really proud of the guys. I had brought blue belts with embroidered names for all the white belts and gave it to them in the hostel that same evening. They had worked extremely hard for them and deserved it more than anyone. Even more importantly, they had become really good friends of mine and I had witnessed firsthand how Jiu Jitsu had affected their lives in a positive direction over the period since they first stepped into the gym.

I was going to miss them all, and I was shit nervous that they wouldn't be there when I got back.

In the time leading up to my departure, I fell into a very focused rhythm. I worked hard in the gym every day, preparing both my physique and Jiu Jitsu for the challenges I would meet around the world.

The timer beeped as the very last round ended on another long Monday night of training. I had just finished off five minutes against one of our seasoned blue belts, who was always a big challenge for me to handle. Training was over, I was soaked in sweat and felt great.

I had been standing up in his guard as we finished. I sat down in a completely normal position when my leg rotated a little bit, and then it hit me.

It felt like someone had stabbed my knee with a knife. A sharp pain ran through my body, and I screamed. Someone came running with an ice-pack that I put on immediately. The pain was horrible, and it felt like something was seriously wrong.

It was just two weeks before I was leaving, and a serious knee injury was the last thing I needed. I was as worried as I had ever been before and right away, imagined that I would have to travel all the way around the world without being able to train Jiu Jitsu.

I immediately sent a text message to my physiotherapist. The next morning, I was lying on the bench, receiving the verdict. A small tear in the meniscus.

There was no time for surgery, so all I could do was to rest as much as possible before the trip, and then hope for the best.

She assessed that I could train lightly, but if I felt any pain, I would need to take a few days to a week off to make sure it wouldn't get any worse. Needless to say, I was devastated. I hated the thought of having to excuse and explain myself in every sparring round I was going to do on the trip. I wanted to go out there and be able to train at whatever level and intensity people wanted to go with me.

My hard preparations for rolling around the world had taken a hit, but at that point, I was more worried about being able to train at all.

Two weeks without training meant two weeks without the opportunity to release the stress building up in my head. Everyone was constantly asking about the trip, and my mind was overloaded with thoughts and worries about how it would go. I got to a point where I just got sick and tired of thinking about it. I wasn't really looking forward to leaving. It was like I had already been through it all in my head a million times during the last year of preparations.

It was frustrating to be on hold with my life, and I just wanted to board that first plane and get going.

It was early in the morning when I got up, the day of my departure. The night before, I had spread out all the stuff I had planned to put in my backpack on the floor. I was afraid that I had missed out on something, and went through the packing list again and again.

Three pairs of shorts. One pair of pants. Five pairs of socks. Seven pairs of underwear. Two gis. One belt. Three t-shirts. One sweatshirt. Small camera. Big camera. Cables. Chargers. iPad. Toiletry bag. Money. Passport.

It was all there. The shiny, new backpack was strapped up and ready to go on its maiden voyage. It was going to see the world.

My girlfriend followed me to the airport with mixed emotions. On the metro train, she kissed my chin, looked me in the eyes, and smiled with a small tear in her eye.

At the security check, she wasn't allowed to go any further. One last goodbye, and I was on my own with a heavy lump in my throat.

I had second thoughts about the whole thing. Was it the right thing to do?

There was no turning back. Everything was planned and I had to go through with it.

It was only going to be a short flight down to Paris. The seat in front of me was taken out to make room for the emergency exit door, so I had lots of space for my long legs.

I bragged a little about my bonus seat to the guy sitting next to me with his standard leg space, also known as no leg space.

He was wearing a pinstripe suit and looked very corporate. Judging from his appearance, I guessed he was probably going on a one day business trip to Paris.

The plane accelerated on the runway, and the wheels released their heavy grip on the asphalt beneath us. The lump in my throat was back. I was not going to be back in my home country for a long time.

Looking out the window down on the city of Copenhagen, it looked so small and flat. Nothing but a small collection of buildings, arbitrarily placed by the water, on what could essentially be any flat island. There was still a bit of snow left on the ground from the long, cold winter. I hadn't been to the beach since summer. The water was frozen, and the sand looked white and hard.

When I had been down in that city, it felt like it was my entire world. Friends, family, past, and future were all compressed into that small place, together with enough opportunities to live a full life from birth to death. From above, it seemed so insignificant.

Why would I want to spend my entire life on that little piece of land? I could have been born anywhere in the world, so why should this exact place be the right and only life for me to live? How many other lives exist out there in the world that I could live, either by chance or conscious decision?

As the plane ascended, we started to hit the thick, winter clouds. The view of my home city—my world—symbolically faded to white, and within seconds, it had completely disappeared before my eyes. Shortly after, we appeared above the clouds. The sky was blue, and the sun hit me in the eyes as the plane made a sharp turn to the right. It was a new beginning. I pulled my hood over my head to try to block the sunlight while still looking out at the clouds that looked like an endless field, covered in snow. I gave up and just allowed the sun to hit my face. It felt warm.

I was sad to leave everything and everyone behind but still cracked a little smile. I was realizing a life dream after almost a year of preparation.

The stewardess came by and asked if I wanted to buy some food. I politely declined with a smile.

I wanted to tell her I was backpacking around the world on a budget and couldn't afford her expensive food, but I kept that to myself. The corporate guy next to me was buying breakfast with his golden credit card. I had brought a few sandwiches from home that I had made late at night in our little kitchen. He was drinking coffee and juice. The smell of the coffee was nice. I had brought a bottle from home and filled it with water in the airport bathroom. It tasted a bit like the apple juice that had once been in it.

He was falling asleep. I wished I could do the same, but there was too much going on in my head. I pulled down the window cover so he didn't get the sun in his face, plugged in my earphones, and pulled the hood over my head.

I was on my way.

CHAPTER THREE

Grass and Bonfire Smoke

When my father was a child, jobs were difficult to find, so my grandfather had taken a boat to Australia, hoping to start a new life for him and his family. Unfortunately, things went wrong along the way and the rest of them never made it there, splitting up the little family and eventually completely losing contact.

It was a huge loss for the three children. Especially my father, who lost not only his own father but also his role model.

It would take many years before the children saw their father again. His sister took the long trip down under and, after much searching, found him in the Danish community in Melbourne. He had traveled around all of Australia, worked as a crocodile hunter in Queensland, gotten married again, and opened up a successful carpet business. The last name Graugart was difficult for the Australians to pronounce, so he had changed it to Jensen.

Eventually, he made it back to Denmark for a surprise visit seventeen years after he had left. Staying with family in the other end of the country to rest for a week before heading to Copenhagen, my father heard through an uncle that he was there. Without a second of waiting, he jumped on his motorbike and drove it directly across the country.

He gave his father a surprise call when he got to the little town. His voice was trembling and his Danish accent was long gone, words now shaped strangely by the land far, far away. He said he was coming to Copenhagen the following week and asked if my father was there, so he could maybe come and see him. If he was welcome. He answered that he was not in Copenhagen, but stood in a phone booth just a hundred meters from him.

There was a pause and probably a skipped heart beat or two.

Years later, newly in love, my parents were on their way to visit the family down under. My mother was a young secretary and my father an electrician. His shirt was often half unbuttoned, and he was wearing a gold necklace with a cross around his neck. He wasn't religious, but I am sure he thought it looked ace.

Australia must have seemed unbelievably far away, back then. Today, going there can be arranged on the couch in five minutes with a credit card and an Internet connection. My parents had to order their ticket by phone through a travel agency on the other side of the globe. It was handwritten, sent by mail, and had seven stopovers on it. I still have it.

My father had brought his gi and black belt, looking for a few places to train. I can only imagine what an adventure it must have been, to sit there in a strange land, flicking through a phone book to look for a gym, then finding the courage to pick up the phone, call them, and try to speak with them in a foreign language of which he had little practice.

April 4th in 1982, I made my grand entrance in the world. My parents moved out of their apartment and spent all their savings on buying a small house in a beautiful little suburb of Copenhagen. It was made of red bricks and had a garden, green hedge, and a playhouse. A red Opel with a back seat I would eventually fill up with Donald Duck magazines and breadcrumbs was parked in the drive way. The summer was warm that year, and the young, new family had high hopes for the future.

Three years after me, my little brother came by. A gentleman challenger—along with myself—in the official competition of "who had the whitest hair in the world."

My life was pretty much perfect when I grew up. I rode my bicycle alone to school every morning, we made tree houses in the forest, bonfires in the garden behind the house, and played football on the many empty streets of the sleepy little town. I always seemed to smell of grass and bonfire smoke.

My class mates were nice, my teachers were inspirational, and I did well in the school that was right across the street from the exciting forest with so much to do.

I couldn't wish for anything more.

The mythical land of Australia, and my family there, played a big role in my early life. Every year at Christmas, I received a big brown cardboard box from down under filled with exciting things from the tropical life I could have lived and heard so much about. Candy, toys, teddy bears, photos, and a blue eraser shaped like Australia with the flag printed on it. I had it in my pencil case for years in school, always saving it and using the other ones I had instead.

Our house was small but filled with exciting things to do for a young boy. There were trees I could climb and secret holes in the hedge to our neighbors' mystical gardens.

Apart from a few appliances and a scary storage room with just a meter to the ceiling where you could only climb on your hands and knees, my father had pretty much taken over the basement of my childhood home. He was an artist, handyman, soldier, inventor, photographer, and a black belt in both Karate and Taekwondo. In my eyes, there was nothing he couldn't do.

In one of the rooms, a heavy bag was hanging from the ceiling and an old, rusty barbell with a few metal plates lay on the floor. Even though I was told it was dangerous for my back to use it, I often tried to lift it anyway whenever I managed to sneak down in the basement alone.

There was a darkroom for developing photographs. The walls were black. Big, exciting machines I wasn't allowed to play with stood in one side of the room. Large, plastic trays were lined up on a long table along the wall, and above my head were lines full of wooden clamps and wet photos, hanging to dry. There was a very distinct smell in that room. The chemicals from the plastic trays couldn't possibly have been healthy for me to breathe in the many hours I spent down there, but it was a fair trade off for a lifelong passion for photography.

I was obsessed with computers. We had our first one—an IBM PC with two 5 1/4" disk drives—when I was around six years old. I tried to learn everything I could about it. It was quite necessary in order to make any use from it, since it was complicated and not very user friendly. Programming became a serious interest for me, and I threw myself into exciting projects such as encryption algorithms and a network chat system for the school's computers. I wrote several issues of a computer magazine at the age of ten, when we got our first printer—sold a stunning fifteen or so of them in school and at my mother's workplace—and made my first website before I had ever been online on that new, exciting thing called the Internet. In fifth grade, I got a job teaching an IT class every Thursday—they paid me a 7UP—but that was only until I hacked their administrator accounts and got banned from using the computers for the rest of the year.

Apart from computers, martial arts was constantly on my mind as a kid. There was nothing I wanted to do more in life. My father had started training in the beginning of the 1970s, when Bruce Lee's movies had created long lines outside of the first Karate school in town. Later on, "Korean Karate" became the new craze, and the rivalry was on between the styles.

He always told me many stories about his training. The competitions back then were full contact, and many times did he have to fight his own friend and roommate. They met in the finals of the Danish championships and beat each other so hard they had to carry one another up the stairs to their shared apartment when they got home.

I must have asked him every single evening, when he came home sweaty from practice when I could begin myself.

At seven, I was finally allowed to start training Taekwondo. My father was teaching in the gym, so I had already been there several times before. I also knew many of the techniques from home, so standing in the back of the class on the hard, wooden floor with my new, little white gi and stiff belt tied for the first time, everything felt very familiar. Already from day one, I was determined to learn this thing. To become really good at it.

Every Monday and Wednesday evening, I walked down the cold, stone-covered stairs to the room in the school's basement. The sound of the big, wooden door opening echoed down the empty hallway. It was scary in the dark when the school was closed, so I always hurried inside.

The gym had a certain smell. A scent of carpet and the wood from the desk and little office that one of the members once had built. On a couple of sofas in the corner, we looked at pictures of Bruce Lee in black and white magazines with beige pages and corners neatly folded at least a decade earlier.

We were more than forty kids in the start-up class that season. After a few months, only half of them were left. There was no way I was going to quit. As the years went by and we progressed in the ranks, it was only me and a handful of the others that were still training. I took pride in not stopping, even though it was boring sometimes.

It was easy for me to learn the techniques and pass the belt tests. On the wall outside of the changing room hung a framed article from a national newspaper about one of the kids from the gym that had gotten his black belt at the age of ten. The youngest in the country. I didn't think about that it was easy for the kids to progress in the belts back then. The amount of dedication and hard work I put into each belt made it worth it to me. White. Yellow. Orange. Green. Blue. Red. The diplomas from each of them—the proof of my persistence—were hanging on the wall over my bed at home.

CHAPTER FOUR

France

The metro smelled strange. Like a mix of sewer and candy. I'd always had an interest in maps and finding my way around unknown places, so I challenged myself to find Jerome without using my phone's GPS.

Sortie. The sign over the stairs I saw as I walked up to exit the metro looked old.

Up on the little Parisian street—light poles with curly details, a smell of baguettes, and light chatter in a beautiful language—a feeling of excitement ran through my body. This was the first time of many where I was going to meet up with a complete stranger that would shape the story of my trip. A fellow Jiu Jitsu enthusiast I had gotten in touch with through my blog, who had invited me to come stay with him.

"Wait for me at McDonalds on the corner," the text message on my phone from an unknown French number read.

It took me a while to spot the golden arches.

Jerome put his hand forward towards me. The 'h' sound of his "how are you" had gotten lost somewhere in the accent. He was tall, had curly hair, and was wearing a leather jacket and a big smile. His English was heavily accented, but it was easy enough to understand with a bit of concentration once I got used to it.

A week earlier, I had no contacts in Paris. After a short blog post about going there on a stopover before heading to Southern France, I had five. I was surprised at how easy it had been to get in touch with people. Suddenly, it seemed like I should have stayed there for more than one day. It was too late for that now.

Jerome walked me to his apartment and handed me the keys. He had to go to work, so I would be on my own for the day. I spent some time just sitting on the mattress on the floor. I was really tired, since I had only gotten four hours sleep before I had to get up and go to the airport. Too many thoughts in my head kept me awake. Now I had arrived at the first destination of my ambitious adventure, sitting in a stranger's apartment in the middle of Paris. A stranger that I had never met in my life before who had just handed me the keys to his home. I was trying wrap my head around the thought that I would not be back in my own bed for the next four and a half months. It was difficult to understand.

A text ticked in on my phone. It was from Arthur, a guy who had contacted me after I posted about my trip online. He had invited me to his gym that evening and said he had the day off in case I wanted to meet up and walk around the city a bit.

I checked my email on Jerome's computer before I headed out. Twenty-five unread mails in my inbox with invitations to come and train.

Arthur's English was good. He was studying the language and wanted to become a teacher. He had a peculiar mix of accents. Bits of British English, American, Irish, and French popped up in his sentences every now and then. He was wearing a hat, glasses, and a shirt that was too optimistic for the weather that day. I was wearing my big winter jacket and a scarf, taking no chances on the flu that had been haunting me for the past two weeks. That guy I fought in the Europeans—his nose looked so red—I was sure he had infected me. 5-2 and the flu.

Arthur was a white belt who had been training for a year and a half. It sounded like Jiu Jitsu was already an important part of his life. He was training in a small gym nearby and suggested we could go there that evening. I felt more inclined to train with Jerome, since he was so kind to host me for the night, so I would have to make a decision. Fortunately, Jerome's gym had no Jiu Jitsu class that evening, so we decided to all go together to Arthur's place and I could postpone the first issue of having to choose one gym over another on the trip.

Jerome and I took the late evening metro for about half an hour to the gym. Arthur hadn't arrived yet, so we waited in a hallway of a public swimming pool. There was a karate class going on. Middle aged men doing katas and a teacher, who was instructing a girl wearing a brand new, stiff black belt to thrust her hip forward as she delivered a punch. Ten meters away from us, a group of guys around my age started to gather. Every few minutes, another one would arrive and shake hands with everyone. They were very loud. Laughing, shouting, and fighting a bit for fun. I was pretty nervous at this point since it would be my first training in three weeks, not to mention my first training on the whole trip. I didn't understand anything of what they said and worried about my knee. I was going into a gym full of strangers and had no idea what kind of guys they were. Ripping up the injury at this point would be a catastrophe for the rest of my trip.

The instructor introduced himself to us. His name was Olivier. He seemed friendly and welcomed us to his gym. He didn't speak much English; every sentence was just a few words.

As I tried to talk a bit with him in the changing room, I could feel the curiosity of the guys on the team, changing into their gis. There were many eyes on me, sizing me up and, occasionally, I could catch a few recognizable words in their conversations such as *Danois* and *centuire marron*. There was no doubt as to who they were talking about. I crossed my fingers, hoping that they would be nice to me and not just a bunch of hungry, competitive purple belts who would try to rip my limbs apart.

We were running around the small room, which was ten by ten meters, at best. Matted walls all around the room and nothing else. Most guys didn't wear their belts, and some were only in shorts and t-shirt. In the corner, three guys had started doing MMA sparring on their own.

The warm up included around one hundred pushups. It made no sense to me to do so many before technique training and sparring, but it was not my class and I would respect the instructor, no matter what he asked us to do. I was the guest after all. We did some light isolation sparring from side control and quarters. I went with Jerome, and after a few minutes, it was time to switch partners. I raised my hand, waiting for someone to pick me. A guy in a white gi, white belt, and a white rash guard approached me and I shook his hand, introducing myself.

He looked at me a little strangely. I figured he didn't speak any English.

I asked him about his name, and he got an even stranger look on his face, like he was really puzzled.

"I'm Arthur?", he replied in near perfect English, wearing an awkward smile.

Arthur looked different in a gi without his hat and glasses. I was embarrassed that I didn't recognize him at all after having walked around town with him all day. I was already confused with all the new faces, and the trip had just begun. Remembering thousands of people around the world was going to be somewhere near impossible.

The accent and voice of the guy asking me to man-dance was easy to recognize. I turned around, and Jerome was smiling, putting his hand on my shoulder.

I sat down to start with him in my guard. He was a big guy, bigger than he looked when he was hidden away in his leather jacket and scarf.

It was my very first sparring round on the trip. I was nervous. I had made a plan of how I wanted to train while being on the road, but I was not sure if it would work. I knew that there would be a pretty high risk of injury if I went out and rolled hard with everyone I met in the gyms around the world. I had planned to visit more than fifty gyms and an injury could potentially ruin the entire trip, so I had to be smart. I needed to pace myself in every single roll, never turning up intensity fully and always trying to relax and rely on technique.

Traveling is hard on the body. Flying, getting up early to go to airports, changing sleep rhythms, time zones, stress, change of food and climate. All factors that wear you out. Training hard with a body that is already under pressure is a potential recipe for disaster. Overtraining could put me out of the game completely for a period.

Also, some people would definitely see me as a challenge stepping on to their mat. Their home. Going hard with them would only confirm the idea in their head that they were defending their pride or testing themselves against "the challenger." The plan was to go light and hopefully break through their hard shell to make them relax and have fun with the training instead. If they didn't get the message, I would just let them submit me a few dozen times and then move on to the next training partner. I was not going out there to compare myself against anyone.

We rolled for a few minutes and he went for the same deep half guard position several times. I defended by going for a kimura on his arm, but he was too strong and I couldn't break his grip. The third or fourth time it happened, his hands slipped, right at the moment, when I tried to break his grip, so accidentally, I pulled his arm behind his back too fast.

He screamed as his shoulder was overextended.

I felt terrible. That was exactly what I hoped would not happen to myself, and now I was the bully. Fortunately, he could continue training.

My knee felt fine during sparring and I was really relieved that I had completed the first training with no problems. Everyone was nice to me and there was no one trying to kill me. It had all been inside my head.

Olivier ended the class like he had started it. Everyone up on a line doing fifty or so pushups, while he was counting. I never do pushups, and I had no energy left in my arms after sparring, so it was really hard for me to follow along. I had to take many breaks and probably only did a total of ten or fifteen.

When I got back to the apartment, it was already half past eleven. I was exhausted from my first day on the road, but I had to wash my gi before I went to sleep. I hung it in the bathroom, hoping it would dry up during the night before I was taking the train down south to Montpellier in the morning.

I was just about to go to sleep but still standing by the window, looking out at the old city, wrapped in a rainy, misty night. The sky was dark, but over some of the rooftops to my left, there was a faint glow from the light coming from the Eiffel tower. I struggled to keep my eyes open, but I was leaving already the next morning so I decided I had to go see it.

It was raining lightly as I walked through the city with my camera in one hand and tripod in the other. No people were on the streets, only an occasional sound coming from the over ground train in the distance. The neon lights from the *brasseries* reflected onto the wet streets.

As I turned a corner, a huge golden light appeared in front of me. I had to stop for a second. When I was in Paris ten years earlier, I had seen the Eiffel tower in daylight, together with a few thousand other tourists with cameras and maps in their hands. Now, I was there all alone on a Monday night in the rain.

I stood there for a few minutes in silence, looking at the tower, listening to the sound of the city sleeping. The usual buzz from the traffic was gone. All I could hear was the rain hitting my jacket and the little pools of water accumulating in the mud around my feet.

I was looking for the perfect angle to capture the atmosphere of the place with my camera. I squatted, resting the camera in the palm of my hand, put my eye to the viewfinder, and for the millionth time, observed the world through that complex arrangement of glass and mirrors that felt like an old friend. Photography had been a part of my life as long as I could remember.

It was clear how I wanted the end result to look. Every detail of colors, composition, and light was right there, inside my head. Now, the art lay in extending my mind out through a mechanical device and capturing that exact expression of my imagination.

My eyes quickly scanned through the little red numbers around the image, knowing by intuition that aperture, ISO, focal length, and exposure time were all set just right.

I adjusted the zoom and moved my body a little to the left and up, positioning the lines and objects of the image. To be able to describe how I know when a photo is composed right would be impossible. It would be like asking a judo player to describe how he identifies the split second where the opponent is in the exact right position to be thrown through the air. There are too many details for the conscious brain to observe and register, so pure intuition takes over.

Everything was set. My entire consciousness was focused on what went on inside the world of the little viewfinder. Full concentration.

Breath in. Wait. The raindrops around me seemed to disappear.

Click-click.

The familiar sound of the mirror flipping, freezing an unimaginably short period of time in the universe to exist forever, had followed me through my entire life. It was comforting.

Since the invention of the camera, a large part of my father's side of the family had been photographers. Some of the earliest memories I have are images of camera lenses in front of my face. For a time, long before digital photography when people started shooting thousands of photos for every week-long vacation, I must have been a highly photographed child.

The first camera I remember owning was a beautiful Nikon SLR with a small 35-75mm lens. It had belonged to my mythical grandfather in Australia, and I had admired it for years and years. It must have been around my eighth or ninth birthday when my father passed it on to me, neatly packed in a cardboard shoe box with a few pages from a newspaper wrapped around it. It was magical. The sounds of the mechanical parts working inside the camera when I pressed the buttons kept me awake in bed at night for hours. The feeling of the soft plastic and the cold metal on my fingers fascinated my young mind. My grandfather had actually used it at one point, and now it was mine to keep forever.

The modern, digital camera I had brought to capture that photo of the Eiffel Tower still somehow reminded me of my grandfather's. A quiet rush of excitement ran through my body. The first day of my trip had already been full of experiences, friends, and training. I had one hundred and thirty nine to go, and I couldn't wait to see what the rest of the world would be like.

I'd been looking forward to the train ride down to Montpellier. I wanted to get into the traveling rhythm and not hurry anything. Three and a half hours through the landscape of France would definitely help with that.

As a kid, I followed the Tour de France every summer and I loved the landscape and small towns the cyclists pass through. My little brother and I got ourselves some bicycles and we saved up to buy those cycling shirts they use in the tour. I remember we wanted our bikes to look a little cooler, so we spray painted them yellow out on the parking lot. When we had raced each other in circles around our building for hours, our mother came home and saw that the concrete on most of the parking lot was bright yellow. We hadn't noticed, so we couldn't understand why she would be mad at us for that.

When I was sitting in the train, I could feel an itching pain in my knee. It was almost like I could feel the bleeding inflammation inside. I tried to find a comfortable position to sit in, but it was difficult. My walk to the Eiffel Tower had cost me at least a few hours of sleep and I was paying for that. My eyes were fighting to stay open. I didn't want to fall asleep and wake up in some city far away from Montpellier.

Apparently, the beautiful Mediterranean city has a dark side. Thomas had been a victim of that, just four days after he moved there from Denmark. He had walked on the street on the way to his first training session, when—out of the blue—he had been hit in the head from behind. He fell over and three guys started kicking him, for what must have seemed like forever. The violence in the area was scary. These people were not attacking their victims just to get their money. They were trying to seriously harm and injure them in the process. Thomas was kicked in the face, on the body and in the groin, again and again, before they took everything in his pockets and ran away.

When he got to his feet, he managed to stumble the last bit to the gym. He entered the door and one can only imagine the look on people's faces there when they saw him. They took action right away—there was no time to wait. One of the guys training was a plastic surgeon and took Thomas through the back door of the hospital to fix the big cut in his face. The rest of the guys in the gym put on their shoes and ran out into the streets to try and find the attackers. They had no luck.

Several people told me that it could be hard to get close to the French people and get to know them. Thomas took a short-cut, and from the first day, everyone knew who the new guy in the gym was. He had just found a very efficient but painful way to make new friends in France. I am sure he won't recommend it to others, though.

I had a few hours to relax before we went to the gym. I was dead tired, but I had to get going with the project of doing as many training sessions as possible around the world.

It was impossible to see what was going on inside through the damp windows of the gym. Thomas beeped a chip in his keychain on a little pad next to the door to unlock it. As we walked in, the first thing that hit me was the humidity. It was like getting punched in the face. There was no air-conditioning, no ventilation, and all windows and doors were closed. I figured I could just as well get used to it, since I would be training some very warm places later on my trip.

A guy was sitting on a cardio bicycle and shook our hand. It was Florent, the owner of the small gym. He was about my size with black, short hair, wearing black fight shorts and a black t-shirt. Thomas shook hands with a handful of guys as we walked through the room. He introduced me to some of them, who tried a few words in English but with limited success.

When the class started, we were seven people on the mat. The coach was Francisco Nonato, a huge Brazilian guy.

We started the warm up and a few minutes in, I realized I was witnessing another "tourist special" workout. Running, sprawling, jumping, rolling, shrimping, pummeling. We took turns jumping over our partner, then crawling through his legs. Twenty times each, as fast as possible. My knee started to hurt a bit and it worried me. I also felt a very familiar pain my left leg. Six years earlier, I had gotten a herniated disc in my lower back from deadlifting that was pressing on the nerve to my left leg. Since then, I had designed my training and life around what I could and could not do. Running and sprawling was on the list of things I normally stayed away from, but being a guest in a gym, I would follow the training, no matter what.

The warm up was brutal, and everyone around me was breathing heavily. Despite the exhaustion from lack of sleep, I was feeling fine. My breathing was still relaxed and the few, short breaks we had in between the drills allowed me to recover quickly. I was looking around at people, fighting to keep up with the rest of the class. All those hard workouts in the gym back home were really paying off and had just saved me from dying on a Jiu Jitsu mat in France, only two days into my trip.

I tried to roll with as many guys as possible. I had a round with Nonato, who must have been way over 130 kilos. It was like trying to grapple with a house. No matter what I did, I couldn't move him. The first roll with a black belt on the trip was in the books, and it wasn't a pretty one.

The one guy was much smaller than me and I outmatched him technically as well. I went slow, loosened up the game a bit, and allowed him to use his techniques instead of just crushing him. I took his back several times, caught him in a few submissions, and every time, I let him escape.

As the timer beeped, he asked me why I didn't go harder on him. He punched his fist into the palm of his hand to symbolize what he meant, assisting his lack of English vocabulary. I didn't think it made sense for me to just tap him out as much as I could. I wanted to play the game on his terms, not just get the win for myself. He seemed a little confused by why I would think like that.

The way I keep progressing and developing my own game is that I have a short list of techniques hanging on my fridge, where I write what I work on in everyday sparring. It is like a written agreement with myself that whenever I roll, I always try to go for those moves. It usually adds up to just two or three things I practice a year, and when I feel like I have them down, I cross them off the list and add new ones.

I had made a little list of things I wanted to work on exclusively for the trip. Wrestling-style sweeps from the guard, guillotine choke, defending myself in guard top, and a specific side control escape would be the only things I would have in mind, no matter who I was rolling with.

I had just caught the first few guillotines and pulled off the side control escape on one of the guys and couldn't wait to try repeat it over and over again against anyone I was going to clap hands with around the globe.

As we walked back home from the gym, Thomas told me that the warm up was usually much easier. I told him about the two hundred pushups in Paris, and we laughed at the similarities. I got a feeling that I would run into these warm ups a few times more during my trip.

In the morning, the weather was beautiful. I opened the balcony door to get some fresh air in. The sun was shining and there was a buzz coming from the street below.

I walked to the supermarket in the mall to find some lunch. The woman at the counter spoke to me in French. *Bonjour. No carde. Merci.* I could guess pretty much what she was saying, and it was a good way to practice some basic phrases, as long as she didn't ask me about anything advanced like, "Do you come here often?"

There was a park next to the mall, where I went to eat my cheap but not very exciting, lunch. The sun was shining. It was the first time I had really felt the sun warm my body for many months.

People were sitting in little groups around the lawn. There was a small, quiet lake in the middle of the park, surrounded by trees, most of them still bare from winter. A few had little green buds on them. Groups of old men were sitting around tables, playing chess. A bunch of students had tied a rope between two trees and took turns trying to walk from one to the other without falling down. A guy was juggling with a football close to a young couple in love.

A girl kissed her boyfriend goodbye. He was texting on his phone as she walked away, making a loud sound as her high heels stepped on the walkway made of stone. She was beautiful. I missed my own girlfriend. It was still difficult to grasp that I would not see or touch her for the next four and a half months.

The next day, I would fly to Bucharest to meet Robert.

"Dress warm", he had ended his last three emails, so I figured he really meant it.

I sucked in the last moments of sunshine and warmth in the park, breathing the fresh air deeply through my nose. I was thinking about spring back home in Denmark, and the smell of trees in bloom from the forest that I lived nearby to as a child. The first day of summer. I was bummed that I was going to miss it but couldn't really complain about where I would be instead.

I trained a few more times in the little, humid gym with the tough Frenchmen. It was like I already knew them all there a bit better, and we had some great rolls, even though many of the guys still didn't make any attempt at conversation.

Florent was one of the few who seemed to know English pretty well.

"I fought this Polish guy at the Europeans. He was so strong, I think something must be 'rong? I look behind 'im... maybe there is two guys, no?"

CHAPTER FIVE

Romania

When I had first talked to Robert about coming to see him, I saw a photo on his blog of an old, brown radio with Russian text on it. That photo had stuck in my mind and somehow defined how I expected Romania to be. My expectations were fulfilled as we drove through town to the apartment. The city was dark and falling apart. Big, gray concrete buildings towered around the wide, empty boulevards. Electric wires hanging everywhere in what seemed to be an impossible knot to solve. A few black silhouettes were walking on the sidewalk, wearing long coats, big furry hats, and shoulders hunched up to their ears. The dim streetlights lit up the heavy snowflakes that fell from the sky. The whole city was covered in snow and seemed depressing in a very authentic, Soviet kind of way.

A distinct smell of urine was in the air as we entered the door to the staircase of the apartment. An old dog was keeping watch, growling at me as I walked by.

Robert told me not to worry. It was only pretending to be dangerous, he said.

The apartment was old. The patterns on the wall and the big, wooden cupboards reminded me of my grandmother's house when I was a kid. Every piece of furniture was in the ultra heavy weight division.

Robert and Amanda were both Americans and a few years older than me. They had met as Peace Corp volunteers in Moldova, working with health education in small villages. When their programs ended, they decided to stay in the area. Not being able to get a permission to live in Moldova, they started teaching English in Romania instead. The language there was the same as in Moldova, and they both spoke it fluently.

I had just arrived, but we decided to go to the gym anyways. The ticket office for the bus had closed at eight in the evening, which basically meant it was free to ride the bus after that hour.

As we walked the last bit from the bus stop to the gym, I noticed a big hole in the sidewalk. It was deep and if I hadn't seen it in time, I could have gotten seriously injured by falling into it. Apparently, people steal the covers for the manhole covers and sell them as scrap metal, Robert explained to me as I jumped over the hole, cheating death once again.

The silhouette of an enormous, unfinished building was hidden behind a long, concrete wall. Pillars that must have been thirty meters tall covered the facade. It looked like some ruin out of a World War II computer game. It was supposed to have been an opera house, one of many ambitious building projects started by the former dictator, Ceausescu, to show off his power. After he died, nobody wanted to finish them, so the half built structures all over the city have been standing there since. It looked a bit like time had stopped.

The gym was located in a military base wrestling room. It was huge. About thirty kids were on the mats at what seemed to be a pretty unstructured wrestling class. Across the room, a bunch of old throwing mats were stacked. They had a fainted camouflage print on them, worn out by the many years of use. In one corner was the weight area. Rusty barbells, some old kettle bells, and a tire lay scattered around the floor.

I took off my shoes. The concrete floor was cold as ice. My ultra-thin travel gi wouldn't keep me warm that night and I hurried onto the mat to stretch and warm my feet a bit.

It was half past nine in the evening, but the room was full of people. I hadn't been sitting twenty seconds on the mat before the first guy came to shake my hand and started to ask me technical questions about Jiu Jitsu. He was very eager to hear my advice on his strategy for an upcoming tournament the next weekend. Many guys came to welcome me. Everyone seemed very friendly and curious. It was different than in France, where I felt it took a little while before people started to open up. Here, they were instantly joking, laughing, and asking questions about my trip.

People asked me to show a few techniques, and everyone wanted to roll with me after class. It was getting late and had been a very long day of traveling, so I was really tired. I agreed to go a few rounds anyways but called it an early night.

The floor was still cold as we changed our clothes. Robert told me that one of the guys from the gym would also be sleeping in the apartment that night. It was one of the kids he had worked with in the village in Moldova. He was twenty years old now and enrolled in the military in Bucharest. He was supposed to be sleeping at the military base that night but had slipped off to Jiu Jitsu and a warm couch instead. The next day, he had the weekend off and would come with us to the village to visit his family. Unlike the Romanians from the big city of Bucharest, the boy from the village had never learned to speak English. I was wondering how it would be to travel so far together with someone I couldn't communicate with.

His name was Sandu, short for Alexandru.

I was doing a seminar in the gym the next afternoon. The place looked different in the daylight. Less scary. I put my bag on a bench in the big training hall and walked around the mat for a minute while waiting for people to show up. Big windows, which must have been five or six meters tall, were covering the wall by the mat. Outside, the snow was falling gently in the little yard between the military buildings. It seemed like a very quiet and peaceful place. I am sure the young recruits staying there might have had a different experience than I.

Sparring with everyone was interesting. I lacked a bit of confidence in my game in terms of rolling with strangers who were eager to try and beat me. Back home, I was training with my own little team of guys only, and was rarely—if ever—exposed to any techniques that I hadn't been teaching myself. Just by rolling with the blue belts that day, it was clear to me that there was still a lot of stuff that I needed to learn.

We got a ride back to the apartment after training. The stark smell of urine in the staircase hadn't gone anywhere.

Robert had cooked up some local soup for us, and Sandu was on the computer again, looking at what seemed like a Russian version of Facebook. He was laughing at some short video clip, eagerly showing it to Robert and saying something in Romanian. I was packing my bag for the bus ride that same evening. Already, I had accumulated more stuff than I needed. A few cool t-shirts had been picked up from gyms along the way, but, still traveling with my big winter jacket, shoes, and sweatshirt, I didn't need that extra weight to carry around the world.

"For you", I said clearly, even though I didn't know if Sandu would understand it.

He held it up, looking at it. The expression on his face showed that he liked it, but he seemed a little confused as to why I had handed some of my clothes to him. Robert explained to him in Romanian that I wanted to give it to him as a gift. His eyes lit up and he quickly stood up from the chair, taking a few fast steps towards me. With a big smile on his face, he looked me right in the eyes, shook my hand and concentrated hard to pronounce "Thank you!" correctly. He turned his head to look at Robert, as in to verify if he had said it right. Robert nodded.

The ice had been broken for the overnight bus ride to Sandu's village in Moldova.

CHAPTER SIX

Moldova

Inside the bus, it was as cold as ice. It was still snowing outside and not many people seemed to be going to Moldova that night. Only a few couples and a young woman with her son had arrived by the time we were about to take off. The bus driver was either saving gas or just didn't bother turning on the heat and light before taking off. No one was talking. The dim light from the Bucharest street outside was coming through the windows, providing just enough light for me to see the silhouettes of the people sitting in the seats in front of me. I was hiding deep inside my big winter jacket, observing my own breath turn to fog in front of me. It stuck on the window by my seat and I drew a random pattern on.

The driver finally got in and, minutes later, we were our way. He made sure to entertain his few passengers by playing some really tacky TV show on the small screen in the front. It was like a mix of James Bond, A-Team, and Walker, Texas Ranger, only in Russian and produced by a 16-year old with a budget of a few hundred rubles. The volume was turned up to maximum to make sure that the guy all the way in the back of the bus didn't miss out on anything. During the ten hour drive, we went through an amazing cascade of episodes, all seemingly having the same plot of everyone trying to shoot each other with toy guns for no particular reason.

Robert told me about Moldova, preparing me for what we might experience there. The small, remote village had some interesting customs. I was expected to shake hands with every male person I met. If I met a group of guys and knew at least one of them, it would be considered an offence if I didn't shake hands with all of them, no matter the size of the group. Shaking hands with women should be highly refrained from, though. All they needed was a small nod and a "hello." Smoking was reserved only for men, and everyone drank lots of alcohol with every meal. It already seemed like a very different place from most other places I would visit on the trip.

Just as Robert was saying something about killing a chicken, I suddenly saw a wall of snow rising outside the front window of the bus, accompanied by a loud sound. It reminded me of the big snowplows in the winter mornings at home. I was not far off, as it seemed like the bus driver had been a little more focused on a shootout on the TV than on driving, and was now plowing full speed into the big piles of snow next to the road. I instinctively posted my hands on the seat in front of me, flexing every muscle of my body, preparing for the impact. Fortunately, the snow provided a semi-soft landing and we all survived. For a little while at least. The piles of snow we had hit on the right side of the bus were so high that we couldn't open the doors and get out.

We were in the middle of nowhere in the Romanian country side. I hadn't seen another car on the road for hours and there was no cellphone signal. Furthermore, we were almost running out of chips and chocolate, and I was starving, so I figured it wouldn't take long until we would have to start eating our first passenger to survive.

Out of nowhere, a tow truck showed up only few minutes after we had crashed. It seemed extremely unlikely that it would be there at that time, but I didn't mind really. It only took five minutes to pull us free from the snow. While waiting in the snow, the TV had been turned off, but the driver made sure to turn it on again as we continued our journey.

Robert told me about his time in the village in Moldova as a Peace Corp volunteer. He had wrestled back in the United States and was eager to do some similar sports while working abroad. Once a year, the villages in the area hold a festival, and amongst many strange activities is the annual wrestling tournament. The first year Robert got there, he was granted special permission to participate. As he got to the finals, it was declared a draw. It wouldn't look too good if an outsider came in and beat the local heroes. He had to share the prize—a live sheep—with the other finalist, and put on a barbecue for everyone.

That same year, Sandu swept the floor in the teens tournament, winning a rabbit. A cute little rabbit. To be eaten, of course.

It was the start of the first ever Jiu Jitsu training in the little village, as Robert got his hand on some old gis and opened up a little gym in the local school.

The bus stopped for a ten-minute break in a nameless city. I walked outside to take a look around. It was getting late, probably past midnight. There was no wind and the snow fell silently on the empty, frosty streets around me. I walked slightly away from the bus. Tall, gray apartment towers were placed in what seemed like an endless row, going down along the street I was standing on. I couldn't see how many of them there were, as the last ones that my eyes could reach started to fade out in the mist of the dark night. A road sign pointing in all directions had seven or eight city names on it in Romanian. I didn't recognize a single one.

For a few cold minutes, I stood completely still and listened to the silence. It felt like I was totally alone in an unknown world, as far away from home as I could be. Another planet—an empty parallel universe. A traveling rush that had demanded effort and courage to achieve was released into my bloodstream. I enjoyed every second of it: It was my drug.

About an hour later, we arrived at the Moldovan border. A few guards were standing outside in the dark, cold night. The snow had stopped. They were dressed for the occasion and looked exactly like I would picture border guards in Eastern Europe to look like. Big assault rifles, long, dark-green coats and large, furry hats pulled down to just above their eyebrows. The place was a eery and could have been any scene from a 1980s action movie, where an agent tries to sneak past the border guards into Russian territory. We made it through without any interrogations or Kalashnikov shootouts, and a few hours later, we arrived in Cahul where we would spend the night.

Getting off the bus, we were supposed to walk a few streets to Robert's friend's apartment. I was too tired to help out with the map and Robert didn't seem to be good with directions, so we ended up getting a little bit lost on the streets of Cahul. It was three or four in the morning and the city was dead. The cold wind was biting my face and seemed to blow right through my thick winter jacket. A lone night club was open, but it didn't look like anyone was in there.

Three young police officers were patrolling the street nearby. They wore long black uniforms going all the way down to their big leather boots. Their shoulders were hunched to their ears and hands dug well into their pockets to keep warm. The sound of their boots patrolling the sidewalk echoed on the walls of the once modern, now faded and worn out apartment buildings on the empty street and could be heard clearly from where we were standing. The orange lights from their cigarettes were becoming more visible as they approached us. Looking at their rough faces, I could tell that they probably had seen a tough thing or two already in their young lives. My guess was that they were around twenty years old or maybe even younger. They looked really scary to me, but Robert didn't think twice about asking them for directions. He had little luck, though.

We finally decided to call Naeema for directions. *Down the small, dark alley next to the night club, then first staircase to the right in the building complex.*

I am sure the place didn't look as scary in the daytime, but walking around the apartment buildings that cold, dark night; going up and down one falling apart staircase after the other—lit up by single light bulbs hanging from cords in the ceiling—listening to the echo of our voices and big, rusty metal doors screeching as they opened and closed, I felt like I was in a first person shooter computer game, out of ammo and desperately looking for a health pack before being found by enemy soldiers.

We finally found Naeema. She was waving a flashlight to signal her location and we walked quickly towards her in a pace that matched our excitement at finally finding our way out.

Naeema was probably the least likely type of person I would have expected to meet in a small Moldovan city that evening. She was a short and stocky African American woman, probably somewhere in her forties. She was from Kansas City and had an accent to prove it; a voice as loud as a gospel choir lead singer; a huge smile and cornrows in her hair. It was in the middle of the night, but she was full of energy and seemed really happy to have guests. Wearing her pink pajamas with little monkeys and peace signs on, she immediately started making soup and sandwiches for us while we inflated the air mattress in the living room.

"There was a cat and a dog and a goose, walking right into the kitchen!"

She was telling stories and laughing loudly from the kitchen while making French toasts on the old stove. Robert was her friend from the Peace Corp. She had been doing social projects in Moldova for two years, specializing in domestic violence, and spoke Romanian fluently. I was really impressed by the energy of this woman, but I had to get some sleep, so I crawled into my sleeping bag and closed my eyes.

It was another long bus ride the next day before we finally reached our destination. There were very few people on the muddy streets of the little village. We stayed in a small, simple house on a hill. It was built with tough materials and made to withstand the rough weather in the Moldovan winter. It was the size of a regular house and functioned as a miniature farm.

In the front of the house were stables with sheep, chicken, geese, and rabbits. They had their own little winery (something almost all houses in the area had). Adjacent to the house was a small field, where they grew vegetables and grapes. An energetic dog lived year round outdoors in the small garden and slept in a little, cold dog house built from old wooden planks.

I stood in the snow with toes freezing, overlooking the field in front of the house. There was a full panoramic view over the area: Hills with small farm houses, a little forest, a river, and small patches of buildings, all covered in snow. I wondered how beautiful it would look in the summer, when everything was green and all the colorful vegetables and grapes were growing. A few small, wooden chairs were placed in the garden, just waiting for summer, where someone would sit in them and enjoy the tranquility.

Tolea greeted us at the door with a strong handshake. He lived in the house with his mother—his father had passed away. He was my age but looked quite a bit older. In general, people seemed to look much older than their age. The rough faces told stories of hard, manual labor since childhood. I had just been playing football and sitting in front of a computer.

We all sat there on the couch in the quiet living room. It was exactly as quiet as the village outside. Tolea broke the silence and asked if I wanted to kill a chicken the next day so we could eat it for dinner.

I had never killed an animal, and the thought didn't appeal to me at all. But I decided that if I could eat meat from animals my whole life, then I couldn't just close my eyes to the fact that I also agreed on killing them. Doing it myself would be a healthy thing. I said yes.

There was a short debate over whether it should be a chicken or a rabbit whose life I would have the honor of ending.

I got a lump in my throat, thinking about my beloved rabbit I had as a kid. No, I couldn't do that. I had to start with the chicken which made me nervous enough. Small steps.

There was a very narrow spiral staircase in the middle of the living room floor, going down to a kitchen and heating room. A big, concrete fireplace was built into the foundation of the house itself, providing heat to the upper floor. I felt cold from the bus drive and the walk outside, so it was nice to lean against the rustic wall enclosing the fireplace and feel warmth return to my limbs.

Now and then, Tolea would try with a little bit of English. He was actually pretty good but obviously lacked training and confidence in speaking.

"In Soviet times, there was no sex, only family. If someone asked where the children came from, people said they got them from the communist party."

An old sports hall had a prominent location in the middle of the village. Tolea had told me that when he was a kid, it was a thriving place with sports events and training going on all the time. There had been wrestling competitions and many tough boxing matches had been fought. He had played football there himself, as a kid. When the Union fell, the funding ended, and the building was left to fall apart. People in the village took whatever they could use from it. When I got there, only the ruins were left of what must have been a magnificent place.

There were no locks on the doors and no glass in the windows. Walking into the entrance hall, it struck me how beautiful it must have looked in its prime. The walls were white and blue. Most of the paint had fallen off. I walked through the main entrance and found the locker rooms. So many athletes must have waited in those small rooms before going into the hall to perform. There were four rooms; two for the home team and two for the away team.

Walking from the locker rooms, a small corridor went into the hall itself. When I first walked this way, I could imagine how it must have been for the wrestlers, boxers, and gymnasts doing the same. Nervous. Anxious. Listening to the sound of the audience inside the hall ahead. Entering the big room, the first thing I noticed was the light coming through the enormous windows on the opposite wall. There was no glass left, just big, rectangular holes. The light must have filled the room beautifully. Above the floor was the spectator balcony with people cheering for the athletes. On one wall was written, "Raise high the flag of sport" and on the other, the Olympic rings and motto, "Faster, higher, stronger."

I wondered how many dreams of young athletes had been dreamed in that building. Dreams of reaching the top; becoming the best they could; making their families and country proud. Standing there was a very special thing to me. It was not hard to imagine the tense atmosphere before a big game or match. When I closed my eyes, I could see how it must have looked. I was desperately hoping I'd gone back in time when I opened them again.

But there was nothing. The paint had still fallen off and the silence was stunning. The wind blew gently through the big windows, silently carrying a few big snowflakes with it. A tree was growing in one corner. The wooden floor was long gone, probably used for firewood many years earlier. There were no more breathtaking seconds of victory and defeat there. No more dreams.

Robert shouted something to me from outside as he came down the hill towards the building.

I shook my head and blinked my eyes a few times, coming back to the real world.

My answer echoed off the concrete walls of the empty hall as I shouted back to him, out through the big, empty windows.

A former theater, now being used as a youth center, was right around the corner in a building connected to the sports hall. A few drunken men were looking out at us through a window. They were probably living in one of the rooms in the building or at least using it for something. We walked up a once prominent staircase to the front door. No shows were on at the theater at that moment and probably wouldn't be for a while. It was being used as a place for young people to hang out. About ten guys in their teens were smoking cigarettes in one of the rooms. The air was thick with smoke. They had a ping pong table and were playing intensely while shouting and laughing loudly, probably trash talking each other. It seemed like they were having a good time. They looked rough. Their faces were hard to see with their beanies pulled down and hands held in front of the mouths to be warmed by their breath. Robert shook hands with all of them, and I remembered the custom of doing the same. They looked at me strangely. It felt awkward.

The boys said there would be a disco in the evening. Before I even got to consider it, Robert had told them we would come. I wondered how the local guys would look at me when I showed up at their party.

In the adjacent room, three guys were playing pool. There was a big scratch in the middle of the table, and the little nets in each hole had been worn out long ago, so the balls just fell directly on the wooden floor with a loud bang every time someone hit the hole.

We shook hands with everyone and I quickly put my gloves back on. The youth center was cold as ice. I wanted to get back to the nice, warm fireplace in the house.

The day after what had been the coldest night out of my life at the local bar—basically just a large freezer with plastic chairs and gigantic vodka shots—we went to visit the school. The kids had a break between classes as we got there, and hordes of them were running around the hallways and staircases. I have never had so many eyes stare at me at once before. It was like every kid running around completely froze as they discovered I was there. Then they just stared at me, like I was some rare animal. In some way, I guess I was.

I met the school principal and all the other teachers. They were excited to have guests. I had shaken a hundred hands and had gotten pretty used to it until I decided to go to the bathroom.

Back at the house, the toilet was a little shed in the garden with a hole in the ground and nothing else. I had been a little hesitant about using it, so I thought that the school must have better facilities. It didn't.

The outdoor toilet was like something out of a "Saw" movie. It was the most disgusting and scary place I have ever been to in my life. I think many of us have bad memories about schoolyard toilets as kids. They were smelly and I was always afraid of the older boys, who could come in anytime and try to play an evil prank on the younger ones, looking over the door or trying to open the lock with a pair of scissors. What a paradise I had grown up in compared to these toilets. I instantly regretted and took back every bad memory I had from my own childhood as I saw the five holes in the stone floor lined up in the small room. Knee high concrete walls divided the holes to provide minimum privacy. There was no running water, no sinks, no soap, and no paper. Only five holes in the ground. Faeces were lying on the floor, mostly around the holes from when someone had missed them and didn't feel like kicking it down. There were brown foot- and handprints on the wall. I didn't want to think too much about how it got there. I felt terrible for the kids who had to go through ten years of school using these.

We went back to rest up before the class in the afternoon when school was out. We met the mayor on the way, who was intrigued by having a tourist in his village and invited us to dinner at his house. Unfortunately, we already had plans to visit Sandu's parent's house. Regardless, we now had enough dinner invitations that I didn't have to kill that chicken anyways. I was relieved but a little disappointed at the same time. It was a challenge I would have to take up again another time in the future.

In the afternoon, about fifteen boys were waiting for us outside the school. They looked a little nervous. They had been looking forward to having someone come from outside their small community to teach them. It was a big thing for them. And for me.

Sandu had the keys for the school. Some old, dirty mats were pulled out from a small storage space. After Robert had left and Sandu had moved to Bucharest, there hadn't been much training going on at the school. They had a big pile of old gis that a friend of Robert's had collected in the United States and shipped over. There was no money for the villages to buy any themselves, so the help from abroad made the training possible. Not a single one of them fit or was intact. They were ripped, dirty, too big, and full of holes. A few belts were actual training belts, the rest were reused pieces of fabric or furry belts from robes. The boys didn't seem to care one bit. They grabbed whatever they could and ran to the gym hall, shouting and laughing, excited to train again.

Walking into the gym hall, I immediately knew that this was not going to be like any other training I would do on the trip; probably not like any other training I would do in my life. There was no heating. It was just as cold as being outside in the snow. The walls were painted green many years ago, and the floor was old and broken. It had big holes in it and some places, entire boards were missing. There was no money for a football goal, so they had painted one on the wall with chalk instead. I couldn't imagine playing football there. More than one kid must have broken a foot, stepping into those holes. There was originally no light in the room, but someone had stolen six street lamps and installed them instead.

The kids were wearing their thick sweatshirts and pants under the gis. I had to keep my socks, beanie, and gloves on, as well as a few t-shirts. Sandu was laying out the mats while Robert showed some of the boys how to tie the belts, and I tried to get a little bit warm. It was impossible. I was freezing to the very marrow of my bones. I took a few photos with my camera, and the boys were eager to pose for me.

I asked one of them to do a portrait. The gi jacket he was wearing reached all the way down to below his knees and the pants had been cut with a pair of scissors so they fit his length. He was wearing a turtle neck sweater, socks, and a thick beanie. He seemed very proud that I would take his photo. Only him alone, no one else in the photo. As he stood there on the broken floor in front of the wall with the green paint falling off, I couldn't really determine if he was smiling or being serious. There was a slight smile on his face, but at the same time, having his portrait taken was something he took very seriously. I clicked the button and immediately realized that it was one of the best portraits I would take on the trip. A split second later, he was gone, playing with the other boys.

I called everyone together and Robert made a brief introduction about me. The boys were completely quiet, sitting around on the cold mats. I tried to do some warm-up with them, but it was impossible to break a sweat so I decided to give up on that.

We started training and I did some of the drills I do with my own kid's team at home. They absolutely loved it. I made squares with belts and did a simple wrestling drill, where two at a time, the kids try to push each other out and the winner stays in. Then I showed them some escapes and simple chokes from mount and back mount. They were having a great time and seemed eager to learn something.

Their physiques were impressive. I could tell they had been doing hard physical labor most of their lives already. Driving through on double legs seemed very natural to them, and they had a lot of power, catching me by surprise a few times. I wish I had the opportunity to work more with them. If only I had just six months with them in my gym back home, they would be absolute monsters in competition.

These were really poor kids, living in such a different world to my own. They didn't have much: No iPods, no cell phones, no fancy clothes, and no heating. But it didn't seem to matter a bit to them. It didn't make any difference at all. For a few hours, they seemed to forget all that and just get lost in training, like we all do every day we go to the gym at home. They were smiling and laughing so much. Every time they laughed, a big, white fog appeared in front of them in the cold air, and it was like I was the only one who noticed the cold. I loved every second of it and was desperately trying to hold on to the feeling they gave me so I could keep it forever.

Only two of the six streetlights on the ceiling were working, so I had to show techniques in the one corner that was lit up. My knee was hurting and I still hadn't been able to warm it up, but I wanted to make sure I rolled with everyone anyways.

When it got too dark to spar safely, we decided to call it a day. My toes and fingers were completely numb from the cold at that point.

It was a big honor to train with those kids and something that I will never forget. That day, I really had my eyes opened to what power I possess to influence people in a positive way with Jiu Jitsu. Giving kids good experiences and being a role model for someone is a huge gift, and it is important to use it right. Although I know that I somehow do the same at home, but this was different. I came from far away lands, completely unknown, and still I was able to have a positive influence on someone; maybe even change their lives a little bit in a positive way. I wished I could do just this on the whole trip around the world. Visiting famous gyms and training with world champion superstars suddenly seemed so unimportant.

It had been the coldest but at the same time, most inspirational training session of my life.

We stayed a few more days in the village and I started to feel at home there. Sandu started to become a friend, and he tried more and more with English phrases. In Romania, we had barely said a word to each other, and I had thought it would have been awkward to have had him with us for so long. I looked back and remembered his face in the Bucharest class. He was one in forty white belts there and I didn't take special notice of him. Now, things were different and we had a special connection. We could communicate little, but it worked out really well when Robert translated. He was young and extremely enthusiastic about Jiu Jitsu. In class, he worked with discipline and sucked in every bit of information he could. Besides that, he was strong as an ox and his base and balance was so good that it was extremely difficult for me to sweep him.

After dinner at his family's house our last evening, we walked home in the frosty snow. I hadn't changed my clothes or showered for four days. Same socks and same underwear. It didn't matter. The sky was clear and thousands of stars were visible. We were far away from any light pollution. It was freezing cold and the air was dry. The moon was out and lit up the snow on the road. No one said anything on the way home. I looked up at the stars, thinking about the kids. I would be leaving the next morning, but they were not going anywhere. They would still be in that gym hall with no heating. I had a tear in my eye: Whether it was from the cold, dry air or from thinking about the unexpected experiences and friendships I had found in the little village, I couldn't tell.

Sitting in the rattling morning bus on our way from the village to Chisinau, the capital of Moldova, I couldn't get a sentence out of my head that Robert had written to me in an email a few weeks back.

"I've been in contact with the guys in Chisinau and it sounds like they are all but rolling out the red carpet for you. That means that they will try and test you. This is kind of the Russian mentality."

I didn't feel like being tested by any crazy Russians. My knee agreed. But there was nothing to do but go there and see what would happen.

Ion, one of the guys from a traditional Jiu Jitsu gym, picked us up at the bus station. I had just had one of the worst hamburgers of my life there and didn't feel extremely well. Having gotten up early and been sitting on the bus all day, all I could think about was rest. The city looked cold and depressing, much like Bucharest. A guy was sitting on a bench with an old scale in front of him on the ground, offering to weigh people for less than ten cents. A woman stood on a street corner and sold colorful balloon animals. She looked sad.

The guys had big plans for my short visit. We were going directly to do a class in the gym, then teach a seminar for a hundred people in a large sports hall. They had even printed seminar t-shirts with my name on them.

I was taken a little by surprise there. I hadn't really thought about what I was going to do in Chisinau, so having to teach two seminars right off the bus just seemed like too much. I decided that training was what I was traveling for anyways, so I accepted the challenge. I could rest the following day instead.

Robert had couch-surfed in Chisinau before, and he hooked us up with the guy he stayed with last time. Sergei lived in a big apartment with his mom, and he was making money buying and selling women's shoes off eBay. He was in his late teens and a bit dorky. When I first introduced myself to him, he was really curious about what kind of Christian I was because he was a catholic himself. I was confused for a second, and it didn't get less complicated when I told him that I wasn't religious at all. I don't really remember how I got out of that conversation.

My brain was fried from traveling all morning, and I tried to sneak around Sergei's many questions. We had to get going. I was teaching fifteen minutes later in the gym, and I almost couldn't keep my eyes open.

Almost everyone spoke nothing but Russian so one of the guys had to translate every time I said something. It took ages to explain the details of every position. Both me and Robert were totally overtired and couldn't stop laughing and joking about everything. We were like kids. I had no idea how I was going to survive a seminar for a hundred people only a few hours later.

Later was getting sooner, and directly from the gym, we went to have dinner and then to the sports hall where the seminar would be. My second class of the day after having been in town for less than three hours.

It was a huge building from the Soviet times. Like the sports hall in the village, it was deteriorating, though to nowhere near the same extent. We walked through the hallway towards the wrestling hall. Old photos of wrestling teams were hanging on the wooden walls. Lots of guys were waiting for us and I was introduced to a bunch of them in the hallway. They looked pretty bad ass, and some of the handshakes were amongst the hardest I had felt in my life. I couldn't stop thinking about what Robert had said in that email. Were they hardcore Sambo guys who were going to test my skills and rip my kneecaps off? I knew they did lots of leg locks and was extremely worried about my injury.

The wrestling hall itself was the biggest I have ever seen. There was at least ten meters to the ceiling and the room fitted three full size wrestling mats. Large posters in Russian from wrestling competitions were hanging on the walls. The ceiling was leaking and buckets were strategically placed around the hall. In one place, the water was dripping down on the wall, making the paint wet and lose. I accidentally put my hand on it and got a hand full of paint that I had to go wash off.

A lot of guys were changing in to their gis and a lot of eyes seemed to be on me. I was starting to get used to that.

I had no idea what to expect. The black belts of the Jiu Jitsu organization looked tough. It could have been a who's who of Russian James Bond bad guys. I was having all kinds of night-mares in my mind about how they would throw me around in crazy submissions and injure every joint in my body. I still didn't feel fully comfortable about sparring with complete strangers yet. My mind tried to play too many tricks on me. It was some-thing I hoped to get better at coping with during my trip.

I started explaining a little bit about what I intended to teach. I usually make lots of jokes when I teach, but it seemed like no matter how hard I tried, no one even smiled. They were just sitting there with stone-serious faces—even the twenty or so kids, who I would have expected to be totally unfocused. I tried so hard, but I just couldn't get a reaction from them. Robert laughed now and then in the awkward silence, and it didn't make our silly, overtired mood any better.

I had people do some difficult body mechanics drills, followed by classics such as the "around the world" drill, where one guy has to climb all the way around his standing partner without falling off. Usually, when people try this first and fail, they get frustrated and start laughing. This time, I didn't hear a sound. People would try hard to do it, and when they failed, they wouldn't have any expression on their faces. They just tried again.

To me, training should first and foremost be fun and enjoyable. If I don't enjoy training and have a good time, I will end up quitting sooner or later. I decided to focus the whole seminar around trying to make people laugh instead of actually teaching them Jiu Jitsu techniques. That part would have to wait.

I explained the rules of a game I play with kids and expected it to make them smile a little bit. They looked like I was explaining how to play a casino card game, where their entire retirement savings were on the line. Eventually, I had forty grownup men play "Jiu Jitsu virus" in a desperate attempt to put a smile on their faces. It finally worked.

Everyone wanted a go at me and Robert in sparring, and we were put to work. My worst fears of Russians dumping me on the head and blowing out my knees were all in my head. There was nothing to be afraid of, and I handled myself well. I wanted to make a point about the importance of positional dominance, so every time I rolled, I made sure to slowly switch between positions and not let people escape them. They would get really tired from trying, and in the end, I could apply a submission with no effort, even on the biggest guys. It was old school Gracie tactics and I think it proved my point.

The head of the organization was a very big, short-haired guy with a worn out black belt. He owned the gym I taught in earlier and was highly respected by everyone in the room. He was incredibly strong and probably about 30 kilos heavier than me. Luckily for me, he had never been exposed to the Brazilian style of grappling before, and I could fairly easily sweep, hold, and submit him.

From my experience, if someone is high in a hierarchy—especially in the more traditional martial arts—then often, they don't feel good about looking bad or losing in front of their own students. I think that in most cases, the guy would have retreated at that point, pretending to be tired, injured, or something, so he wouldn't have to lose more. This time it was different. He wanted more.

He concentrated to pronounce the English word "again" right.

I couldn't get him off of me. Everyone in the room had started to sit in a circle around us on the mat to watch as their master was submitted by a much smaller guy, again and again.

As we got home from the seminar, I was completely done after the long day. I had nothing left in me. Sergei kept asking questions about everything in the world it seemed, and I didn't want to just come and take advantage of his hospitality so I politely answered as many as I could.

He didn't understand how the triangle choke technique worked. He had seen it in the UFC but never used it in his Karate training and wanted me to demonstrate it for him.

It was way past midnight and I was triangling a guy I had just met on the living room floor in an apartment in a former

Soviet Union country. I'd had enough impressions for one day. It was definitely time to go to bed.

Robert had planned a day trip for us to Transnistria, a place, people told me, is located somewhere between Dracula and Tsjernobyl. I was honestly a little nervous about going to a country that—according to Wikipedia—didn't officially exist. If something happened there, would I be able to get out again? A quick look online made it sound like a lawless place, controlled by ruthless, Russian military warlords. Robert was, as usual, not bothered at all by this and seemed to be able to move around freely in any dangerous and unknown territory without even thinking twice about it.

We went to the little local market to buy tickets for the bus. They handed us customs papers that we needed to fill out for the border control.

I once again found myself in a cold, small van and the drive would take about forty-five minutes. Robert told me that some guys had built a homemade raft and used it to cross the river to Transnistria to steal some watermelons. They got caught and are probably still in jail. I guess they really felt like having watermelons that day.

As we arrived at the border, a uniformed guard entered the van and collected everyone's passports. We waited about twenty minutes before he returned. He said something in Russian, and a few people from the bus walked out. We didn't understand anything, but a guy sitting next to us spoke a little English and explained that all foreigners had to go to the customs office to apply for a tourist visa.

There was a long line in the small building without any windows. Different forms were lying around on the tables and instructions in Russian were posted on the wall next to wanted posters of criminals. They were probably more water melon thieves, I thought.

Through a small hole in a window, a very serious border guard was processing the visa requests from people in the line. He was taking his time. The room he was sitting in was about five times the size as the small one we were waiting in. It was completely empty except for his desk, an old, beige computer with a CRT monitor, and one of those old keyboards with a curled cord and a click sound for each key press. The walls were mint green and the only thing on them was a big Transnistrian flag with hammer and sickle hanging in the back of the room, reminding everyone who was ruling this border. There was absolutely no expression on his face as he typed in the information from the passports. I slowly moved forward in the line and was feeling a little nervous about the whole situation. Would he be suspicious that I was a tourist? And what about Robert, who was American?

I handed the border guard my passport and the form, hoping I had filled out correctly. He didn't look up from the screen as he picked it up. Rarely had I seen such an expressionless face. He started entering my information in the computer. It seemed to take forever.

Then he suddenly asked me, with a deep voice and a heavy Russian accent, if I was going back the same evening. I was.

Still not looking at anything but the screen, he put my passport back on the little desk in front of me, together with a stamped entry visa for the day.

"Good luck", he said with a voice so deep and rough that it could make even Arnold Schwarzenegger shiver with fear.

What? Why would I need luck? For a moment I was a little confused and at the same time, it was hard for me to not smile or laugh at the absurdity of the situation. I took a photo of the little piece of paper with the stamp on, proving that I could enter the country of Transnistria for one day and one day only. I hoped that I wouldn't be late for the last bus back to Chisinau.

Driving into the city of Tiraspol, I noticed that surprisingly many buildings and shops had a big sign saying "Sheriff." Apparently, some super rich guy owned most of the country, including the football team, gas stations, and supermarkets. To make everything easier, he decided give everything the same name. It was a strange place.

We got off the bus by the Sheriff Supermarket, located right next to the Sheriff football Stadium. Robert had stayed in Tiraspol with a guy called Andrei for a few days and we decided to go visit him. After walking around a little bit, we found the area where he lived. It was a bad ass Soviet ghetto. Naked trees in the snow were lined up between a handful of identical concrete buildings with rusty, caged windows and faded yellow balconies. Laundry in all colors was hanging to dry outside the windows and there was no one on the streets.

We found Andrei's apartment. It was on the fourth floor and very spacious. He had a kind wife, a kid, and a small dog. They invited us in for a cup of tea in their simple kitchen. It was cozy and didn't feel at all like what I had in mind after reading Wikipedia the day before.

Andrei had studied German, which allowed him to travel to Switzerland. He worked as a translator and ran a German Internet radio with news from Transnistria. I only spoke German when I was drunk. He told us that in Soviet times, translating any movies in a foreign language was illegal. The translators were arrested and prosecuted. People still wanted to watch American and European movies, so to hide their identity, the underground translators held their noses while recording.

Visiting a home in such an isolated country in a world so different from my own felt like a very big privilege. Having guests like me and Robert was their window to the rest of the world, as we came from a place that was impossible for them to visit themselves. I thought about how lucky I was that I didn't need any visa or have any worries if I wanted to go somewhere in the world. I took the freedom of travel for granted, but it was ignorant of me. For Andrei and his family, traveling anywhere outside of their miniature country was virtually impossible. They had to let the world come to them; so with the Internet radio and inviting people into their homes through couch surfing, they got a glimpse of the world outside and were able to hear about it from people who lived there. They were extremely hospitable and very interested in hearing about Denmark. I felt sad for them. They hoped for a better and freer future, especially for their young daughter, Andrei told me.

I would never take my freedom to travel for granted again.

The whole little family—with all their dreams and visions for the future—were standing in the falling apart doorway, waving goodbye to us and offering for us to come back any time as we walked down the stairs from the apartment. I wished I could have taken them with me to see the world. The only thing I could do was to make sure I went out there and took in all the experiences I could, getting the absolute most out of it, being open to everything and not taking anything for granted. Anything else would be a disgrace towards those people who were unable to do it; people like those I had just met.

We met up with Ion at a cafe. He was really excited about his first experience with Brazilian Jiu Jitsu the day before and couldn't stop talking about it. Coming from a traditional Jiu Jitsu background, it seemed to have been a real eye opener for him. There was a lot of information and thoughts for him and his training partners to process, but I had a feeling that when I would come back one day, things would be very different, and Brazilian Jiu Jitsu would be a fast-growing sport. The seed was planted, now it was just a question of time.

Robert took the bus with me to the airport. People would jump on and find a seat. Then they would tap the shoulder of the person sitting in front of them and ask them to pass on their money for the driver. If someone got the back seat, their little handful of coins and notes would be passed through the entire bus before reaching the driver. He would then send the change back through the bus. Since I was sitting in the front, I was being tapped on the shoulder the entire way.

The airport was almost empty when I got there. It felt like they had built it with shops and everything, just for me to fly to Turkey that day. No one else seemed to use it. An empty cafeteria had a TV showing "Banged up abroad," a show about people getting caught in airports smuggling drugs and thrown in scary jails. It was almost like a message to the passengers not to try anything stupid.

Sitting in the plane, I wondered how the rest of the trip could possibly top what I had seen and experienced in Eastern

Europe. It had really changed my view on how I would travel in the months to come and even for the rest of my life.

I needed to stay focused on getting out and seeing the real world, not just the big cities with airports which are often just a variation of the world I already know. I had to seriously push myself to see another side of the world and experience the lives of real people in real places. It was too comfortable to travel safe. I could easily go around the world like that, but I wanted more.

With an overwhelming excitement to see what awaited me out in the world, I put in my earplugs and curled up under my little blanket on the airplane seat. I felt at home in planes and fell asleep right away.

CHAPTER SEVEN

Turkey

It was late in the evening, and we drove straight to a hotel where Eren had booked a room for me. I didn't mind at all sleeping on a couch or similar, but he insisted since I would be teaching in his gym every day. After having spent many nights already in plane seats and on uncomfortable couches, I had to admit that having a quiet hotel room with a nice bed all to myself was a great luxury.

I threw my backpack on one of the beds and went to lie down on the other one, enjoying the silence. There was no need to turn on the TV or my computer. I just enjoyed being alone in my own room for the first time since I left home. I knew this was something that would not happen often on the trip, so I savored every second of it. The bed felt like heaven. I had only traveled for two weeks and had more than four months left but already, I missed the feeling of having my own bed to sleep in.

I hoped that I would get accustomed to sleeping weird places during the trip and forget about my nice bed at home.

Only three guys had showed up for the class in the morning. I could tell that Eren was a bit disappointed. He was working hard to build up the sport from complete scratch and would naturally meet a lot of challenges on the way. At that moment, all his focus was put into just trying to create a core group of dedicated guys and build from there. It was a lot of work, which I had been through myself when building up my own gym. I understood his frustrations.

To me, it didn't matter if there were two or twenty people on the mat, though. I wanted to train with anyone on the trip, no matter the size of the group or the skill level. In my world, the interesting thing was to meet the people behind the Jiu Jitsu, and even if there was only one complete beginner, he also had the potential to become a great friend. White belts are real people too, after all.

The guys were enthusiastic and had a pretty good game for beginners. Eren had put a lot of emphasis on breaking grips and defending the neck, and it had paid off. Even though they were white belts, they were hard to handle and submit because of this.

Eren likes food. So do I. Visiting him was like half Jiu Jitsu and half food adventure. As eager as he was to train, he was equally eager to show me around to his favorite places to eat.

"Do you like intestines?"

I stopped for a second. It wasn't a question I was asked very often. I wanted to be adventurous about food on the trip, but intestines just sounded wrong (especially after just having enjoyed a kebab so delicious, I felt like I could eat only that for the rest of my life).

But I had to try everything. It was a rule I had made for myself, so I said yes while admitting to being a bit nervous about it.

We drove down town to Eren's favorite intestine joint. The brown, unrecognizable mass was rolled up like a kebab, sliced off, chopped, and fried, then put in a sandwich bread. I decided not to think about what it was and took a bite. It tasted like spicy, fat, tender chicken. I was surprised at how good it was and ate the whole sandwich happily, though I concentrated on believing it was chicken.

The flight on to Cyprus took only about an hour. It was a bumpy ride at low altitude, flying just above the clouds all the way. It was evening when I arrived. The same second I got out of the plane, I noticed a certain scent in the air that reminded me of vacations with my parents in the Mediterranean when I was a kid. It was warm and dry, similar to pine and grass.

Selman, who ran the only gym on the Turkish side of the island—dividing Turkey and the country of Cyprus—had told me to take a bus to the university, where he would pick me up. As I got off, he wasn't there. A young Turkish guy got off at the same point and we stood there quietly in the night by the roadside for a few minutes before he asked me where I was going. He was an electrical engineer trying to get to the United Kingdom to find work, but it wasn't easy. He offered me a cigarette as he told me about his life while we were waiting. Him for a taxi, me for Selman.

I kindly replied that I had never smoked in my life.

He was friendly and it was interesting to hear the story of a complete stranger I had just met. I wondered how many thousands of interesting stories I missed every day from people I walked past on the street but never talked to.

Selman showed up. He had gotten me an apartment in a girl's only dorm house and made some joke about hoping that I was ok with that.

No one else stayed in it during that time, so I had four beds, a kitchen, bathroom, and living room to myself.

I slept like a baby in the small bed. The next morning, I stood out on the balcony, enjoying the morning sun. For the first time since I'd left home, I really felt warm. The cold weather in Romania and Moldova was far away, and it seemed like my days walking in snow with freezing toes in my big winter jacket were finally over. In front of the house was a small field with a windmill and in the distance, some big mountains. It was early March, and I had started summer a little earlier than my friends at home in cold Scandinavia.

A small, matted room in the university's sports hall—the classic photo of Helio Gracie hanging on the wall—was being used for the training.

The twenty or so guys had a few technical questions I helped them out with, but most of the time, we just rolled. The room was so quiet. I always play music in the gym at home, and I hadn't trained one place on the trip yet with music. I really missed it.

It was all beginners on the mat, who had only a few months of training. Selman had studied a little longer than the rest and had a good understanding of the game, but obviously lacked experience in executing it. He needed higher level sparring partners in order to grow at that point, but with the enthusiasm they put into the training, it would only be a matter of time before they had a strong group there.

I rolled to submission with everyone in the class. Being inexperienced beginners, they were going really hard to try and beat me. In return, I tried to prove a point of technique beating strength by going slow and relaxed. I lay down on my back and played an easy guard against all of them, letting them go all out to try and pass while I spent little energy defending, sweeping, and submitting. The thought crossed my mind that it maybe wasn't a great thing for my knee injury to have someone pull my legs so hard, but I didn't feel anything going wrong at that point.

The next morning, my body was tired from the long sparring the day before. I stumbled to the shower in an attempt to wake up. As I reached up for the shampoo, I stepped forward a little bit and my leg buckled under me. A strong pain shot through my meniscus, right where I had the injury.

Biting my lip in pain, I was reminded how stupid it had been to let those guys go so hard on me the night before.

I was starting to get pretty worried about the knee and felt a pain every time I bent my leg. It was a very real threat towards ruining my whole trip, and I couldn't cope with the thought of not being able to train like I had planned to.

To fly from Cyprus to India, I had to do a stopover in Istanbul, so it was an easy choice to stay for a day and check out a gym there.

As the plane descended towards Istanbul, I couldn't believe my bad luck. The whole city was covered in snow. In Cyprus, I was sure that I had finally put winter behind me, but it looked like I was going to have to deal with it for another day.

Burak had emailed me the day before and said he would pick me up in the airport. He arrived just as I got through customs. It was pouring down as we ran to his car. The snow had melted quickly on the ground, and running over the parking lot got my shoes soaked in no time. The cream-colored cabin was cold, making me shiver for a few minutes before it heated up.

Burak laughed and told me I had chosen to come the only day a year there was snow in Istanbul.

I had gotten in touch with him online, a brown belt who was running one of the few gyms in town together with his friend, Ertan, a professional MMA fighter. They were training and teaching full time and working hard to try and make a living out of it.

After showing me around town a bit and lifting weights in a super luxurious fitness center, we went to the gym in the late afternoon. It was one of the best looking gyms I had ever seen. Ertan was teaching the first MMA class of the night. I wanted to join in but had to be disciplined about my knee. It was still sore.

The training was intense and the technical level pretty high. During a roll, a heavy guy tried to slam his way out of Ertan's backmount. Ertan got up and started shouting at him. I didn't understand the language, but it was obvious what was going on. He had a fight coming up and couldn't afford any injuries from inconsiderate training partners. He was furious and the big guy almost started crying while apologizing. Ertan threw his water bottle across the mat and everyone was completely silent. He took a breath, slapped the big guy's hand, and it all ended with a hug and a laugh.

I went outside for a walk. It was dark and the snow was still falling. The sound of the prayers could be heard from the speakers of a nearby mosque. I was thinking about how it would be in India the next day, hoping that my knee would allow me to train there.

Burak came outside and asked me if I wanted to teach a little bit. I couldn't do anything else so that suited me fine.

I did a class on passing the guard. For a few years, I had been working on conceptually understanding how my friend Martin Aedma from Estonia did his brutal pressure passing—also known as the guard passing from Hell—and I had finally boiled it down to a recipe I could understand myself and even better, teach to others. It was a good group of guys and there was some serious talent in between. I sat out and watched the sparring. There were some tough rolls. It was a different training culture than what I knew from home but nevertheless, interesting to witness.

That night, I was lying on an air mattress in Burak's apartment. I was dead tired, but there were so many thoughts in my head that I couldn't fall asleep.

Would my knee ever get better? Where should I go after the Philippines when I had used my last plane ticket? Would I stand a chance competing at the World Championships in California, or should I just skip it?

I enjoyed the fast pace traveling, only staying a few days each place, but on the other hand, if I got injured, I would quickly miss out on training opportunities like I'd done in Istanbul.

CHAPTER EIGHT

I Will Never Talk to You Again

I was eleven years old, coming home from a trip to the neighboring town with my mother and little brother. It was sunny, and I remember we hadn't been to school that summer day. My brother and I sat in the little hallway and took off our shoes while our mother unloaded the grocery bags from her bicycle.

The letter was on the table, my mother's name written in my father's beautiful handwriting.

He had worked as a sign painter before technology took over, and I had spent years trying to emulate his graceful strokes with a pen.

I knew immediately that something was not right. My mother was sitting on the couch in the living room, reading the handwritten letter on the already creased paper between her nervous fingers. She was trying hard not to cry, but she couldn't hide it from me.

"Go play some football in the garden, boys," she said.

My little brother was three years younger than me and too young to know that something was going on. I knew that I had to get my hands on that letter and find out what it was about. I had my suspicions, but it was hard to believe it could be real. From the garden, I observed my mother through the windows to our living room, crying. I saw her hide the letter on top of our tallest cupboard.

I wasn't stupid. I crawled up to grab it later when no one was in the living room. Then I sneaked it out to the green tiled bathroom, locked the door with the little metal hatch that had always safely hid me from the world, and sat down to read it.

"Dear Eva. This is very hard for me to write."

The tears of my mother had landed on some of the letters and faded them. My father wanted a divorce. He had met someone else and was too much of a coward to tell it to her face.

From that moment on, it was all over. The first crack had been made in the dam holding our family together. It was the end of our perfect life as we knew it.

I was in my bed as my father got home from work in the evening. I could hear my mother cry and scream at him from downstairs. He was trying to calm her down.

He walked up the stairs and slowly opened the door to my room, whispering to see if I was still awake.

I lay under my blanket, staring into the wall.

I hated him. I knew exactly what this meant. We would have to move out of the house, maybe even go to another school and start all over. I loved my life, my family, and our home. Now, he had ruined everything.

Despite my young age, I was completely aware of the situation and what I intended to do about it. I wanted him to feel the pain. He shouldn't get away with this without tasting the bitter consequences of his actions. The most powerful thing I could do was to rip his own son out of his life.

"These are the last words you will ever hear me say to you," I said inside my head.

Then I told him out loud.

He sat down on the edge of my little bed and tried to tell me something. I hid under my duvet and screamed at him to get out of my room.

And so it was. I never said a word to him again.

It all seemed to happen very fast. Everything fell apart that summer. My mother almost attempted to take her own life and was admitted to a closed psychiatric department. She'd lost so much weight and cried so much that I couldn't recognize her anymore. There was also a lawsuit, but I don't remember much of it. It was pretty bad. My father tried to talk to me, but I ignored him and never answered.

Many of my classmates' parents were getting divorced in those years, and it was often hard on the kids. I think the one I went through was definitely on the rougher side of the scale. Of course, compared to the lives of children all over the world, living with poverty, war, hunger, and disease, it was nothing. But in my reality as a kid, it was tough, and it affected me a lot.

I couldn't concentrate in school. I had always done my homework and was way ahead of everyone else in class. When I finished kindergarten, I had solved the last math book in a series that was going all the way to the seventh grade, but it all fell apart, and I paid no attention to what went on in class anymore. I didn't do my homework, and in the breaks between classes, I just sat and looked out the window or drew on a piece of paper. I was completely introverted—often disappearing into some impossibly complicated piece of programming code on my computer—and didn't have any connection to the world around me. My classmates could feel it too. I was alienating myself, and they saw my life take a turn for the worse.

My brother and I lived with my grandmother for a while. For every day that went by, where I saw my mother sink deeper and deeper into depression, the hatred towards my father grew.

The house I loved so deeply—our home—was being sold. It physically hurt inside of me the day my mother told me that someone had finally bought it. She couldn't afford it alone on her low salary as a secretary.

There were only villas in the town we lived in, and we didn't have anywhere near the money needed to buy any of them. Eventually we found a small, shared house, right across the road from the forest. It had a little garden with a pond, and for the first time, we felt like something positive was coming our way. It was a stroke of luck that no one had bought it before us. My mother was smiling and so was I. My little brother was smiling too. It was just few hundred meters from our old house, a stone's throw from the school and the forest I loved so much. I had already planned where I would put my bedroom furniture.

Then it all fell to the ground again. After we had signed the contract, we found out the roof was full of mold, and the deal had to be canceled. The real estate agent had known all about it but still tried to sell it to us, well aware that we would have to move out within the near future and replace the roof. He knew we were weak, desperate, and he was trying to take advantage of us. It was pure luck that we found out in time, as it would have been a financial catastrophe for us.

It looked like we would have to move to an apartment in another town. It was the worst case scenario for me. Not only were we moving out of my childhood home, my brother and I would also have to go to another school and move away from all our friends. In that age, it was the worst thing I could ever imagine. And it was all entirely my father's fault.

We couldn't find anywhere to live and had to ask for help at the social office. My mother had yelled at them, so everyone in the waiting room could hear that she was under no circumstances moving her kids to another town. I never told her, or anyone else, but I was grateful that she fought so hard for that.

With a stroke of luck, and at the last possible minute before we were put on the street, we managed to get a tiny apartment in the small town we loved so much. There wasn't much room for the three of us, but at least we could stay in the same school and still only be a bicycle ride away from our friends.

I was crying as I lay down to sleep the first night in the new place. I had gotten a new bed; it didn't smell right.

There was only one bedroom, and my mother and brother slept there too. All three of us cried as the lights were switched off that very first night. It must have been horrible for her.

I missed our family and old house so much. I couldn't understand how my father could do this to us. I was in complete disbelief at where things had ended. My life had been so perfect, and in the blink of an eye, it had all vanished. I could never go back.

My brother was still little, and my mother wasn't much stronger than him, mentally or physically. I was the man of the house, doing all the stuff that my father had used to do. I fixed the TV, installed the electrical devices, carried heavy stuff up the stairs, and put together our new, bland furniture from IKEA.

My mother was working hard to make our daily life run smoothly. She was struggling with her own problems and at the same time, trying to fill out the role of two parents for me and my brother. We couldn't afford a car, and I remember her coming home, pale and tired, with the bicycle full of plastic bags with groceries. One day, she crashed it and punctured her liver, nearly killing her. The doctors said that she only survived because she was in good shape from running. I was glad that I didn't lose her there and can't even begin to imagine the consequences that would have had on our lives.

My brother was a bit too young to really understand everything that was going on, I think. He just kind of followed quietly along with everything and was seeing my father every second weekend, waiting for him out on the street Friday afternoons. I didn't want to look out the window in case I would catch a glimpse of him. I didn't want anything to do with him. There was never a nice vibe in the air when my brother came home those Sunday evenings. My mother was always half sad, half angry and I guess my brother felt guilty that he—as the only one—still saw my father. It saddened me very much that he should have to bear those difficulties on his shoulders. He was just a kid who was suddenly caught between two parents in a tough situation.

We were relatively poor, my mother was depressed, and every now and then, adults around me would ask me how I felt. I went to see a psychologist, but she couldn't get a word out of me—it became almost a sport for me to refuse talking. That way, I felt powerful and in control.

"It would be healthy for you to talk to someone about how you feel, Christian."

I heard that so often, but I wasn't interested. I wanted to show everyone that I could do things on my own. I had made the decision not to see my father and was determined to prove to myself and everyone else that I was strong enough to handle the pressure that came along.

"I don't have a dad anymore," was the only thing I told those who attempted talking with me.

Along the way, it eventually became clear to me that I was sliding in the wrong direction. I was keeping a lot of anger inside and dark clouds had started to gather over me as I locked myself more and more into my own little world. I began to see how the person I had expected to become faded away. I no longer knew what I would end up like, and it scared me.

So I decided to fight it.

I wouldn't let the emotions, the anger, get to me. I wouldn't allow it to control my thoughts or my actions. I was deeply hurt, and it would be easy for me to project that into bad behavior or to shut everybody out. I was going to do things differently and I started to work on keeping the tsunami of emotions far away, not letting them affect my mind.

The ambitious plans I had lain down for my life were not going to be ruined by my selfish father. I wanted to make something out of it, not get sucked into depression and lack of confidence like I had seen happen to other kids in school.

My life would be exactly as amazing as I had imagined it to be.

I felt a strong determination inside me to pull myself together and do something with my life; to crawl back out of that black hole I was about to fall into. A combination of anger and determination set my mind on a straight line towards the goals I had set for myself. I wanted to create opportunities for myself in life. If I leaned back and hoped for the best, I was afraid that I would get pulled back into realizing my new, scary, unknown destiny. Instead, I developed a powerful focus on long term planning and creating a life of independence, freedom, and opportunities to do what I wanted to—the very same focus that drives my everyday work as an adult.

Twice a week, I caught a ride to training in the neighboring town. There was a big, happy Taekwondo-family with three kids and a big dog. Everyone was going to training, crammed into their refreshingly dirty black Volvo. One of the kids was the youngest black belt ever in the country. He was always competing and winning the Danish Championship every year. I admired his courage and confidence. He was usually a calm boy, but I guess he one day had enough of being bullied and kicked another kid in the head during football practice. It wasn't too good.

Myself, I had competed just once when I was about ten years old. A kid with a green belt back-kicked me in the stomach, so I lost all my air. I still remember the pain, when my entire body seemed to retract in one big cramp. I had a tunnel vision and the helmet strapped around my chin made me feel like I couldn't breathe. I was crying in the corner when my trainer lifted my arms over my head to try and open up my lungs. The emotions were overwhelming.

It wasn't a nice experience, and I quickly decided that it wasn't anything for me.

Since I didn't give a shit about being like my father anymore, I was looking for something else to pursue in my training. Getting kicked in the stomach wasn't doing it for me. One of the older kids was going to a forms tournament and convinced me to join him. Three judges gave points for a choreographed series of movements, just like ice skating or talent shows on TV. I won the Danish Championships in front of thirty other kids the first time I tried it.

When I got that first gold medal around my neck, I remember thinking that it was a much more fun way of competing than getting beat up.

My new focus in training became a way for me to channel all the pain, sorrow and anger out of my life. I put more determination and power into every session than I'd ever done before. When I had seen my mother cry, or the sad look on my poor, brother's face when he got home from spending the weekend at my father's place, I got all of that out on the wooden floors. Every time I kicked the pads, it was with grinding teeth and white knuckles. I remember some of the kids were afraid to hold pads for me in case they caught me on a bad day. I really got things out of my system that way.

Even though it had absolutely zero resemblance to actual fighting skills against a resisting opponent, I found an interest in training for the forms tournaments. The same movements were being practiced again and again to absolute perfection. If a certain kick wasn't high enough, I would stretch every day to make it easier to perform. The sports halls with the cold floors were completely silent when I and the other competitors stepped onto the mat for the finals. I didn't win every time, but I usually always reached the final rounds. There, I would have to show the most difficult form I knew while everyone was watching.

I certainly did not learn how to fight, but there was a ton of practice in concentration, immersion, focus, and performing under a lot of pressure.

Training was an efficient way for me to get rid of the bad things in my head and focus on the healthy stuff instead. I was a troubled kid and often wonder what kind of person I would have become if I didn't have that vent to let all that stuff out.

Every summer, when the the beech bursts into leaf and the whole forest is neon green, I take the train out there with my mountain bike. The quiet beauty is just like I remember it from my childhood—leaves whispering in the wind, the sun filtered by the tree tops, and little branches cracking under my feet.

I always drive down through the small town, turning the corner on the little street with the green hedge and the red brick house. I would give everything to sit in that garden again and smell the grass between my fingers; to touch the sloping walls of my room; feel the steps of the wooden staircase; smell the walls of the basement; and just one more time, look out at the garden from the living room.

Every summer since the divorce, I've been standing there on that street with my bicycle. I never find the courage to ring the doorbell.

CHAPTER NINE

India

At home, I had done my best to try to search out Jiu Jitsu academies in the most unlikely places. It was difficult to do online, but I managed to find a very simple website from India with sparse information about a gym and thought it would really be a different place to travel for training. I sent them an email and got a short answer back that I was welcome and just needed to let them know when I would land. That was it.

It was a long shot, but I booked the ticket from Turkey to Mumbai and sent them my itinerary. I'd had lots of thoughts about how it would be to train with people there. The only thing I had seen was a group photo of some mean looking Indian dudes in an old gym. Now, I was actually going there, and there was no way back.

At the passport control, the immigration officer was looking thoroughly at the little visa sticker I had gotten from the Indian embassy back home. Never really knowing what else to write, I had written "sports coach" as profession.

A few years earlier, as I was entering the United States on a different trip, the immigration officer was a very seriously looking American guy in uniform.

"What kind of sports is it you are coaching?" he asked me as he checked my arrival form.

"It is something similar to wrestling or judo," I replied as I usually do, not feeling like explaining about Brazilian Jiu Jitsu to people who don't train themselves.

"I will ask you once more," he said with no sign of facial expression, "what kind of sports are you coaching?"

"It's called Brazilian Jiu Jitsu, sir."

He paused for a few seconds, flipping through my passport.

"Please look to the right."

I didn't know why he wanted me to do that, but he seemed so serious that I thought it would be best to just do whatever he asked me.

"And to the left."

There was a pause again.

"Cauliflower ears are looking good. BJ Penn or GSP?"

"BJ Penn, sir"

He handed me the passport back with a grin.

"Welcome to the United States of America. Enjoy your stay."

It was my first long, overnight flight with a time difference. My brain was confused as I woke up in the afternoon in a little bedroom in the middle of Mumbai. Strange smells and sounds were coming from behind the white curtains that were moving gently in the wind. A woman I didn't know came in with a cup of tea. She told me that someone had come to pick me up and was waiting for me downstairs.

And there I suddenly was, hardly awake, on the back of a motorcycle in India, driving on a dirt road through a small market filled with people, animals, children, and vehicles. I felt like I had been teleported from the dark, cold, and snowy Istanbul, directly to the back of the motorcycle in the burning hot Indian sun, as if all the traveling and sleep in between had not existed.

People were, on average, about an hour late for the class I was teaching. It was a different culture than at home, where I would be annoyed at someone being ten minutes late for my class and miss out on the warm up drills. In some way, I enjoyed that people didn't seem to be in a hurry with anything, and with the temperature that day there was no need to warm up anyways.

Alan and Jitendra, the two coaches, introduced me to everyone. It was a very mixed group of guys, both age- and size wise. I had no idea as to what level they were or what to teach. After some body mechanics drills for warm up, I had them roll to see what they could do. Alan seemed like he had a pretty good game, and I spotted a few others around the mat that had some skills. They were still beginners, and it was obvious that they lacked some solid fundamentals to build their game on so I taught a class on holding the mount position.

My knee was still somewhat hurting, but I had run out of patience and had to go a few rounds. It seemed like the guys were all on a level where I could control the pace of the roll and not jeopardize my knee with any surprise moves from my partner that I did not see coming.

It was a pleasure to roll again, and the knee held up fine. Alan was talented, but he obviously lacked higher level guys to roll with on a regular basis. I iced up my knee after class and crossed my fingers that I hadn't done any additional damage to it that day.

There were six or seven people from the gym going out for dinner that evening, and we parked the car outside a building with a few restaurants inside. Tons of motorbikes were parked around us and hundreds of people were running around the streets, in and out between the cars with drivers trying to find parking lots. It was hectic and noisy. Walking up the stairs to the restaurant, the atmosphere changed. It was warm; people were chatting at tables; the light was dimmed and there was a wonderful smell of spices and herbs in the air.

The food was as good as I could imagine. Even though it was my first day in India, I almost felt sad because I knew I would have to leave that food less than a week later.

"I don't like the company of that animal," Mastveer said when he was offered a goat curry.

He was a huge guy who had grown up in Sweden and now lived in India. He had an impressive beard, a gold chain around his neck, and lots of tattoos, including a machine gun on one of his arms. He looked like a hardcore gangster, but when he opened his mouth, I couldn't stop laughing. His razor sharp Scandinavian sarcasm was completely out of place in India but right up my street.

It was difficult to find rest in the warm bedroom with all the impressions, not to mention jet lag. I had only been to five countries so far, but still my head was exploding with the thoughts of everything I had experienced. Falling asleep was really going to take some practice.

After working out in the morning with giant Indian bodybuilders and going for a swim in a pool, Alan and I went to his apartment to wait a few hours before we had to leave for Nashik, another city roughly four hours out of Mumbai. We took the elevator to the ninth floor, where he lived with two others. A guy, who Alan introduced as his brother, was sitting in the sofa, watching a movie on a big screen TV with the volume turned up really loud.

I was tired from working out all morning and sat down in a comfortable chair by the window. Looking out, I could see what seemed like an endless, dust-colored city. Construction workers were sitting on a scaffolding outside a building, having a break. It was put together by what looked to be bamboo sticks and rope. They were at least as high up as I was on the ninth floor, sitting there with no safety harness on a wobbly wooden scaffold.

Alan was about to take a nap and had put out a mattress for me as well. Thinking about the long drive to Nashik in the evening and the training next day, I decided it would be a good idea to get a little rest. I lay down on the thin mattress by the window on the hard, tile floor in Alan's room.

I asked Alan about his family, and he told me his story. When he was a young wrestler, all he dreamed about was to become a fighter. His parents had other plans with him and wanted him to marry and get an education. They ended up presenting him with an ultimatum. If he chose to pursue a career as a fighter, they would not accept him as their son anymore.

So he left.

He had nowhere to go until his coach Daniel took him in as one of his own. Since then, they have been living together for sixteen years in Nashik. In the weekdays, he went to Mumbai to teach and stay in the apartment. He had found a new family that accepted him.

"I don't share blood with those people in my life, but I consider them to be my real family", he said.

The whole thing was hard for me to grasp. I was coming from a privileged world where I could basically pick and choose whatever I wanted in life and not having to sacrifice much for it. Alan had given up everything to follow his dream. I was amazed by his determination—especially living in a country with so little opportunities to become a professional fighter.

With a gentle and peaceful aura and always a smile on his face, Alan didn't look anything like a fighter on the outside. If I didn't know it, I would never have guessed that he had given up his biological family for a career of training.

I lay there in the silence, thinking about what he had just told me. There had been a pause in the conversation for a while, and Alan had fallen asleep. He was snoring. A pleasant breeze from the window touched my face gently. The buzz from the dusty city, nine floors below, seemed so distant. My eyes got heavy and I felt like there was no other place in the world I could be more comfortable or relaxed at that very moment than right there on the thin mattress in a Mumbai apartment.

We woke up late in the afternoon when Jitendra came to pick us up. We were filling up the car before driving to Nashik. I had been looking forward to see some of the countryside, but it became dark early, so I missed it. The guys were telling jokes in the car all the way. I was really tired and didn't say much, but it felt nice to be with them.

They spoke a strange mix of some local Indian language and English with a heavy Indian accent. I understood most of it, although sometimes I really had to concentrate. During a stop at a gas station, Jitendra was telling me a joke where the crucial punch line word was "rubber," and he had to repeat it to me about ten times before I understood it through all the rolling r's. At that point, the joke was kind of dead.

The traffic was insane. People were overtaking like they were suicidal. Apparently, a driver's license only cost a few dollars to get. A few bucks more, and you can skip the test, Jitendra told me, as everybody laughed.

I wished I had time to go and get an Indian driver's license. With the price of a driver's license and cars in Denmark, I hadn't gotten one yet. Having an official Indian license with photo and everything would be the coolest ID I could possibly have for getting into night clubs and picking up packages at the post office.

Nashik was a small city about four hours outside of Mumbai. Small cities in India hold the population of half an average Scandinavian country: This one over two million people! It was so spread out that it didn't feel like a big city, but just like everywhere else I had been in India, it was packed with people.

We arrived late in the evening at Daniel's house, a former kickboxing champion that had now created MMA gyms in both Mumbai and Nashik, organizing competitions and managing fighters from around the country. Alan was his most talented and successful student.

It was a big house, and I had a whole room almost to myself, only sharing it with a handful of mosquitoes. I hadn't given malaria much of a thought on the trip so far, but it was hard not to think about it just a little bit at that point. I had decided not to take the expensive pills to prevent it, so I was completely vulnerable to being infected. The large fan in the ceiling sounded like an old propeller airplane. I put in my earplugs and covered my head with the blanket. It was quiet. I couldn't hear the fan and the mosquitoes couldn't get to me. A strategy game on my phone diverted my thoughts from all the stuff going on in my head about how the rest of the trip would unfold.

Five hours later, I was woken up and told that we were going to the gym. I couldn't believe it; I needed at least double that to recover from all the traveling and training. While the Indian people never seemed to hurry with anything, they were suddenly in a hurry to get to the gym early in the morning.

I felt so tired when we got to there. It was on the first floor of a building on a busy road in the city. Posters of the Indian fighters were plastered all over the walls, and the facilities were nicer than I had expected when I sat at home a few months earlier trying to imagine how training in India would be.

Alan was teaching an early class, but I couldn't keep my eyes open.

Daniel asked if I wanted to take a nap in the office. I saw it more as an extension of my night's sleep than a nap. He had a thin cotton mattress I laid down on the tile floor of the small office. I fell asleep immediately. All the noise from the street outside made me dream that I was lying on the backseat of a taxi, driving around town, because it was a much cheaper place to sleep than in a hotel room.

A lot of people had showed up for my class in the evening, and I was feeling like I could go lots of rounds of sparring. My knee felt pretty good, and I went a few rounds with some very skilled guys, both big and small. I had considered giving some of them blue belts, but despite having trained very hard, they had only been going at it for about a year and a half without real instruction. They definitely had the level, but they also planned to go competing in the future so I thought it would be better to wait and accumulate a bit of experience as white belts first.

Alan had a beautiful classic motorbike that we drove home on. It was similar to the one I had been picked up with on the first morning in Mumbai. It was a long drive back to the house from the gym but I enjoyed every second of it. It was late in the evening and the streetlight was sparse, as in non-existant. The traffic and amount of people in the streets was much less intense at that point, and I could just lean back and enjoy the ride. Alan drove at a nice, slow pace. There was no hurry. The air was hot and dry. All I could hear was the smooth sound of the engine, the little clicks when the gears were changed with perfect timing, and the song of the cicadas coming from the bush around the dusty street. We drove past one area after another with small, simple houses built out of whatever people had been able to find. Occasionally, light would come out from the cracks in the walls and hit the street in front of us. The smell of steamed rice was in the air.

I admired Alan very much for what he was doing. He had all the odds against him and still, he worked so hard towards becoming a professional MMA fighter.

We had driven out of the city. There was no light on the street other than what came from the motorbike. No other cars or people around us. It was dark, and there were no houses there. The warm air blew gently in my face. I was far, far away from home, but it felt nothing like that. I was completely relaxed and didn't think a second about being anywhere else.

Alan put his hand out before making a left turn, and I asked him why he didn't use the indicator.

He told me that in India, no one uses the indicator. So if he turned it on, people would just think he was crazy and then ignore it.

"If it was invented in India, it would have been abandoned right away as a useless device," he explained while laughing.

In the morning, Daniel had ordered a taxi for me to take me to the airport. It was a four-hour drive, and would cost me around fifteen dollars—it was the best taxi deal I had gotten so far on the trip and probably in my life. When it arrived, the taxi driver was obviously disappointed to see me. He had expected a local guy, so he had charged local price. If he knew I was a tourist, it would have cost ten times as much.

There was trash all over the streets. People just threw it there and eventually, someone would gather it and set it on fire to get some heat. These were the filthiest streets I had ever seen in my life. A woman washed clothes outside her little house while five goats slept on the sidewalk next to her. A tiny barbershop was full, having two costumers sitting in chairs getting haircuts. The hand- painted sign on the wall must have been fifty years old, and I could barely make out the word "BARBER" from the flakes of paint that desperately clung to it. A dead dog was lying in the middle of the street, and no one seemed to care. They just drove around it, like nothing had happened. The taxi driver was just as reckless in his driving as everyone else, and I held on to the seatbelt with white knuckles every time he did one of his patented overtakes from hell. At least, if I survived the traffic in India, I could survive the traffic anywhere in the world.

I needed a break from the high pace traveling and all the hustle and bustle of the big cities in India and Turkey. I had originally planned to go to Kuala Lumpur, but I just didn't have the energy for yet another crowded place. I had to get away for a few days and recharge my batteries before moving on.

I looked at a few of my favorite backpacking sites to try and find a place to go near Kuala Lumpur. There was a small group of islands only a short flight and boat ride away that looked exotic and relaxing. I decided to ditch the big city—even though I had been looking forward to seeing the Petrona towers—and spend a few days on a beach instead. It was the first time I strayed off my original travel plan and was more spontaneous. The feeling of freedom to go anywhere I wanted with a few days' notice was great. The Philippines—my last planned destination—was closing in, and I started to look forward to see what spontaneous decisions would come after that and just how far I could go planning everything on the road.

CHAPTER TEN

Malaysia

Coming straight from busy India, my body thanked me for taking a break and sunk into a deep state of relaxation as I leaned back on the boat, closed my eyes, and let the sun hit my face.

I spent three days on the island without doing much. Most of the time, I hung out with three Brits on the beach whom I had shared a taxi with from the airport, or lay in a hammock with a view over the sea and read a book. It was really nice to forget about Jiu Jitsu for a few days and just recharge my batteries in the sun. My knee agreed.

The waves picked up one of the days, and I rented a body board to try it out. It was difficult, and the current was really strong. When I later lay on my towel on the beach, I saw someone getting pulled out to sea and saved by locals, who swam out after him.

In the evening, I was sitting on the beach in one of the two bars on the island, and I met the local lifeguard. He was a short, skinny Rastafarian guy, who had lived his entire life on the island. He had 19-year-old, thick, heavy dreadlocks all the way down to his butt. If I wasn't in Asia, I would think he was from Jamaica.

They looked like an impractical accessory for being a lifeguard and having to jump in the water every day. He blew out the smoke from his joint and told me about how stupid people were, panicking in the currents instead of just floating and waiting for the sea to take them back to shore again.

He painted with his finger in the sand how the waves and currents worked. I never knew anything about that and found it quite interesting. Being in the ocean had always scared me, and with an idea in the back of my mind of trying to surf sometime on the trip, I thought I'd better learn as much about this stuff as possible.

Drying the dreadlocks took a whole day, so if someone was calling for help, he would first shout to them to relax or swim parallel to the beach. Only if they started swallowing water would he bother jumping in and saving them. I was glad I hadn't been sucked out earlier that day on my body board.

The waves were still high in the evening when we were sitting on the beach and looking at the stars. One guy told me that it was usually calm, but since the Tohoku earthquake in Japan—the most powerful known to have ever hit the country—there had been abnormally large waves coming in.

Japan.

I still had half an appointment with my old friend Ryan to visit him there, but the natural disaster had probably put a stop to that. I reminded myself to check out the news to see how everything was looking.

After a three day break in paradise, I packed up my backpack and headed back with the boat. It was a great feeling to have gone somewhere unplanned. I had feared ending up being alone there, but that had far from been the case, and I gained a few points in social confidence. Back on the mainland, I didn't think twice about asking people at the harbor to share a taxi to the airport and ended up with an American guy in a very old, wrecked car. Both our flights were three hours delayed, and we spent the time playing on his guitar in the airport together with a guy that looked—and played—like he could be some sort of an Asian Jon Bon Jovi.

It was late when I arrived in Kuching airport in Borneo, and the humidity hit me as soon as I stepped out of the building.

Albert had emailed me many months earlier about his little gym there, and now I was standing alone in a parking lot on a late evening in Borneo, trying to guess what he looked like. The white t-shirt with blue "South East Asia BJJ" print on it blew his cover.

He took me out to get some food in an outdoor market and then to a small hotel, where he had booked a room for me. A big, nice king-size bed, bathroom, and a TV all to myself. After sleeping in a falling apart, five-dollar-a-night bungalow on the island, a real hotel room with a real bed felt like heaven. I couldn't wait to get a full night's sleep and be rested for training the next day.

It turned out to be one of the worst nights of my trip.

I woke up two hours after falling asleep, feeling dizzy and nauseous. I could feel the grease of the barbecue sauce as a lump in my throat, and my stomach was turning.

Food poisoning.

When I left for the trip, there were a few things that I was mentally prepared to happen. I assumed that I would most likely get robbed, sick, lost, and get in a fight. So getting sick from food poisoning did not come as a surprise. However, it didn't make it any more fun.

A lot of people before and during the trip had been talking about how I would most likely get food poisoning in India or Turkey. In fact, everyone I had talked to who had been to India had gotten sick there. I went straight through those places with not a single problem, eating only local food and gaining a lot of confidence in my hardcore stomach's game. Getting through India felt like an accomplishment. I had just proved that it was possible and I didn't have to be afraid of street food.

One day out of India, and hell broke loose.

It was horrible to be alone that night, feeling so bad. I missed my girlfriend and my own bed. Everything seemed to make me feel bad. The mess of my backpack caused my brain to overflow with stress. Just grabbing the water bottle on the table next to the bed felt like an impossible task. The whole room was spinning and I had to run to the toilet again and again. Deep inside, I knew that it would pass and I would enjoy being on the road again, but at that point, for the first time, I really wished I were just at home.

After a long and tough night, I felt a bit better the next morning as Albert picked me up. The nausea had almost passed, but my stomach was still rumbling.

Albert's gym was beautiful. Big windows from floor to ceiling surrounded a large, matted area. The windows stood wide open, and the warm, tropical air flowed through the room. Being on the second floor, the top of lush, tropical trees and blue sky dominated the view from the mats, where people rolled.

I weighed myself on the scale. Only 77 kilos and I had just drunk four liters of water. The food poisoning was hard on my body. Training was difficult. My brain was working in slow motion and I was catching my breath every time I had been demonstrating a move that normally would demand no effort. I felt dizzy and had to run to the toilet every fifteen minutes.

It was a small group of guys, who all seemed dedicated to learn Jiu Jitsu. Albert was the only blue belt; everyone else wore white around their waist. I only had energy for one round of rolling and went with Ivan, originally from Hungary but who was now teaching English in Borneo. He had been a white belt for three years, and his game was solid. Everyone else in the class had stopped to watch the roll, and as we finished off the round, they all clapped. I did my best to hold everything in and not run to the bathroom till at least a few seconds after they stopped clapping. It would have been a weird scene to run out there while being applauded.

I bought some food in a small supermarket on the way back to the hotel. I was looking forward to relaxing and feeling a little better. I lay down on the bed, turned on the TV, and unwrapped the chicken sandwich I had bought for myself. My stomach was empty and my body felt drained from having been so sick. I took a bite and immediately felt my stomach turn. It was the same sauce as the hot wings that made me sick. I spat it out, emptied the bottle of juice in a few seconds, and in desperation, filled my mouth with a whole pack of chewing gum, in an attempt to press the reset button on my taste buds. I gave up on the cozy evening I had hoped for and, disheartened, decided just to go to sleep instead.

We were going on a kayak tour the next day, Albert and I. I packed a lot of diarrhea pills. Despite it having rained a lot the night before, the weather was perfect that morning. The sky was a bright blue and not a single gust of wind could be felt. We had two kayaks, one for me and Albert, and one for the guide. We were the only ones doing the trip that day, and it felt like we had the whole jungle ourselves.

We paddled out in the shallow, quiet river, the kayak floating slowly through the water. The rain from the night before had upped the flow of the water just perfectly, so most of the time, we didn't even have to paddle but could just sit and steer. It felt like the river took us on a guided tour through the dense jungle. There were a rustling sounds from the trees around us, but I couldn't see any animals. I am sure they were watching us closely, though.

Sometimes, Albert and I talked about life, training, and traveling. Other times, we were quiet for what seemed like an hour, just taking in the impressions around us and the loud silence of nature.

I stopped paddling and leaned back, almost lying down. I looked up at the trees above my head that moved past me quietly. There wasn't a single human-made sound around us, and I felt at one with nature. I let go of the past and future and found myself lost in the moment. It took an effort to understand that I was actually sailing on a river in Borneo's jungle at that very moment. My idea of traveling and seeing, experiencing, touching, smelling the world at first row was happening right there. In a parallel universe, another version of myself—that hadn't made the brave decision to break out and travel the world—was waiting for the train on his way to work on a cold, gray, and rainy April morning.

Training was much better that evening. I was teaching a class again and only had to run to the bathroom every half hour at that point. The nausea was almost gone, but I was still low on energy. Finally, I got to roll with Albert. He had a great game for a blue belt—very fluid and technical. With his smaller size and my food poisoning, we were almost equal on the mats. Rolling with constant focus on whether or not I had to run to the bathroom was difficult, but I was desperate to do something and with such short time for my visit, I didn't want to sit on the sideline, watching.

Everyone in the little gym was always laughing and joking and it seemed like they were such good friends. It reminded me of my friends in my gym at home. I missed hanging out with them every day like these guys did. I was left with hanging out with new friends every week instead of the old ones. Both were good, but I was also looking forward to be back home on my own mats. It would have to wait a few more months.

The effect of the pills I had taken for the jungle trip was really wearing out, and my evening at the hotel became more desperate than I had hoped for. I really wanted it to be over, but it seemed like the diarrhea had picked up and became worse than ever. Luckily, I wasn't nauseous or throwing up any longer, but sitting in the toilet that evening had to be on my top three list of most intense defecation experiences of my life. Number one was in Jamaica.

Hands down.

After a two week trip with my friend in Mexico in 2008, he was going home and I was going to New York to train for ten days. A few days before we had to split ways, I was looking at the weather forecast for Manhattan. It was twelve degrees Celsius and raining every day. Going home to the beginning of a Scandinavian winter didn't sound very appealing, so to much despair of my bank account, I made a quick decision to visit to Cuba and Jamaica instead.

I spent Halloween in Havana with two Norwegian guys—as probably the only ones celebrating it, even dressed up as Cubans with hats, cigars, Mojitos, and the works—then a week alone in a small hut on the edge of a cliff in the Jamaican jungle. It was built from bamboo sticks, had an outdoor bathtub right next to a 30-meter straight drop off the cliff to the ocean. An outdoor bathroom was complete with shower, sink, and toilet, but no roof. The door was a blanket and it took a few days to get accustomed to the sounds of the jungle in the night, but after that, I felt completely at home and slept like a baby. In the mornings, I sat naked in the bathtub, looking at the sun rise in the horizon over the sea. Making a spontaneous decision to spend a week there instead of rainy Manhattan was one of the best things I had ever done to myself, and it was the first baby steps I made towards being comfortable in non-planned travels. It just made sense to do it.

One night, it had been raining quite a bit when I went to bed. In the middle of the night, it had turned into a full on tropical storm. I was woken up by rain that was blowing horizontally through the cracks in the bamboo wall of my hut and straight into my face. For a second, I was confused about where I was, being woken up like that with rain in my face and the sound of a roaring storm over my head. I could move away from the wall a bit so I didn't get more wet, and from there just lie and listen to nature's violence ripping through the jungle around me. Thunderclouds were coming in from the ocean outside the hut, and flashes of lightening lit up the hut, coming through the cracks of the walls and the front door where the carpet was blowing around in the wind.

I was sleeping in the nude; both because it was really warm but also because being so isolated and alone, it didn't really make sense to wear clothes anyways. As I had lain in bed listening to the storm for a while, I noticed that I had to go to the toilet. It felt a bit urgent and quite heavy. I could hear raindrops the size of walnuts hit the outdoor bathroom and initially thought it would have to wait till the next morning when the rain had stopped. Then I realized that it might be one of those once in a lifetime opportunities.

I gathered the courage to crawl out of the elevated bed and stood naked in the doorway, looking out on the toilet. I almost couldn't see it from the dense rain, even though it was just a few meters in front of me. The wind was brutal and throwing the trees above the bathroom around. It looked like they could snap anytime, but I guessed that they had many storms in the area and the trees were still stood there for a reason. My short hair was pushed back by the wind. I was still a bit dry, but was about to change that. There was no need to run to the toilet. I would get completely soaked, no matter what.

And then I sat there, naked on the porcelain toilet with my bare feet on the small rocks and branches on the ground. The rain had drenched me in seconds and I almost couldn't see out of my eyes. I was shivering, the trees above me were roaring, the wind was whining and the thunder right over my head was as loud as a bomb attack.

"IS THIS ALL YOU GOT??!!!", I felt like shouting to the sky while raising my clenched fist.

I was experiencing the ultimate rage of nature while taking a tremendous dump, naked, in the middle of the night in a Jamaican jungle.

When I finally got back inside the little hut, I curled up in the fetal position on the bed with a towel around me, shivering from the adrenaline pumping through my veins from the powerful experience I just had. What a rush.

CHAPTER ELEVEN

Singapore

I had talked to Jonathan from Kauai Kimonos for over a year about my trip. He had been excited to sponsor me and we had been on Skype numerous times to talk about the design of my gis. I had never actually met him in real life, but now he was waiting for me in Singapore airport. He lived in Bali but was traveling around Asia for business and had made sure to be in Singapore to hang out with me.

We met up in the arrivals hall. Erik and Liam, my two friends from home who were supposed to meet us there, were nowhere to be found. An hour or so later, there was still no sign of them. Their phones were off, so I assumed they had run out of battery and gotten too tired of waiting for us. Singapore is a small place, so we could find them later.

We took the train to the city and sat on a bench at a small burger place. I was still badly dehydrated from being sick in

Borneo, and the diarrhea pills made me nauseous. The city looked really nice and clean, and tall skyscrapers of glass and mirrors surrounded us. It was like a cleaner, tropical New York.

Jonathan spotted a tall, Brazilian guy walking past us in the crowd and got up to catch up with him. It was Gordinho, one of the instructors at the Evolve gym.

He shook my hand but didn't seem very friendly towards me. I was wearing a Brasa t-shirt I got from Turkey and wondered if there was some politics involved there. Or maybe it was just inside of my head.

He invited us to come train with the instructors in the noon class the next day. It sounded like a good opportunity to get tapped out, and we were not going to let that pass so we agreed to drop by.

A few hours later, Erik finally called back. They had given me the wrong dates and were still in Amsterdam. It sounded like they had just woken up from a mad party and were desperate to reach the airport in time.

Jonathan stayed at a friend's apartment. I would be staying with an old friend from Denmark. He was working and wasn't off work until the evening, so we had some time to kill. The place where Jonathan's friend lived had a pool, and we decided to jump in the water for a bit.

We sat by the pool and chatted for an hour. Jonathan had grown up in California, then moved to Hawaii and fallen in love with surfing. After having seen enough photos of Bali in surf magazines, he finally decided to move there permanently. That's where he set up a small factory producing super light rip stop gis, great for the warm, humid weather and easy to travel with. They fitted my trip perfectly.

Erik and Liam looked very tired from the long flight when they met me the next morning on the corner of an exceptionally clean street. I gave both of them a big hug. It was so nice to see someone from home, and I couldn't wait for them to join me on the adventures in Singapore and Bali. They had been playing a big part in the competition team I had set for the European Championships. Six months earlier, they had been hobbyist white belts, but joining the competition project, they had upped their training to a whole new level, and I was really proud to give them their well-deserved blue belts after the Europeans.

Now, they were taking their skills to the test in the big world, and I was eager to see them on the mats of the gyms we would visit. They were too tired to join in on the first training and decided just to watch and rest.

We were only eight guys on the mat. I read Gordinho, Brodinho, Ximbica, and Magrinho on the collars of the black belts' kimonos. I have never been following Jiu Jitsu competitions much, so at that point, I didn't know who they were. They looked at me with no facial expressions, making me suspect that I was in for a tough afternoon. I was right.

Mentally, I was struggling with the intimidation of being on the mat with the seasoned black belts. Physically, I was still low on energy after the food poisoning from Borneo. The diarrhea pills made me feel dizzy, but there was no room for whining. The least I could do was give it my best and not waste their time. After all, they had been kind enough to invite me to train for free with them.

After a short warm up, we went straight to the positional drills. Brodinho, one of the smaller guys, got in the top mount position on me. It was my job to try and escape, and his to submit me. We clapped hands. I tried with a little smile, but got no reaction back.

"Fuck, here we go," I thought to myself.

Immediately, he slammed on a cross face and squeezed my face with his chest. He was way smaller than me, but the power of his grip was immense. It felt like I had been falling through the ice on a winter lake and my body had gone into shock after hitting the freezing water. I tried to regain my focus, but all I could think of was how my nose was getting crushed by his chest, and that I didn't want it to break. I reached my hand up to defend my face, and it was just the mistake he had been waiting for. He trapped it with his arm and punched his fist into the muscle on the side of my neck. It was nowhere near being a choke, but the pressure on my nose and neck was so hard that it felt like my head was going to explode. I tapped out frenetically and realized that the whole thing had taken under four seconds.

We clapped hands, and I went to the back of the line at the wall. I didn't really want to be on the mats at that point, but I knew that it was training and experiences like that I would gain a lot from. I manned up and looked at the clock on the wall. It would be at least an hour more of beatings, and there was no way around it.

The rest of the training pretty much continued like it had begun. The Brazilians tried their best to end my life and I tried the best to survive. It was exactly like that TV show *Survivor man,* just with black belts instead of sharks or bears.

Ximbica, a big heavyweight with long, curly hair, went harder on me than any of them. It seemed like he was doing Jiu Jitsu as if he were weightlifting. Before every move, he accelerated his breathing and then exploded into a full speed, full power technique while shouting really loud. I started in mount top on him, and it was like sitting on a rodeo bull with a big count down timer and a giant spring in the seat. There were no surprise elements in his game. I knew exactly when he was going to explode, and there was nothing I could do about it but just enjoy the ride as I literally went flying through the air from his escape. It must have looked like a cartoon.

The strength, technique, and experience these guys possessed were light-years ahead of me, so it became an exercise in keeping calm under pressure. At home, I didn't have anyone to push me that much, so as the class progressed, it became more and more obvious to me that I was really getting a lot out of the beatings. My cardio felt fine, and I focused on defending, finding my happy place, and not panicking. There was no way I was going to succeed in any offensive moves against them anyways.

I tapped more times than I could count that day. At the end of the class, everyone was friendly. They were laughing and talking to me. Training was over—the lions had eaten.

I was glad that I had joined in on their small, closed class and I walked out of there with a few souvenirs. A big, black bruise on the nose—my first ever—and a nice, clear, red stamp of Brodinho's fist on the side of my neck, knuckles and all. My first training in Singapore was officially in the books.

There was no time to waste. After training, we had a quick lunch, then went on to the next gym and from there, directly to the third of the day, teaching a seminar to about thirty people in a crammed, boiling hot gym.

Singapore had been conquered in record time.

CHAPTER TWELVE

A New Beginning

My training in Taekwondo had first served as a way to follow the inspirational footsteps of my father, then later as a way to channelize my anger towards him. At seventeen, when I started in high school after finishing ninth grade, I hadn't seen him for six years, and the aching memories of the divorce seemed further and further away.

My mother had re-married, and we had all moved, together with her new husband and his daughter, into a beautiful, big house. It took me a little while to get used to not being the oldest man in the house, but my stepfather was a good man and a highly respected local politician for the Social Democrats. His views on life, society, and the people around him were similar to mine and inspired me a lot.

Life was easy again. Starting in a new school was fun, and I made a lot of friends. My fourteen-year-old little brother was growing up, and we enjoyed every single afternoon on the football field, pretending to be the superstars of the 1990s Manchester United team. For years, we played every day from the minute we got home from school until the sun went down. In the summer, we had half time dinner in the evening, then went out again and could play almost till midnight before it got too dark.

The anger towards my father and the pain he had caused us all had slowly faded into the background. I was even starting to consider forgiving him and maybe one day seeing him again.

With all the new things happening in my life, I was looking forward towards the future more than backwards towards the past. The therapeutic purpose of my training started to become irrelevant as I realized I had nothing I needed therapy for anymore. Then, other interests took more and more of my time, and eventually, I decided to quit after more than ten years of kicking pretty holes in the air.

I spent a year trying to balance party, sleep, and schoolwork without doing any exercise other than kicking a ball with my brother. He was playing in a club on an increasingly ambitious level, whereas I was more interested in just juggling around with the ball and hanging out with him. Eventually, I realized that my body was deteriorating from all the drinking and lack of sleep. I was tired of seeing myself going in the wrong direction physically, and I knew I needed to do some real training again.

When I started in high school, I was really skinny. At 17, I weighed only 63 kilos and stood 1.85 meters tall. Drinking at least once every week for a year hadn't helped the state of my body, and with the social pressure in that age, gaining some weight was something I wanted to do. With my usual methodical approach, I started reading everything I could find on bodybuilding online. Going to a gym didn't really appeal to me, so I cleaned out some furniture in my small room to fit a training bench that I had bought used online. Within a year, and with a lot of help from natural hormones in just the right age, I weighed 75 kilos and had finally rediscovered my passion for training and taking care of my body.

I was enjoying my new feeling of confidence from having gained weight, and it reminded me of how good I felt about myself when I trained Taekwondo. Lifting weights at home in my room became boring in the long run, and I started to think of other things I could do.

It didn't appeal to me to go back to Taekwondo, and having grown up with it the way I did, it was really the only martial arts to me. I knew about Judo, Karate, Kung Fu, and such, but the thought of actually trying it had never crossed my mind. It had nothing to do with a sense of pride or feeling that I was only supporting one style, my mind was simply hardwired to the strange fact that standing up and kicking was the only way to train martial arts…

Until one day, when I saw a flier in the local supermarket with a picture of Bruce Lee.

"Learn Jeet Kune Do, the scientific fighting art of Bruce Lee. Call for a free trial."

I had watched all the old Bruce Lee movies a hundred times as a kid and read all his books from the local library. I ripped off a slip with a phone number and put it in my wallet. Weeks went by where I just looked at it. I got my hands on some of the old books again and practiced lead jabs and sidekicks in front of the mirror in my room in between sets of bench presses and bicep curls. I even bought myself a foam nunchaku to train with. It only lasted about four days before I smashed a glass cupboard with it while doing my best "Enter the Dragon" reenactment.

I finally gathered the courage to call the number and ask for that free trial lesson. The guy in the other end asked about my prior training experience, and I told him that apart from ten years of Taekwondo, I had also been training Bruce Lee's techniques intensively at home for about a month.

He laughed a little bit but tried to hide it. I must have sounded like the most goofy teenage Bruce Lee fan ever. Or probably just exactly like every other guy who reacted to an ad like that and called to hear more.

I convinced a few of my friends from school to join me for the trial lesson. I told them it was the ultimate street fight training invented by Bruce Lee. We were shitting ourselves from nervousness when we found the sports hall and entered the door with the little sign saying, "Jeet Kune Do." I had imagined how we would be training in a back alley, hitting pads with nunchuks and clinching against garbage containers.

Jacob was shorter than me but at least double the width. He had light blond hair and was wearing a tight, white tank top, revealing some serious guns. He seemed really nice, and we immediately felt more confident about the training.

There were only two other people in the class. One of them was warming up with some shadow boxing and impressive flying kicks. He was muscular, wearing silk Kung Fu pants, running shoes, small Vale Tudo gloves, and long hair that was just covering his eyes so he had to flick it away every other second. We all agreed that he looked exactly like Ken from the Street Fighter computer game.

Jacob went on to demonstrate the curriculum we would be going through if we signed up for the training. Boxing, kicking the legs, elbows, knees, trapping, clinch, stick fighting.

My mouth must have been wide open in awe for at least half an hour. I had no idea that training like that even existed. Just the concept of grabbing hold of someone was completely new to me. My mind was just about to blow out from pure awesomeness overload as Jacob dropped the bomb on me.

He indicated to one of the guys to get in the mount position and made a small speech about how it was no problem to be on bottom there. I am not sure exactly what techniques he showed to demonstrate an escape, sweep, and submission from there on. Partly because I had no idea what was going on; partly because my world had just been hit by a dinosaur-extinguishing-sized meteor of amazement.

The guys were fighting *on the ground*. I couldn't believe my own eyes as I saw the attacker fly through the air, then get caught in arm locks, chokes, and foot locks that rendered his face in pain and forced him to give up. Jacob hadn't even broken a drop of sweat and even more amazing—he hadn't thrown a single spinning high kick the whole time.

I was sold. The striking training and clinch were interesting, but the ground grappling was absolute love at first sight. From that second on, I have never looked back and can honestly say that I have been thinking of grappling every single day since.

And at the time of writing, Street Fighter Ken has been my training partner and friend for thirteen years and counting.

I was more passionate about learning martial arts than ever. It felt like I was seven again and had just started training, eager to learn as much as I possibly could. Restitution was never an issue at that age. I could easily train hard several days a week, sleep just a few hours at night, go through school in the daytime, and have Friday and Saturday nights out with my friends.

We had a lot of fun those years, and there wasn't a bar or club in Copenhagen we didn't try to sneak into, even before most of us had turned eighteen. One late night, I thought I recognized a beautiful blond girl standing in line outside the bathroom. There was something about her, but it took me at least half an hour to be certain. It was my beloved cousin, the daughter of my father's sister. We were almost exactly the same age and she had been like a sister to me ever since we were little. When I stopped seeing my father, I lost contact with that whole side of the family.

I had missed her and we started seeing each other again, trying to catch up on all the years that had passed. I felt we had a special friendship, a connection to our childhood together. Through her, it was natural for me to be reunited with a few more members of my father's side of the family. It felt good to see them and I sensed where it was all starting to lead for me.

I had a job a few days a week after school, working at a small company updating their website and maintaining their computers. It was a sunny summer day when I sat there and gathered the courage to send an email that would change my life.

"Hey, Dad

It has been a long time, and I was thinking that maybe we should start talking a little bit again.

I don't feel like rushing anything, but I am open to perhaps seeing you again one day. I hope you are doing well, and that we can have a future together again at some point.

-Christian"

It had been a long time and I started to miss the father figure that had inspired me so much as a kid.

It still felt like a long way to go before I wanted to actually meet him and even longer before I could meet his new family. He had married the woman he left my mother for and had a son together with her. It was a big pill for me to swallow and I wanted to take it one small step at a time.

I looked at the send button for a very long time. All day, I had been thinking about whether it was the day when I would finally contact him again. I hadn't done much work that day and couldn't concentrate in school either.

Click.

Adrenaline rushed through my veins. The sound of clicking that button only lasted for a split second but defined a sharp turning point in my life. I had let go of the last bits of my anger and was ready to forgive and move forward.

"Christian, there is someone here for you."

The woman working the reception knocked on the door to the room I was sitting in and said someone had come to see me.

It had only taken about twenty minutes before he stood there. Just like he had immediately jumped on his motorbike and driven all the way across the country to meet his own father as he heard he had returned from Australia, he dropped everything when he received my email and drove straight to where I was. As a kid, I had always admired him as a man of action—someone who got things done right away instead of just talking about it. If he had an idea or dream, he would start realizing it right away. There would be no waiting. While everyone else was talking about what they wanted to do, he was already out in the back yard with all his tools spread out on the grass and had begun building right away.

He was wearing a blue work jacket over a white t-shirt. It was full of screwdrivers, pens, and other tools for his job as an electrician. His shoulders and arms looked strong. He had less hair and more wrinkles than I remembered. Seven years had passed, and there he stood. My own flesh and blood.

"I've missed you", he said with tears in his eyes.

I wanted to be mad at him for not respecting that I needed time. On the other hand, he did exactly what was necessary to break the ice and went straight for the kill like he had been doing his whole life, and I myself had done with everything I had set my mind on. I immediately understood that he had done the only right thing.

My legs were shaking, and it felt like I had been buried in quicksand as I tried to get up from my chair. I gave him the longest hug I had ever given anyone. It was all the hugs I had missed for so many years combined.

He smelled exactly like I remembered from when I was twelve years old and had seen him the last time. My colleagues were looking confused at us through the door from the other room. I hadn't told them that I had been away from my own father for so long, and in the blink of an eye, he was back in my life.

In that second, everything was forgiven.

CHAPTER THIRTEEN

Indonesia

After the hectic time spent in Singapore, the pace of our days quickly slowed down on the lazy island of Bali. We spent most of them just relaxing in a big house we had rented and then going out in the evenings. We would stay on the island for a while, so we were in no hurry with getting on the mats. It felt nice to have a little vacation with my friends.

Eventually, the busy city and nightlife of Kuta—the largest city on the island—became too much for us, and we decided it was time for a bit of adventure. We had rented some motorbikes and felt really comfortable on them, so we thought it would be a great idea to go on a little road trip.

A girl in a bikini and white sunglasses passed me at high speed as we drove out of town. Her long, brown hair was blowing in the wind as she pulled the throttle, and she had a pink surfboard attached to the side of her bike.

"We need to try this surfing one day!" I shouted to Erik and Liam behind me, who were also finding it equally hard to focus on traffic.

It took us four days to make it all the way around the island. We spent hours and hours on the bikes, driving by beautiful rice fields, through dense forests, and along deserted beaches. A gang of monkey thieves stole the keys to my motorbike at a roadside temple, and it was pure luck that they—fifteen minutes and two sweaty palms later—dropped it from the tree they were lounging in.

We found cheap rooms along the coast where we spent the hot nights with no air conditioning. One night, while Erik and Liam were sleeping, I went out to find an Internet cafe. I needed to get in touch with people in the Philippines to plan my visit there. On my way to the little bamboo hut with the few, old computers, I drove along a deserted road with no lights. I stopped in the middle of it and turned off the engine. The inky black night was pitch dark, and I couldn't see my own hands in front of me. There was no sound of either humans or machines to be heard. The wind had completely stopped, and a few animals in the plants around me were the only thing that broke the silence.

I was seriously far away from home. At the same time, I didn't feel away at all. I searched for the slightest bit of home sickness inside myself, but there was nothing. I was totally comfortable, right there in the middle of nowhere.

Driving back to the place we stayed, a bat hit me right on chest and flapped around on me with its disgusting, hairy wings. I screamed like a little girl, instantly regretting everything about feeling comfortable and just wanted to go home right away.

A guy called Hoky had emailed me. He was on vacation in Bali, and following my blog, he invited me to pay the mat fee for us for an open mat training session.

We got up early and raced the last piece of road back to Kuta, driving behind big trucks for hours and hours, zig zagging past them.

We made it to the gym just in time and met up with Hoky. He was a nice guy who just got his blue belt and was really interested in Jiu Jitsu.

He asked me after a round of sparring what I thought he should work on. I often feel like someone is better, not so much because of their technique, knowledge, or physique, but because they have the tactical overview to always stay one move ahead of their opponent. Getting that is only a matter of spending time on the mats and maturing in the game. Hoky was like that. He was on the right track and just needed more time.

Danny—a friend of Jonathan—came by, together with a Japanese guy that had a great wrestling game. It was nice finally to be back on the mats, but my cardio felt really, really bad from breathing in all that dirty exhaust on the roads for days.

A small, Portuguese guy, Quico, was giving me a really hard time on the mats. He was strong and fast with very good technique. He tapped me with an arm in guillotine, and I asked curiously how he had done it. He had a lot of details on it that I had never seen before, and I couldn't wait to get home and share it with my fellow guillotine nerds in the gym.

After a few more rounds, I lay flat on the mat, trying to catch my breath. Quico and I talked for a while. Like most of the other guys we had met, he had moved to Bali for the surfing and turned out to be a super cool guy. He promised to take us out in the water one day. Surfing was on my to-do list for the trip, and I knew it would be a challenge for me to get in that scary ocean.

The local black belt had just finished a small class next to us and asked me if I wanted to go for a round. Everyone was watching, and I sort of expected that it was going to be a tough roll. I had just tapped everyone in the house, and now I had reached the boss of the level. He was a tall, slim guy who had started training with Rickson all the way back in 1996.

I sat down in my guard and started out really easy, going for a few sweeps but never following through. His base was great, and his legs very flexible. His shins felt sharp as he pressed them into my thighs and put pressure on my guard. He passed and grabbed my wrist in a weird way I had never seen before that completely ruined my side control bottom game. Then he took my back and crammed his forearm across my teeth before I had a chance to tap out.

I was bleeding from my mouth and went to the bathroom to wash it. I looked myself in the eyes in the mirror. My teeth were dark red. The pressure across my mouth had pressed them into the flesh beneath my lips and made three deep holes. I cleaned it with water and went back on the mat.

Hard rolls with risk of injury have their time and place and were inevitably going to be a part of my trip. There was no way I was going to get around it, and so I might just as well accept it. I was riding out the storm for a few more rounds, and—of course—came out alive on the other side.

We shook hands. My teeth hurt, and I imagined how it would be in Brazil. There would probably be a horde of hungry, aggressive black belts taking turns on cranking my joints in all thinkable and unthinkable directions, not caring a bit about when I tapped out.

I would have to train hard to prepare for that.

Erik and Liam were lying in front of the big fan, totally exhausted after a few rounds. Erik had only slept for two hours in the warm room we had rented up on the west coast.

Beaten and tired, we drove back to our house and jumped straight in the pool.

"I just realised that I haven't washed or changed these shorts for a full week today," Liam said with a definite sense of pride in his voice as we stood there in the water.

It was a beautiful anniversary.

Next day, it was my 29th birthday, and what better to do on a day like that—on a beautiful, exotic island—than go training.

We met up with Quico and Danny in the gym and rolled for a few hours. The weather was great, and my body felt much better than the day before. I had rested and been breathing primarily fresh air during the morning. Red Hot Chili Peppers were playing loudly on the stereo, and the warm, tropical air flowed through the big, open windows onto us on the mats.

Everything felt better.

Danny asked me what my plans were for my day as we sat around on the mat after a few hours of hard rolls. I hadn't planned anything but when he suggested that he could help us try surfing down on the beach, I didn't need to think twice about it.

There was no need to shower. We jumped straight onto the motorbikes and drove through town to a spot on the beach where we could rent some boards.

Danny pointed out a young local salesman on the beach who was trying to impress a Japanese couple in beach chairs with his language skills. He had taught himself English, Russian, and Japanese just from working on the beach, and the couple looked like they would definitely buy a bracelet from him after that show.

Danny picked out a few boards for us at a local rental place.

I looked at the water. The waves weren't big, but I didn't feel safe about going out into them.

Swimming had never been my thing, and definitely not in the ocean. As a kid, I was always extremely skinny, so staying afloat demanded a lot of work for me. We had weekly swimming lessons in school but it was so hard for me that it never caught my interest. I had always envied those who enjoyed being in the water and I knew that feeling confident in the ocean was a life skill I needed to acquire. I should have learned that twenty years earlier, but I guess it was never too late. My plan was that surfing could maybe be a good way to learn to be confident in the ocean.

Danny lay the boards down in the sand and showed us the basics of standing up and how to position ourselves. It felt simple on land, but I knew it would be nothing like that in the water.

My heart was pounding. The shallow water would have a very hard time killing me that day, but I was still afraid to be out there. I had been in the sea only a few times where I couldn't touch the bottom, and I never felt good about it.

There was no way around it.

"Baby steps," I told myself, and walked out into the water with a pounding heart.

The little waves crashed in front of us, and I desperately tried to jump over them so I wouldn't get water in my eyes or mouth.

Danny explained that we should stay away from the red flags that indicated the position of the currents that could pull us out to sea. My eyes were fixed on them for a good thirty minutes after he said that. I remembered the Rastafarian life guard in Malaysia who told stories about the people who got sucked out by the rip current. I didn't want any of that, so I made sure to stay near Danny, who was an experienced surfer and swimmer.

My feet could touch the bottom where we stood, and I appreciated that. I could feel the currents under me, pulling my feet along the sand, together with empty chips bags, used condoms, and all sorts of other trash.

I looked at Liam on his board about twenty meters away from me. Danny gave his board a push in front of a wave coming in. He tried to stand up but slipped and fell under. His head popped up with a big smile. He laughed and waved to me. I couldn't hear what he shouted to me.

Suddenly, Quico told me to quickly get ready. I scrambled to get onto the board, looked back, and saw a wave coming towards me. I paddled as much as I could and focused on keeping my balance on the board.

The wave felt fast and powerful as it hit me. Even though it was only a small children's wave, I had never felt the power of nature like that before, and it stunned me for a second.

I could hear Quico shout behind me that I should try and stand up. I had forgotten all about that. I put one knee up but couldn't keep my balance and the board flipped, throwing me into the water.

Immediately, I thought I had to try that again.

And we tried. Many times. Every time, I slipped, went for the wrong wave, or couldn't keep my balance when I tried to stand up.

Then suddenly, it happened.

The wind hit my face as the wave pushed me forward. My knuckles were white, holding on to the board, and after a few seconds of trying to keep it straight in the water, I went for it. One knee up. Front foot. Back foot. I held my breath and stood up.

The wave gently slid me about seven meters towards the beach before parking my board in the sand. It was the shortest, smallest surf ever but still, my heart raced in excitement to the extent that I almost couldn't breathe. I turned around. Danny was clapping and gave me a thumbs up. I was super proud.

It felt like I had just hit my first submission in sparring as a fresh white belt who had only trained for a week on another white belt who had only trained for a day! It was utterly amazing.

I had never really thought much about surfing, other than how insane it was that people were sitting on boards in shark infested waters, making themselves look like delicious seals. In that moment, I realized that this thing would haunt me, like Jiu Jitsu had haunted me since the first time I ever tried to roll.

It was the best birthday present I had ever given myself.

Feeling high on my newly found hobby and hopes of becoming less afraid of the sea, we were back in the house, getting ready for our last night out.

Jonathan wrote to me on my Skype chat. The connection was too slow for calls. He had arranged to come to the Philippines and hang out with me on his way to Hawaii. He had a lot of friends in Manila, so it would be no problem to find places to train there. A guy called Stephen had also emailed me and invited me to come to his gym. I could even sleep on the mats if I needed a place to crash.

Danny went out with us and brought a few of his local friends. I had bought a colorful cap saying "Jiggy-Jig." I had no idea what it meant but assumed it was just some surf brand. That was only until one of the guys told me that it meant "fucky-fuck," then I decided right away to buy five more the next day.

Danny's friends were pro surfers, and it was hard not to admire their life. I had never really thought of surfing as a sport, but these guys were like black belts who had trained since they were kids and put enormous amounts of time into learning their craft. I was really inspired by my experience in the water that day and was eager to see where it would take me on the rest of my trip.

CHAPTER FOURTEEN

Philippines

Someone was waving at me from a small window in the basement as I tried to find my phone in my backpack. I figured it had to be the place I was looking for.

As I entered the little room, the humidity hit me like a wall. It was even worse than in Montpellier, and I immediately felt a sweat break on my forehead. There wasn't any air conditioning or open windows; only a few fans that moved the warm, sticky air around the small room.

A man of around fifty years old, built like a rock with an Australian accent and a firm handshake, welcomed me. Stephen was the black belt who owned the gym. He had invited me to come train and offered to let me sleep in the gym. It was nice to have a place to stay for free, and sleeping in a gym was something I had expected to do a lot on the trip but hadn't had the chance to do yet. What would a round-the-world Jiu Jitsu backpacking trip be without sleeping in gyms?

With the long flight all day, I mostly felt like going to sleep, but I was going to be on a tight schedule in Manila so I thought that I might as well get some training done. I could sleep in the summer when I got back home to Denmark.

I did a small class on guard passing. The material was really starting to fall into place for me after having taught it so many times. Jonathan was supposed to come and join, but he was nowhere to be seen.

One guy asked how I would escape the rear naked choke when it is already locked in.

It was a classic question. How do you prevent something when it is already too late? The answer is obvious; you don't get in that situation. If the guy has locked in the rear naked choke, that probably means he took you down, passed your guard, took your back, and got the choke. You already fucked up big time, way before the submission, so there are a lot of other things to work on than the submission defense. My finest analogy for these questions—if I should say so myself—I came up with while teaching a seminar far out in the countryside in Russia. How do you prevent your country from being destroyed when the nuclear missile is already launched and on its way to hit you? You don't—it is too late. You should have shot the guy who pushed that big red button. Same thing with the rear naked choke. Just don't shoot anyone.

When we started sparring, I got caught in the moment and forgot how tired I was. Getting warm was no problem, and it was nice to go a few rounds. During the rolls, I didn't think too much about my surroundings but was just focused on the task at hand. It wasn't until the second the timer beeped that I realized I almost couldn't breathe because of the heat and humidity.

Stephen claimed that it might be the warmest gym in the world. I was sweating like a rapist and tempted to agree with him.

Every time a round ended, everyone would immediately jump up and literally run out of the room to get a breath of fresh air from the hallway. I had never seen anything like it, and it was quite an entertaining scene to watch.

When the training ended, we sat around on the mat and talked. Wrapping up my gi in my belt was a ritual I had been doing for years and years after training. I sat down on my knees and folded it with perfection while the sweat dripped down my scratched face and bare chest. The pants, the top, then tighten the belt in a knot around it.

Jonathan walked through the door a good two hours late for class due to traffic. He was staying in a love hotel and asked if I wanted to share a room with him there. Sleeping in a gym or a love hotel. Both sounded like great adventures, so it was a difficult decision. I thought to myself that I would get the chance to be a bum and sleep in a gym another time, so love hotel it would be. I said goodbye to everyone and thanked them for the training and offer to sleep over.

They were eager to have me back for training the next day. I would love to train more with them, but I would only be in Manila for a few days, and I had a ton of invitations from different places. I almost felt bad telling them that I probably wouldn't make it back. It was my mission to visit as many gyms as possible on the trip and train with as many different people as I could. Despite wanting to be that guy who is friends with everyone and trains with everyone, it was sometimes difficult to turn people down because I had to train somewhere else. Getting emotionally attached to one place could happen very quickly, and then going to their competitors the next day was sometimes difficult. I didn't want to feel guilty about it, but it was hard not to.

Things shouldn't be like that. Everyone should train with everyone, and politics are childish and stupid. I needed to get rid of those thoughts in my head and just go train everywhere as much as possible.

Four more gyms were already lined up for the coming two days in Manila—a schedule as busy as the afternoon traffic I had just been caught in coming from the airport. It was going to be hard work, but I could look forward to a little vacation on the tropical Island of Boracay when it was over.

The hotel Jonathan had found was called "So Good, So Clean" or in short "SoGo," and it was exactly like I imagined a real love hotel would be.

People in the lobby and elevator were whispering, looking down at the floor, trying to not be seen. Jonathan had already spent a night there in an all red, all velour-padded room. When we asked in the reception to change for a double room with two beds for a few days, they were clearly confused. No one came to that place to stay in a room with two beds. And no one stayed for more than a couple of hours at a time.

Next to the hotel was a little convenience store. It had a door in the back that lead through a small hallway to the reception. It was a secret entrance for those who didn't want to risk getting seen walking through the main entrance. Needless to say, we thought it was über cool to have a secret entrance that we right away decided to never use the main entrance again.

It was difficult to not laugh when standing in the elevator together with several very embarrassed couples. I had to try not to catch Jonathan's eyes in the mirror, or I would crack up. A small TV screen on the wall was showing cheesy, romantic scenes of couples on the beach, having dinner, getting married. It was probably in stark contrast to what was really going on in that place.

The hallway smelled funny, and spanking noises could be heard coming from one of the rooms next to ours. We had two beds. It was the only "family room" they had in the entire hotel. There were no windows, and the beds had rubber sheets under the cotton ones (easy to clean from being soaked in bodily fluids several times a day). When flicking through the channels and realizing that there was nothing but porn on the TV, it suddenly became very clear to me that I didn't feel like touching the remote anyways.

A guy who had invited us to come train in his gym was taking us to a party that night. Both me and Jonathan only owned sandals, but a 24-hour shoe shop down the street—which was actually more a pile of shoes on the sidewalk that some guy was selling from—saved us. Despite not really moving at the party due to exhaustion, both our new, shiny pairs of shoes had completely fallen apart before we made it back to the hotel in the night.

The small front desk looked messy in the first gym we visited the next day. So did the matted area in a room with a few fans on the walls and in the ceiling. I didn't mind at all. I felt at home in any gym.

A big brown belt named Ali was teaching guard passing. He had some good details that fit my game perfectly, and I made mental notes of it to bring back to the gym at home. Despite being a heavy dude, his movement was smooth and light. I listened interestedly to every detail he explained, making sure to remember it.

After five or ten minutes of drilling the moves, we did a round of guard passing, winner stayed in. There were a lot of blue belts in the class. They all worked hard and looked really athletic and competitive, so I assumed I was up for a few challenges.

My first round was against a small purple belt. We clapped hands, and I slowly rolled to a lazy inverted guard. As always, I tried to signal that I would be going nice and easy, especially with the small guys, who I had no intention of trying to bully with size. He was having none of it though, and within seconds, I felt like I was inside a tornado. He went all out to pass my guard with full speed and power. His grip on my pants seemed incredibly strong for his size, and I was trying to figure out what was up and what was down as he pulled me around.

I weathered the storm and eventually, managed to sweep him for top position.

"Alright, so this is how we play," I said to him, laughing.

It didn't bother me. People train differently in different gyms, and I wanted to respect that and go along with whatever style they had.

The next many rounds, I had the pleasure of rolling with both strong, aggressive and small, easy going guys, all on a high technical level.

A small stereo in the corner played some nice and relaxing music. It was awesome. In my own gym, I always train to music. There is nothing better than listening to good tunes during good rounds of sparring. This was the first gym so far on the trip that did the same, and I enjoyed every moment of it.

I gave Ali a thumbs up when he asked me from across the mat to roll.

My observation of his movements from earlier were correct. He was fluid, strong, and highly technical for such a big guy. The pressure he put on my guard was immense, and I struggled to defend his pass, only to fail again and again. Ralph, a tall, lanky guy, was next. His game was impressive: Smooth, powerful, and really tight.

I didn't stand a chance to attack the two guys, but working on my defense against such high level offense was great for me. Mentally, it didn't feel nice to get smashed and outclassed in sparring, but I figured it was probably only because I wasn't used to it. I knew I'd better start getting used to that, because there would undoubtedly be a lot of guys out there for the rest of the trip against whom I would stand zero chance.

After class, there was no time to hang around. We had to get to the next gym. I quickly said thanks for the great training to everyone and bought a "Pray for Japan" t-shirt they had produced for charity.

Jonathan and I were both intense Jiu Jitsu travelers, but combined, we would reach unseen levels of madness in terms of training schedules. For some reason, it seemed like we were trying to break the Singapore record of three gyms and an all-night party in a day and a half. This time, we had five gyms scheduled in less than 48 hours. *And* a party. The Manila Marathon was on, and we were already in the taxi on the way to the next training session. Wet gis in the trunk and no time to shower.

We made it to the class just in time.

I recognized the face of one of the guys standing in the reception. He was a big, bald guy wearing small glasses and a polo shirt. It was Francis, one of the first guys to email me and invite me to come by when I posted around forums about my idea. What a great feeling it was to shake his hand after talking for over ten months about coming over.

I had little energy left for training after the hard workout earlier, and my mind was completely zoned out as I tried to survive the hour and a half on the mat.

The shower after training was one of the best I have ever had. It was warm, luxurious, and had three different soap dispensers.

I was done. Beaten. My face was all red.

I stood quietly under the steaming hot water for a long time, almost sleeping. I was so tired, I felt like I was in some sort of trance.

When I had changed, I used two alcohol wipes on my arms to kill whatever bacteria that might have survived the shower. It stung badly when it touched the many bruises and cuts I'd gotten from the three training sessions since I arrived in the city less than 24 hours earlier.

Francis took us out for dinner. Delicious pig face was on the menu.

He told us that because of the traffic situation, there were small branches of Jiu Jitsu gyms all over town. Living more than a kilometer and a half away from a gym, it would be impossible to make it there in time for training. And walking is out of the question due to the air pollution.

Back at the hotel, I felt like I had been hit by a truck. As my body cooled down, my knee started to hurt again. I could feel the inflammation start to grow. Fuck. Three training sessions in 24 hours had been hard on my body.

I was too tired to fix the cotton sheets on the bed, so I just kept my clothes on and lay down directly on the rubber mattress instead. The red light from my little bed light was on, and I couldn't lift my arm to turn it off. It was not like it was going to keep me awake anyways. Jonathan was speaking Indonesian with one of the workers of his factory in Bali, and the sweaty smell of our gis hanging to dry in the bathroom had filled the little humid room that had no windows.

I was knocked out for 14 hours straight.

First stop of the day was to visit Wacky, a professional boxer who had emailed me and invited me to come train with him. He had recently started training Jiu Jitsu, and was an eager white belt following my blog.

The Philippines are known for their legendary boxers, so I thought it would be cool to do some boxing while I was there. I had trained several years of striking in Muay Thai and MMA, but it had been a while since I decided to dedicate my full attention to Jiu Jitsu.

Despite looking good on the heavy bags, my timing was way off. When I trained MMA, my trick was to look really good when I was striking. In reality, I could never hit anything but instead, I gave my opponent an illusion of being skilled just so I could get a chance to take him down.

Wacky was all over me. It was like rolling with a really good Jiu Jitsu guy, always being one step behind. Whenever I thought I had found an opening to hit him, he already knew it was coming and elegantly slipped my punch to follow up with a hit to my stomach.

Eventually, my instincts took over, and I accidentally hit him right on the chin with a perfect knee strike. I didn't even think about it but just lifted my leg as he tried to close the distance. Everybody in the gym was watching, and they laughed and clapped, as I caught him with the, in boxing, very illegal technique.

I spent the last minute of the round running away and shooting for double legs, to the amusement of the old boxing veterans who were standing around the ropes of the ring.

It was great fun to do some boxing again. I had missed it with all the Jiu Jitsu nerding I had done for so many years.

We had an appointment to go train at a place called BAMF (short for Bad Ass Mother Fuckers). I didn't know what to think about that name, but I kind of liked it. Peewee was our driver for the day—a fun guy who talked a lot. Having lived in the states, his English was perfect. It seemed like most people spoke fluent English—even the Jiu Jitsu classes were in English.

The front street with the little sidewalk shoe shop was bad, but the backstreet was horrible. It looked like a serious ghetto. On the corner, a guy sold hotdogs for thirty cents. There was music playing, people were sitting around on the dirty streets in old plastic chairs, kids were skateboarding, and the buildings looked like they hadn't been renovated in decades. A small restaurant stood out as the most well maintained property on the street. It had dark curtains and neon signs in the window. I guessed that if you wanted to go to the nicest restaurant in that neighborhood, you probably didn't want to look out onto the street anyways.

It was strange to sit in an expensive car with darkened windows and drive right through the area. No one could see us inside the car. We were spectators to their world, completely separated despite being only a few meters away from each other.

The motherfucker guys trained in an enormous building. It looked like an old warehouse that had been rebuilt and was one of the biggest gyms I had ever seen. The light was dim, and a cold concrete floor convinced me to keep my socks on for a while.

I was too tired to concentrate and found myself zoning out as the instructor explained exquisite details of passing the half guard. I just followed along like a zombie; a really bored zombie.

It had been more than two hours of pushups and technique repetitions before it was finally time to roll. It was my last training in Manila, and I thought I might just as well use the last bit of energy I had in me.

I finally got to roll with Jonathan. His game was good and he felt really strong. It was the eighth gym we had visited together but the first time we actually got to roll.

As I left the mat to look for the showers, a small guy with a dirty white belt and a patched up gi caught up with me and reached out his hand to shake mine. He was an avid reader of my blog and asked if I had energy for a roll. There was absolutely nothing left in me, but I somehow still managed to go one last round with him before my body finally said stop.

Once again, Jonathan and I had completed a Jiu Jitsu marathon. In Singapore, we did three gyms in 48 hours, but in Manila, we managed to do five in the same amount of time.

It had been really interesting for me to roll with so many guys that had different games than I was usually exposed to at home. Lots of guys had played reverse De La Riva, 50/50, and deep half guard on me, which I wasn't used to dealing with. Back home, I was basically only exposed to whatever I had been teaching people. In 48 hours, I had gotten more practice in defending new moves than I would in a year at home.

I realized that I had to do this more; expose myself to different games of Jiu Jitsu. I needed to train more with different people, compete more, and study more. It was easy to get accustomed to only rolling with the same 20-25 guys who are all doing roughly the same game. If I ever wanted to be successful in competitions, I needed to be able to handle all the different moves that were out there so no one could surprise and puzzle me with them.

Home was still very far away, but I was excited to get there and study Jiu Jitsu with my training partners there again. There were so many challenges for us to work on together.

My friend Søren and I had bought tickets for the football World Cup in Germany in 2006, but when Denmark failed to qualify, we had to figure out something else to do with our money and vacation time. We put our minds to finding the tropical beach we had been dreaming of, and through lots of research and a long, long flight, we ended up in the little Philippine island of Boracay.

I immediately knew that it was the right one. So many years of wallpapers on my Windows computer of tropical beaches and islands, and at the age of twenty four, I finally made it to one.

We spent almost three weeks there and enjoyed every second of it. With about a week left, we heard that a typhoon was going to hit the island straight on. We joked about going to the beach to play extreme badminton—flipping a coin to determine who would have the wind in his back—and were a bit excited and silly about the whole thing.

As we woke up in the middle of the night, it suddenly wasn't so funny anymore. It sounded like someone had placed a jet engine right outside our little bamboo bungalow and pulled the throttle. It was one constant, powerful wind that made a loud, steady whistling sound, like when you blow into the top of an empty bottle. We got up and opened the door. It looked like it was raining sideways. Palm trees had fallen down all around our hut and coconuts were flying through the air like missiles.

We slammed the door shut again and went back to bed, trying to fall asleep, hoping that our bungalow wouldn't blow away in the meantime.

The next day, half of the island was destroyed. Boats had been thrown up on the beach, and the roof of the little bar in the place we were staying had blown off. The beautiful palm trees on the beach had lost all their leaves and looked strange as they stood there, all bare. We heard rumors that a few fishermen had drowned and that it had been the biggest typhoon that had hit the island in fifteen years.

Now, I was back on that same beach, and it looked like nothing had ever happened.

My eyes were blinded by the light from the setting sun as I walked out in the sand to find a spot to sit. The view hadn't changed from what I remembered. My photo of it had been the background image on my computer for a long time after I got home.

It had only been three days since I talked to Jaguar for the first time. I got his number from Stephen at the boiling hot Manila gym, who told me he was on the island of Boracay for a couple of months, going through job training as a chef in a hotel.

Being a Jiu Jitsu geek, he had found some mats and was holding a daily open mat for anyone in the area wanting to train. He was twenty three and Taiwanese but grew up in the Philippines. His dad had apparently had a big love for the Jaguar cars, so he named his son after them.

He had been following my blog for some years, and told me that he had pulled off one of my moves in a competition. It was pretty interesting to have had an influence on a complete stranger's game on the other side of the planet.

When Jaguar's girlfriend, Ruby Ann, was off work, we picked her up and took a little tuk-tuk to their apartment. They lived at the end of the long beach in a small studio apartment on the top of a hill.

It was a beautiful view from their apartment. The island was as exotic as it gets and resembled anything you would see in a Bounty commercial. At the bottom of the hill was a little beach with a few local fishing boats anchored.

I sat on the small balcony and looked into the apartment through the big windows. Ruby and Jaguar were lying on the bed, talking. They spoke a strange mix of Filipino and American English. Ruby Ann was seventeen years old and had a summer job as a waitress. I was once again amazed at how Jiu Jitsu had dropped me straight into the everyday lives of some locals. These were experiences that I would never have had a chance to have as a conventional tourist.

The apartment was really small and barely had room on the floor for the mattress I was sleeping on. As I lay down and tried to rest, pain in my knee from all the training in Manila kept me awake. I must have lain there for an hour. A fan and a gecko were the only things to be seen in the white ceiling.

It was interesting to be back in Boracay. It had only been five years since my last visit, but I felt so much older. I had never noticed that I had changed, but coming back to that place again and seeing it with different eyes made me realize that I had matured a lot since then.

It was hard to put a finger on exactly what was different. Maybe I saw myself differently in contrast to the young couple. I had definitely become way more confident as a traveler, and—unfortunately—less affected by the beauty of tropical, exotic islands. Since visiting that island for the first time, I had been to many of the most tropical destinations around the world, and for each trip, they felt less and less special.

The week before I arrived, Jaguar had borrowed some puzzle mats from a hotel that had Yoga classes. They needed them back now, and the guys he had rolled with had returned to Manila.

We had no mats and no one to train with. Jaguar had the day off, and we walked around the beach, thinking about how we could get to do some training. The only thing to do was to build a whole new gym from scratch, so that was what we did.

We needed mats, and since we were on a small island, getting real grappling mats was not an option. The back road running along the beach was full of little shops, selling anything you could imagine. We found a hardware shop that had a large roll of blue, plastic canvas. We bought five meters of it and hoped we could fix it on the sand with some big rocks.

It cost something like three dollars and must have been the cheapest mat space any BJJ gym in the world had ever gotten.

We decided that our gym needed some sort of a sign to make it more legitimate. We walked up and down the back road to look for the place that made them, but it was closed. Right next to it was a building lot. The workers had gone home for the day, so I went treasure hunting and found a nice, big piece of plywood and a sharp-tipped board with some rusty nails in it.

A few minutes later, we had also stocked up on spray paint and walked back to the beach to find the right spot for founding the island's first Brazilian Jiu Jitsu academy.

A heavy rock doubled as a hammer to put the pieces of wood together, and while Jaguar tried to find something to pin the canvas to the sand with, I painted a nice sign, complete with a beach and sun on it.

"BJJ BORACAY. OPEN MAT."

We fixed the sign in the sand and were all set. The sun stood high in the sky, the palm trees above us gently swayed in the wind, and the crystal clear blue water next to the mats was completely calm. It was probably the coolest Jiu Jitsu gym I had ever trained in.

Now, we just had to wait for someone to come and join.

So far, it was only me and Jaguar, and we wasted no time getting to roll. Within minutes, we had sand all over, and about twenty people had gathered around us as we scrambled around on the blue canvas, trying to take down and submit each other. I had missed rolling no-gi, and what a place to do it. It was intense, warm, and full of sand. As I stood up in Jaguars guard, I noticed his face was covered in sand as he lay there on his back. Despite that, the only thing that was on his mind was to give it everything to try and sweep me.

Every three minutes, we had to get the sand off. Water breaks had a different meaning in the BJJ Boracay gym. Instead of drinking water, we ran into the water for a quick dive to clean ourselves off. The hot sun dried us in a matter of seconds, and we were back on the mats for another round.

Many people stopped and watched, and several of them asked Jaguar about the training. Unfortunately, no one dared to join despite being offered free private lessons in the most tropical Jiu Jitsu gym in the world.

Eventually, we got tired of having sand in our faces and decided to try skim boarding. It was hard work, basically like interval cardio training. Every two minutes, I had to sprint as fast as I could in the water before jumping onto the board. Carlos—a local skim boarder—could keep going, but I needed a break. I sat in the sand with my bottle of water and the sweat running down my face. The sunscreen lotion on my forehead got into my eyes and itched. It was enough practice for the day, I decided.

Carlos came and sat down next to me. He was interested in hearing about my life and my travels. I was more interested in his, and even though he didn't seem like he was eager to tell his story, I persuaded him to do it anyways.

He pointed to an island in the horizon, where he was born. It had been impossible to find work there, so he moved to Manila and waited tables twenty hours a day for less than fifty cents an hour. It had been tough to serve food all day and still not have enough money to use some of it for himself, his wife, and his kid.

His story gave me a lump in the throat. It was hard to imagine a life like that, but having seen the poverty in Manila with my own eyes, I believed every word he said. When he was attacked one day on the street and had all his money stolen, he decided it was time to change his life. Tired of his job and the pollution in the capital, he finally moved to Boracay, where he invested in a skim board and learned how to ride it. Practicing every day for a few years, he was good enough to give lessons to tourists like me now and then.

I liked the guy, and I could see by the look in his eyes that he was definitely not making up his story.

In many ways, we were very alike. We had both learned and fallen in love with a simple skill and were now trying to make a living out of sharing this passion with others. I did it at a very big scale back home and he alone on a beautiful tropical beach, but still, we basically lived the same life.

In the evening, I lay on the mattress on the floor and looked at where to go next. The ticket to the Philippines was the last one I had bought from home. Now, I had reached the point where nothing was planned anymore, and I had to find my way around the world one step at a time.

People from different places in the Philippines had invited me to come train with them. It was easy to just lean back and enjoy tropical Boracay without going anywhere else, but I had to make a decision at some point. I had three months left to make it all the way to the United States and down through South America to Brazil.

I found an interesting email from Taiwan in my inbox and made a quick decision.

CHAPTER FIFTEEN

Taiwan

The guys in the Taipei gym had arranged a hotel room for me for the first night in exchange for teaching a few classes. I would gladly help a little bit, and a nice, private hotel room felt like the perfect exchange. It was clean, modern, and had a very comfortable bed.

I still had no idea what would happen the next day or how I would get to the gym. I had WiFi in my room, and checked a few emails before I went to bed. Daniel, a Scottish guy, was training in Taiwan for three months and suggested we could meet up and train, or maybe he could give me a lift to the city down south I had planned to visit.

I looked him up on Facebook: "Dan Tastic" was his name. At that point, I already knew that a road trip with that guy had to be a cool one, so I wrote to him right away.

"Savage," he replied and promised to come pick me up the next day.

I had dark circles under my eyes when I was standing outside of the hotel in the morning, waiting for Daniel. He had some problems with the Chinese road names, but finally, he pulled up to the front of the hotel in a small, yellow car.

Daniel was a tall, long-limbed guy with brown hair, a short beard, and a Scottish accent that was hard to understand. From the first handshake, we had an instant connection. He had been trying to make the Taiwanese people understand his humor for months without luck, so when someone finally laughed at his jokes, it was like he couldn't stop them coming. I had missed having someone to act silly with, and the chemistry was there right away.

Signs were in Chinese everywhere on the busy roads, and I really felt like I had come to a very different place compared to where I had been that far. We had no idea what to do, but since the only thing I knew about Taiwan was that it had one of the tallest buildings in the world, we decided to go check it out.

On the bottom floor, we tried to find some food in the food court. Everything looked really strange.

"You handsooome, you very handsooome," a women in her sixties working at a little noodle shop told us, which somehow convinced us to pick her food.

At the top of the tower, they served a stunning view and draft beer with vanilla ice cream. I wanted to concentrate on being amazed about how far up in the sky we were, but the ice cream beer took most of my attention.

For most of my life, I have been fascinated by skyscrapers and have made it my project to be able to say I had taken a dump on the top floor of each and every one of them. The Empire State Building, CN Tower, Rockefeller Center, and the Eiffel Tower had already been conquered by my ass, and now I could proudly add the Taipei 101 to the list.

In the evening, we went to the gym. A few guys from there had emailed me and invited me to come train with them. The sign on the second floor of the building was difficult to see from the sidewalk, and we knocked on a few doors before we found the right one.

Coming up the stairs, I was met by the distinct, internationally standardized smell of sweaty gis. We had come to the right place.

I said hi to a few guys who were sitting on the mats, talking and stretching. I had heard a lot of good things about the head instructor of the gym, a Japanese guy named Makoto. Unfortunately, he was not in the country that week, as he had gone to Japan to do a seminar. He had left a message for me on the white board, hanging on the wall:

"Welcome to Taiwan BJJ!!!!! BJJ Globetrotter Mr. Christian!!!"

He seemed excited. One of the guys gave me an envelope from him with a letter and a set of keys.

"Dear Mr. Christian! I am in Japan for a seminar. Very sorry cannot be there to meet you. Please take keys to the gym if you need place to sleep or train!! Thank you! - Makoto!"

I was bummed that I didn't get to meet that guy. I already liked him.

After me and Jaguar's few rolls on the beach canvas, I was looking forward to training in a real, indoor gym again. It looked like there would be plenty of folks to spar with there. A few purple, lots of blue belts, and the mandatory Swedish guy were on the mat. Swedes are everywhere in the world.

Many people from my trip had told me about how good this particular gym was, and I couldn't help feeling a bit uncertain about my own level. I still wasn't completely comfortable about rolling with strangers who could potentially make me feel like I was nowhere near brown belt level. I was not at all the type of guy that ever worried about belt colors or ego, but suddenly being an "internet BJJ celebrity" made my mind play tricks on me, and I didn't like it.

I told myself to forget it. I shouldn't be afraid to wrestle with other adults because of some imaginary hierarchy. Why should it stop me from just having fun with it?

It really doesn't make sense to try and sharply divide the skill level of individual athletes into so many categories anyways. Imagine a ranking system like that in any other sport, like maybe tennis, golf, or basketball. Measuring your expectations of performance against whoever you clap hands with through these nonsense visual indicators is impossible.

Despite being a cute idea, belts symbolize many other things more than just how you are "supposed" to do in sparring and competition. We are each on our own journey.

I knew this, but it took some work to ignore the negative thoughts my brain created.

I taught a class on the guard passing concepts I had been working on. It was an extremely narrow room, and people kept bumping into each other. Only around twenty people were on the mats, but it felt extremely crowded.

My fears about performing were—of course—only in my head. I did well, and so what if anyone tapped me out? It was the fight or flight syndrome. My brain was trying to convince me to run away from the "dangerous" situation, but as soon as I jumped into it, there was no fear at all. It was all enjoyable to roll with the very cool and skilled guys.

We went a full hour of solid sparring. Daniel had a great game. He was athletic, flexible, and had a strong grip. Because the room was so small, people took turns, standing around the couples rolling and holding puzzle mats up so they didn't hit each other. It was like rolling inside a private moving cabin with guards standing around it. It was kind of weird in a cool sort of way but still didn't top the ice cream beer.

Daniel was staying with Irene, a Taiwanese girl he met in Texas who had invited him over to visit for a few months. She offered me to stay in her guest room and since we were leaving for our little road trip the next day, I thought that was better than to sleep in the gym. The place was designed for people whose average heights were lower than mine or Daniel's. I got to train my standing guard passing posture in the shower, as I had to hip forward and heavily lean back in order to get my head under the water. Then I checked out my chest in the mirror while drying my hair.

We ended up in an all-you-can-drink bar with the guys from the gym. The floor was sticky, gripping our shoes, making sure we didn't fall off the face of the earth. It was difficult to get to the bar, so when we finally made it through the line, we needed to order a lot.

Daniel asked for two triple rum and cokes and two of the same shots as the guys before us had just had. Double size. They looked like some kind of glowing candy shots.

We said cheers to a good trip the next day and downed the shots.

Immediately, my throat closed and my eyes opened up wide.

It was double absinthe shots. It took me a few seconds to recover my thoughts and resurface from getting kicked in the face by my own stupidity.

Daniel suddenly looked really pale. The smile he had been wearing since I met him the same morning had drastically faded. Then came one of the strangest moments of my life when he looked me straight into the eyes, and—without moving, bending over, or making any sound—he opened his mouth a little bit and slowly threw up into a small glass he was holding in his hand. It had a muddy, gray color, and was flowing in a steady, wide stream, down in the glass, and out onto his hand.

His face was like stone, not revealing to anyone around him in the crowded bar what was going on. He was still looking me in the eyes and hadn't even blinked yet as he realized that he couldn't stand there with a glass full of gray vomit and do nothing about it. In a nonchalant move, cold as a Siberian assassin, he turned the glass upside down, spilling the contents out on his own shoes; then he swiftly grabbed the newly ordered triple rum and coke and poured it into the sticky and smelly glass in his hand. Like a boss.

I was speechless and decided it was maybe time for us to leave. We just needed to get some food on the way. The guy from the gym explained to us that there were no fast food places, but we could go to a regular restaurant that was open all night. We had duck breast and steamed rice in a fine restaurant, dirty drunk at five a.m.

I like to eat when I am drunk. Once—in my young, irresponsible teens—we crashed a family party of one of our class mates. They had finished the dinner hours before, and I found a whole, roasted ham in the kitchen. I cleverly snuck it out and hid it in a gutter by the roof outside, thinking that I would get hungry later and could eat it on the way home from the party. My secret little hideout was—to my big surprise—pretty dirty, and I broke my tooth on a little stone, when I greedily tried to eat the ham while waiting for the night bus home. Karma lesson for me.

With a dose of heavy hangovers, I threw my backpack in the back of the little yellow car in the morning. Daniel only packed a toothbrush and a pair of shorts for training.

"What the fuck are we doing here?" I said to Daniel, as we found ourselves in the middle of an empty boulevard, surrounded by tall, dark buildings, way past midnight.

We had promised to drop off a microwave oven on the west coast of the island, which ended up sending us on a massive detour and we had to find a place to stay for the night.

Only a few people were out on the streets. Young kids were sitting around on street corners, looking at us like we were aliens from another planet. It felt like we were just that, so I couldn't blame them.

We found a hotel for the night. The lobby was all covered in marble, and there were at least ten meters to the ceiling. We got a room on the 20th floor, and it wasn't too expensive.

Daniel had spotted a nightclub from the window and suggested we go there and check it out. I only had sandals, so the chances of them letting us in were slim, but there was nothing else to do in the official middle of Asian nowhere.

We tried to look as casual as we possibly could as we crossed the street. I concentrated hard on trying to look like someone who was wearing shoes.

The bouncers had spotted us a mile away, and we hadn't even gotten to the door before one of them said something really mad in Chinese, and pointed at my dirty, old sandals. They didn't understand a word of English, but we still tried to convince them to let us in. Eventually, they got too annoyed with us, and we decided it was time to give up.

We went for a walk down the empty streets to see what was going on in our newly found mystery town. Around the corner was something equivalent to a dollar store. It sold all kinds of strange stuff, and everything had the same price.

Daniel told me he once succeeded in getting into a nightclub by pulling black socks over a pair of sandals, so it looked like shoes in the dark. There was no way we were not going to give that a shot.

I put on Daniel's shoes, assuming that they would be looking at my feet if we came back. And after about fifteen minutes of non-stop laughing on the sidewalk, we finally got three pairs of socks pulled over my sandals on Daniel's feet.

It looked absolutely ridiculous, but in the dark of night, it was surprisingly difficult to tell. The biggest problem would be to not laugh when we got back there.

We failed.

The bouncers had almost let us in, but then as one of them bent down and lit up Daniel's feet with his flashlight, we broke out laughing and gave up. The bouncers didn't find it nearly as funny as we did, but—despite the language barrier—I could tell they were impressed with our effort.

We ended up hanging out in a small bar, the only one we could find. We spent the whole night hanging out with the owner—a very gay guy who thought we were professional wrestlers from the WWF and whose daughter worked as a waitress dressed up as a nurse—drinking his hundred year old Japanese whiskey and betting on whether or not he would sing along on the chorus of Jon Bon Jovi songs.

It was one strange night out.

We drove for hours and hours the next day through small villages and along vast stretches of beautiful coastal road with black sand beaches and green mountains before finally making it to our destination in the late afternoon.

A text message from Val beeped in on my phone. He was waiting for us by the entrance to the university.

After half an hour of trying to enter the address of the place using Chinese characters on the GPS and a detour going literally through a rice field, we found Val waiting for us by the gate to a gigantic campus area. It was the weekend, and the place was totally deserted. One big, gray concrete building after the other were spread over a vast area, surrounded by nothing but fields and dirt roads. In the humid mist, it looked like something out of a post-apocalyptic Hollywood move.

I had no idea what to expect there. Val had said there would be some training and asked if I could teach a class.

As we walked up the wide stairs of the empty building, he showed us to the door of the training room. I expected it to be a small place, like many of the other places I had been to.

I couldn't believe my eyes. From driving hours and hours into the Taiwanese countryside, a place like this was the last thing I had thought I would find.

It was by far the biggest mat I have ever seen in my life. It was a professional-style Judo gym with something near 1,000 square meters of tatami mats, at least fifteen meters to the ceiling, weight lifting equipment, climbing ropes, and big wall-to-wall windows in each end of the room. The first thing that came to mind was that it reminded me of an airplane hangar. At least two hundred or more people could easily train on the mat at the same time and have plenty of room to throw each other around.

Daniel had just broken the world record for saying "savage" most times in a day as we both stood there and looked at it with our mouths open in awe.

More people started to show up, and we ended up with a solid little group of about twenty people. I did a class on sweeps, and then attached my iPad to the stereo and played loud seventies rock and roll music for a good hour of sparring.

There were a handful of Judo girls there. They were smaller than the kids on my kid's team but obviously training at a really high level.

After training, I lifted some weights for a bit. I really missed the physical training that I'd had no time or energy for on the trip. There was no chance I was going to win the season's Gun Festival—a highly prestigious, annual summer competition in my gym, where everyone measures their arms, pumps the guns for two months, then finds out who grew the most and should receive the honor of being that year's champion.

Val introduced us to Gray, an American guy from Arkansas, whose house in the mountains we would be staying at. He was tall and lanky, moved around in a very relaxed way, and used the word "bro" a lot.

"What's up, bro," he said.

After an interesting dinner at an outdoors aboriginal restaurant—consisting of snails and other strange stuff the locals had found in the jungle—we drove up a steep mountain road to Gray's place.

He had married a Taiwanese girl and was teaching English in a local school. His house was built in concrete by a simple design and located next to a big stream, surrounded by the dense forest. A few chickens were sleeping behind a fence, his two little dogs were very interested in the guests, and he had a classic, old motorbike parked in the drive way. A tin roof covered an outdoor area from the rain. Under it stood a couch, a few plastic chairs, and a wooden table. Bananas and passion fruits were hanging in the trees all around us.

I went to sleep in the guest room. Daniel and Gray were drinking beers outside, but I was too tired to do anything but sleep.

It was a bedroom with a small bathroom, solidly built in concrete. As I brushed my teeth, I observed myself in the mirror. I looked very different from when I had left home. My hair was getting longer and curlier. My skin was darker and I hadn't shaved for a while. I felt different too. Something inside of me was changing.

Lying in the bed, it started raining heavily. The sound from the drops hitting the tin roof were loud. I put in my earplugs and tucked myself in under the small blanket. I felt a bit lonely and sent an expensive text message to my girlfriend. She didn't feel far away when I was online, but in the Taiwanese mountains, my only option was a text message now and then, and I couldn't afford to send many of them. I hadn't talked to her in almost two weeks, and hoped I would be able to find an Internet connection somewhere that was fast enough to call her from. She texted me back, and the little 160 character long connection to home made me feel good again. I was looking forward to see her when I finally made it to New York, even though it felt like it was still ages away.

The rain had picked up. I hoped it would pass before the next day so we could go surfing.

The chickens outside the window woke me up in the morning. They sounded exactly like "Angry Birds," a game I was playing on my phone, and I couldn't help laughing a bit.

I was sharing the double bed with Daniel who had been up late, drinking beers with Gray. He wasn't really sharing, since he was lying diagonally from one corner of it to the other. I realized that I had been curled up like a ball, crammed up against the wall in a corner of the bed all night.

He was out cold, impossible to wake up, and I almost had to butterfly sweep him in order to move him to his own side of the bed.

Gray had already packed the surfboards on the car and was ready to go. Daniel worked hard on the project of opening his eyes as Gray told us we needed to get going before he had to work.

The crazy Scotsman and I took our little yellow sports car and drove behind Gray down the mountain. He had warned us that the dogs might try to follow us when they figured out we were going to the beach.

Going down, we noticed the dog standing out on the road, looking at us leave. As we got around the first corner, it had started chasing us. Gray, in front of us, was already driving at reckless speeds and Daniel accelerated the yellow lightning, trying to catch up with him.

I shouted in panic for Daniel to floor it as I looked through the back window and saw the little dog literally fly down the hill to catch us.

I have never in my life seen a dog run so fast. It only touched the ground every ten meters or so. The rest of the time, it was hovering over the road, speeding after us like a bullet.

Despite driving as fast as we possibly could, the dog finally caught up with us as we got to the bottom of the mountain. Gray got out of his car and let the dog in on the backseat, not wanting it to keep chasing us on the highway amongst the other cars. It was so tired, it looked like it was about to cough up its lungs from exhaustion.

As we drove along the mountains down to the coast, Gray stopped at the side of the road to tighten the straps holding the surfboards a little bit more.

The front door of his car was open and Jack Johnson was playing from his stereo. It was an old, white Ford Fiesta. And by white, I mean brown. It was dirty, falling apart, and in general, not very well kept. It didn't seem to be important though. Gray lived the life he wanted: The life many people in the world dream about but never have the guts to go for. A quiet, simple home, out in nature with good friends, surfing, Jiu Jitsu, a mean-ingful job, a beautiful wife, and soon, their first child. He had broken out of the norms and expectations of modern, western society and followed his intuition.

It had taken him all the way to the mountains of Taiwan in an old, dirty car with his wife in the front seat, a dog hanging out the window, and three surfboards strapped to the roof. That vehicle that day seemed to contain everything he needed to live a happy life. It was difficult not to admire as I observed him standing next to it, leaning over the roof reaching for the surfboard straps.

The beach was wide and deserted. The sand was black, and green bushes and trees had hidden it from the road.

"We gotta paddle all the way around that break to get to the outside, bros," Gray said and pointed out into the water, explaining about the direction of the currents.

The clouds above our heads were heavy, and it was eerily dark for that time of day. The water looked wild and scary. I had only been surfing in shallow water in Bali so far, and paddling out into the dark, big sea frightened me.

I had to do it.

The water felt cold on my legs as we walked out. Daniel and I had big beginner's foam boards that floated easily, which calmed me a bit. I got on mine and started to paddle towards the waves. The first one was big and crashed right on top of me. I could see my board go flying through the air, milliseconds before I tumbled under the water and rolled around on the sand bottom.

When we finally got out past the break, it was quiet. The three of us were sitting on our boards and waiting. The water was still, and there was no wind. The scenery was stunning. In front of us was the wide, empty volcanic beach and behind it, majestic green mountain walls stood straight up for hundreds and hundreds of meters, right in front of us. The water was perfectly clean and looked black from the volcanic sand. I could see my feet clearly but beneath them, it was pitch black. The contrast looked strange, almost like a black background of a studio photograph. It started to rain a slight drizzle. The drops landed calmly on the water around us. Right there, I felt a connection, a meditative feeling of being at one with nature.

For a moment, I forgot my fear of the ocean and was totally comfortable just sitting there, far away from land, relaxing.

The silence was suddenly broken by Gray shouting like a maniac.

"Here it comes, bro! Paddle like a motherfucker, bro!"

Daniel and I turned around and started paddling. My shoulders were burning from doing military presses in the Judo gym the night before, but I gave it all I had. The wave was too big for us, and we were thrown around in nature's big washing machine.

The current was strong, and we had to constantly paddle to stay in the right place. Eventually, my sore shoulders had had enough, and it was far between the waves so I decided to paddle in and rest a bit.

Halfway in, I sat on the board and took a break while looking at the guys. They were far out from where I was sitting and waiting for the waves to come. Suddenly, a wall of water started to lift up behind me. It was dark but crystal clear, and I could almost see right through it.

I held my breath for a second before I came to my senses and realized that this was my chance.

I quickly turned the board around and started paddling. The adrenaline pumped through my entire body, and the mountains in front of me disappeared in my tunnel vision. The wave crashed behind me with a large roaring sound before hitting me with a vicious force that pushed me forward, like a horse had just kicked me in the ass.

The speed was intense, and I could feel the wind in my face. My body froze, and I held on to the board as hard as I could, concentrating on not falling off. I didn't want to be rolled around by a wave that size. I raced forward through the water and forgot all about standing up because of the frightening speed I had gained. When I finally put one knee up on the board, it was too late and it had lost its power.

The intense adrenaline rush made me forget everything about being tired, cold, and having sore shoulders, and I ended up spending at least an hour more, catching more and more waves.

It was time to make a decision. I had to find an Internet place and get myself some tickets for my next destination. I was in the middle of nowhere in Taiwan and I had only two and a half weeks to work my way to New York, where I would meet my girlfriend. I liked the spontaneous planning but not the rush. Originally, I hadn't planned on going to Taiwan for more than a day or so, so I was already pushing my schedule quite a bit, having been there for four days.

We found a cafe down town with a fast Internet connection. I had postponed the decision of going to Japan or not for too long. The situation there had been too much for me to think about, but unless I went to Hong Kong, Shanghai, or Korea first, Tokyo seemed to be up next. I had to make a choice.

There was a lot of information online about the situation in Japan, and it was difficult to figure out what to believe and what not to. Someone had set up live webcams filming Geiger counters around the country. As far as I could see, the radiation was twice the normal level, but still way below dangerous levels. It still scared me though. What if the Japanese government was hiding something and I risked my health? I am definitely planning to have kids one day. I could jeopardize my own health, but what about my future kids'?

I'd gotten several emails from Japan from people writing about my concerns on my blog.

The only real danger seemed to be the big earthquakes. Apart from the aspect of people losing their lives and homes, I have always been fascinated by natural disasters. Hurricanes, earthquakes, floodings all had me glued to the television screen if they were on TV. In a time where mankind controls so many aspects of nature and the earth, it is fascinating to see and feel that we are still completely helpless and incredibly tiny when nature decides to show its real powers.

Experiencing an earthquake in Japan—as stupid as it may sound—was a very intriguing thought to me. I wanted to feel nature in its rawest form. A few years earlier, we had one in Denmark. It was the only one in a hundred years or so and really small, although big enough to be felt. It was in the morning, and it was the only time ever that I was sad that my Jiu Jitsu life allowed me to always sleep late.

We discussed it back and forth. I decided that I had to do it. I was on the adventure of my life, and I had to take risks like that. I couldn't allow myself to play it safe.

Many people at home had been worried whether I decided to go to Japan or not. I could understand that sitting at home and watching the news, it looked like the obvious choice to skip a dangerous place like that. It was hard for me to explain to anyone why going there was important to me. I had promised to push myself to the limit on the trip, to go the furthest I could and never turn down any opportunities for special experiences. It was a very special time in Japan's history, and all worries about my safety aside, everything inside me urged me to go there.

I booked a one-way ticket, leaving Taiwan two days later.

Val walked into the cafe. He was already wearing his gi pants, ready to train.

My knee hurt, and I was tired from surfing all morning, but I definitely wanted to roll. After having such a great training the day before, I was psyched to get back on the mats. Daniel had given me a good challenge, so I wanted to spend some more training time with him.

It looked funny when Val raced through the dark streets on his little scooter in front of us. He was wearing a winter jacket and held a big fan in his hand that was rotating in the wind.

The gym was basically a small garage on a street corner in a dirty part of a dirty town. The walls were made of metal. A few puzzle mats where lain out in the corner, and a thick blanket was placed under a heavy bag. On the walls hung a handful of Thai pads and mits, and from the ceiling, a homemade pull up bar made from rope and an old tire.

The place was a mess but had a very authentic look to it and could easily be the gym of any bad guy in a Van Damme movie.

It took me a while to warm up. My body was really tired from sitting in a car for so many hours, then training and surfing. Reggae music played from a small stereo standing on the table and we were five guys, taking turns to roll on the small, matted area.

Everyone wanted to go a round with me, and when I was warmed up, I got into a good rhythm and felt great. An American guy, probably around his late forties or early fifties, introduced himself as Peter.

He was in good shape for his age, had a gentleman's mustache, and a great southern accent. He was a former wrestler that had been living in Taiwan for twelve years, running a pizza shop. He hadn't trained for ages but heard I was in town and wanted to come and check it out.

We clapped hands, and I sat down in my guard. He grabbed my wrist and ankle, and I immediately noticed that he had quite unusual grip strength.

I let him pass my guard to see what his game was like. He obviously didn't really know what to do with me but just sat on his knees next to me. He grabbed both my wrists and pinned them to my chest. I was still relaxed and thought I would pull guard in a second and then look for a light sweep to get on top.

That's when I realized that I couldn't move.

His grip was so strong, and even with his arms straight, sitting on his knees and pinning my arms to my chest, I couldn't get out. It was crazy.

Val coached Peter from the sideline.

"Use your wrestling!" he shouted.

It was like a light bulb went on in his head and he was taken back to his young days. He grabbed me in a strange headlock pin and grapevined my legs in a sort of a half guard, compressing my lungs to the size of a tennis ball, and making it impossible for me to move even an inch.

I was being totally dominated by an old wrestler that had showed up out of the blue in the middle of nowhere in Taiwan.

With much effort, I finally managed to escape and catch him in a guillotine.

He hadn't wrestled for twenty years and was interested in learning about Jiu Jitsu. I spent a little time explaining to him about passing the guard using hip pressure. He would have to get my legs in position and obtain the right angle.

"…and then you just do a sprawl on my hips," I said.

He reacted like a robot. As soon as he heard the word "sprawl," in the blink of an eye, his legs disappeared behind him and his hip slammed into the floor. As if the long forgotten movements of wrestling were programmed into his mind and the right keyword would wake them up twenty years later.

I hope anyone won't accidentally one day yell "sprawl" when he is standing in line in the supermarket or something.

When evening came, I couldn't sleep. One of the purple belts I had trained with for many years at home had written on his Facebook status that he had decided to stop training. Losing someone from my team, who I had been through so much training with, was a big thing, and it bothered me a lot.

The thoughts raced through my head. Was this one of the consequences of me leaving the gym for so long? Before I left, I had been starting to get really nervous about whether everything I had built up would be gone when I got home; wondering if people would go to other gyms or the kid's team would dissolve. Had I been too selfish in leaving everything and everyone behind like that?

I had to talk with him when I got home. I knew there could be lots of reasons for him to quit, but I couldn't stop feeling that it was somehow my fault.

It was time to hit the road and get back to Taipei. We packed the car and entered the destination on the GPS. After six hours of zig-zagging through mountain roads, the light from the Taipei 101 tower appeared in the horizon, and we had successfully driven all the way around the country. It wasn't really our initial plan, and it ended up being the biggest detour anyone in the history of the world had ever taken, just to drop off a micro-wave oven.

I was leaving Taiwan, and the experiences there had really planted some thoughts in my head.

Originally, I had planned to spend just one day in Taipei in case I could get a cheap ticket with a stopover there before going to Japan. I didn't, however, know anything about the place, and therefore assumed that there was nothing for me to find there. Even one day there seemed like it would take a lot of valuable time out of my tight schedule, so the thought didn't really appeal that much to me. I ended up spending five days in Taiwan, and I don't regret it for a second.

If I knew beforehand what experiences were waiting for me there, I would have been crazy to—even for a second—consider not going. I have amazing memories from other places on the trip, but the difference is that these destinations and connections were all planned out well ahead of time from home. Taiwan was a decision I took only a few days before going there. I ended up spending my entire stay with Daniel, who I didn't even know before I set foot in the country.

I realized that adventure is everywhere and became confident that I could buy a plane ticket to any place in the world—no matter how foreign, strange or dangerous it might seem from a distance—and it would contain friends and experiences that I would treasure for life. My mindset definitely took a turn to—if possible—an even more adventurous state and I intended to try out my theory.

CHAPTER SIXTEEN

Entrepreneur

I was a goofy teenager when I went to high school and trained in the Jeet Kune Do gym. Having lost interest in Taekwondo and then spent a year of doing nothing, it was an amazing feeling to re-discover my passion for martial arts.

Jacob had a solid foundation to teach from, and we explored every aspect of fighting we could think of: Striking, wrestling, grappling, weapons, sport, self-defense. It was all there, and a hell of a lot of fun.

We bought VHS tapes online and studied them in the gym on an old TV with a VCR machine. One guy had a few left over scooter helmets that we put on and we went all out, hitting each other with head-butts, knees, and baseball bats home made out of duct tape and old foam mattresses. During the summer breaks, we would put on our gear and beat each other up in our parent's gardens or in the hallways of a dormitory, where one of the guys lived.

We had no idea what we were doing, but through hardcore trial and error, we acquired some actual hands-on fighting skills those years.

While I was fascinated by learning striking in a completely different way than I'd done in my childhood, my interest in the grappling aspect grew stronger. With lots of VHS tapes and lots of confused rolling, I began to get a decent grasp of the game. Choking people in their own clothes became a weird fascination for me, bordering on a fetish. Gi, t-shirts, or hoodies, it all was all wrappable around necks for me.

Jacob, the trainer, started noticing that people rarely tapped me out in sparring anymore, and one day, he pointed out that he hadn't seen me tap for two months. I didn't like that he was keeping track of it, but on the other hand, I was young and immature and with a bit of ego involved, it pushed me even more in my pursuit to learn more about grappling.

I took a job with a public school organization, teaching self-defense courses to young teens twice a week. I had such a passion for training that I started to consider whether it could one day become a job. I wanted to evolve my own teaching skills and started at the bottom, trying to pass on my sparse knowledge to rogue teenagers for little money.

Having trained in our small group for a few years, I and a bunch of the guys slowly started to get an idea of what we wanted to do. We didn't know much about MMA or Brazilian Jiu Jitsu yet, but we had a vague conception about the route we were on and the direction our training was going. The self-defense part of the training had started to seem a bit silly—the sports aspect was much more interesting to us.

Training to hurt someone just appealed less and less to me. Denmark is a safe place, and getting into a fight is highly unlikely if you are not consciously or unconsciously looking for it yourself. The fear I'd had as a young teenager of getting into a fight was disappearing as I matured and saw the world around me in a different light. I realized that I was probably never going to need to use my skills in a real life situation, and it started to make little sense to train for something that would never happen. The young urge to test myself and my training was big, but I was not going to start a fight just for that. That's where sports entered the picture.

A gym in another city about an hour and a half away was at a similar place in their progression as us. They had taken the initiative to invite a guy from the United States to come teach a seminar. His name was Matt Thornton and he was a Jeet Kune Do instructor that had put a heavy emphasis on sports style training with sparring, resisting opponents, and competition. He was shaking up the community and was very successful at traveling around the world doing seminars. He was a Brazilian Jiu Jitsu brown belt and a very clear thinker that had hit the nail on the head, business wise. Most of the people who had been seeking out JKD probably really wanted to do something more like MMA. Unfortunately, at that point, MMA training didn't really exist as we know it today, so JKD was the closest they could get. Needless to say, when Matt came around and taught real fighting skills such as wrestling, boxing, and Brazilian Jiu Jitsu, these guys—who had been caught up in weird Kung Fu and stick fighting pattern training—would see it as the revelation they had been looking for.

That included me and my friends from the gym.

I sucked up every bit of information I could get from Matt. It was everything I had been looking for: A solid system of actual, applicable skills and an intelligent and safe way of training them. The progression of our skills went through the roof in no time.

In 2002, Matt visited Denmark a second time to teach for a full weekend. He had attracted people from gyms around the country who came to get some material to take home and train. This was way before YouTube and the only other source of instructional material were rare VHS tapes that circulated the community.

Sunday, after the last training session, I was sitting and talking with a guy named Kenneth who was training in one of the Shootfighting gyms that had started to pop up around the country. He was already an avid competitor with many fights in full contact Karate, Muay Thai, and Shootfighting. At that point, the Shootfighting rules were the closest people could come to MMA. They fought with open hand strikes standing, and if they hit the ground, it was grappling only. Kenneth wanted more than that. Like the rest of us, he had been watching the UFC and knew it was the future.

He told me he was planning to go to Oregon and train with Matt for a few weeks. I had never before thought of traveling somewhere to train but suddenly, it made perfect sense to me.

I decided to join him, and so, the BJJ globetrotting had begun.

I had been with my girlfriend a few years, and we had both been traveling without each other a few times but never for this long. It wasn't easy to gather up the courage to tell her that I planned to go. I eventually did, and it all worked out. We were definitely a bit nervous about being away from each other for almost three weeks, but we both had a strong belief in not standing in the way of each other's dreams. Looking back on it now, it seems silly to be worried about being away from each other for such a short time, but we were young and still had many experiences to gather from life. Personal freedom was important to both of us, even though the thought of letting go for a while hurt a little.

Six months later, Kenneth and I set our feet in Portland, Oregon. It was my first time in the United States, and we were both very excited about it.

From watching the videos and imagining Matt as this super famous instructor, we had imagined the gym to be huge and filled with hardcore ultimate fighters around the clock. We had seen Randy Couture, Dan Henderson, Nate Quarry, and other big stars on all the videos. I think we were both a bit disappointed when we arrived and realized that it was really just a regular, small gym like any other. The classes had about 10-15 people in them, just like home. Randy and Dan had moved on to open Team Quest, so they were nowhere to be seen.

The training was good though, and I took in as much as I could from Matt and the other guys. I remember the young, goofy me, fascinated by freestyle wrestling—a sport that is virtually non-existing in Denmark—asking one of the instructors how to dump someone on their head.

I did fairly well against most of the guys in the gym and was a bit surprised that only a few of them could really put me under pressure. Kenneth had razor-sharp Muay Thai, and in the boxing ring, he manhandled every guy in class, one after the other. We trained every day, and the guy we stayed with was awesome. He took us to bars and out trekking in the mountains. The countryside was beautiful, and sitting in the sun on the top of a cliff, looking over the Colombia river, I knew that traveling like that was something I needed to keep doing.

The last training session of our trip was a small class of only five or six guys. We did a lot of sparring, and at the end, Matt put me in the middle and had me rolling against a new, fresh opponent every five minutes. I didn't know how belt promotions were being done, but I had an idea about what I was up for. After about half an hour of constant sparring with everyone in class, I got a break. Most of them were blue belt already, and I held my own really well against them, even submitting a few. I was still at the point of my training where I constantly compared myself to others and was eager to try and get a submission of a higher belt on my "record."

Everyone in the small class clapped. Blue belt had seemed like an impossible milestone to reach for our small training group back home. I felt really proud that we had accomplished that together and couldn't wait to get back and see where this would take us. I was only the third blue belt in the country, and the race to learn BJJ was now officially on.

Coming home from the training trip to Portland, I had seen how modern combat sports like MMA and Brazilian Jiu Jitsu had a huge potential to become the next big thing. There wasn't really anything like it back in Denmark. A few training groups had popped up here and there, but none of them seemed to have a clear direction of where they were going.

As our training in the Jeet Kune Do gym became more and more sports oriented, it seemed to make less sense that we were a part of the place. I and a handful of other guys had basically completely rejected the self-defense part at that point and were only interested in sports training. Jacob was doing a really good job with the gym, and it came to a point where I felt bad about influencing new members too much with my philosophies on sports training that somehow clashed with the whole street fighting theme of the place. Jacob was excited about our project to become pioneers in MMA and BJJ, but his interest was still in self-defense.

Some of the other little gyms that had popped up around town were already boxing, wrestling- and grappling-based. The most promising of them had been started by a group of instructors from an extremely successful Wing Tsun academy that had over a thousand members at the time. The time of Kung Fu self-defense training seemed to be at its end, and many of the guys had—like myself—gotten a taste for Brazilian Jiu Jitsu. They had teamed up with some established guys in Sweden, who were already brown belts and going to Brazil on a regular basis to train and compete. A few Brazilian black belts had just moved to Denmark and started setting up training groups of their own. Things were happening everywhere, and even though I could have joined any of the growing teams to train with a black belt, I decided to go my own way. The training philosophies and mentality I had gotten from Matt had already settled too strongly in me, and I couldn't find the training environment and atmosphere I wanted for myself in any of the other gyms.

In the fall of 2003, I made a decision to try and set up my own gym and split with Jacob on the best possible terms. I was only a novice blue belt, and I knew it would take much longer to progress than if I had chosen to train with any of the black belts who were around at the time. However, I never felt in a hurry and had a clear vision of exactly how I wanted my own gym to be.

A few months earlier, I had talked to a guy on a Danish martial arts Internet forum that I had set up as a hobby project to practice my programming skills. The debates about sport training vs. street fighting systems—such as Wing Tsun—were heated, and many offices around the country must have lost tons of work hours from people reading the hundreds of posts written there every day. I was an avid debater, fighting daily keyboard wars against the established, traditional self-defense masters. It was still a time when we could spend months debating whether kung fu chain punches could stop a double leg takedown.

Carsten had no experience with MMA or Brazilian Jiu Jitsu training himself, but training on the national Judo team and competing at the highest, international level in Sport Ju Jut-su—basically a mix of Karate and Judo—he saw the values of sport training.

He invited me to come and train with the Sport Ju Jutsu team and share my knowledge about Brazilian Jiu Jitsu. He had never heard about it before but was interested to see how it compared to his own style.

I showed up one evening for their training. They were big, strong guys, training in heavy Judo gis. I had almost exclusively trained without a gi, so it was something very different for me to try and clinch and grapple with them. Training and competing full time, they were all in much better shape than me and really gave me a hard time. They had a big training facility sponsored by the Danish government and sports association, complete with springy mats and weight lifting equipment. Guys with cauliflower ears and six packs carved in granite were doing Olympic lifts with more plates on the barbells than I could count.

It was a whole different atmosphere of focused and professional training, and I had no idea it even existed in my own city. It immediately struck me that with facilities and focused training like that, the possibility of pioneering my own sport was grand.

The Judo team finished training every evening at eight. After that, the mat was empty and Carsten had a plan to rent it and make it a public gym where people could come and train all kinds of styles.

It was as obvious as it could be. I didn't really know the guy, but within weeks, we had made the blueprints for opening a new gym together. The name was Combat Sports Academy Copenhagen—eventually shortened to just CSA.dk—and the vision was clear.

We wanted to create the best possible training environment in order to produce high level competitors in different combat sports. To make that happen, we would offer a variety of training at all levels. Getting people through the door was going to be the main focus. If we could create a foundation of members who loved to train in our gym, they would keep coming back, and in the end, a few really serious athletes would hopefully come out of it.

We decided to forget all about creating results in the beginning. Our only focus was to create the world's best training environment. That would come through a heavy emphasis on social life in the gym. A pleasant physical environment and the right selection of enthusiastic instructors.

The schedule was filled with classes. We had MMA, BJJ, Sport Ju Jutsu, Karate, Kickboxing, Muay Thai, Capoeira, boxing, Judo, submission wrestling, and kid's classes on the program when we launched the training on September 29th, 2003. Our idea was to offer as much as possible in order to attract as many members we could and get things running.

In the beginning, things went really slow. We had a core group of around fifteen guys to begin with, a few from Carsten's Ju Jutsu team but mostly guys from the Jeet Kune Do gym. Street Fighter Ken was there as well. Financially, there was no rush. We had all the facilities we needed, and the rent was so cheap that we could easily pay it with the few members we had. The rest of the money went to pay the instructors we had hired. Paying them well from the beginning was a very important issue to us to keep them as motivated as possible to inspire the new members.

I was working hard on the website and doing promotional fliers, and it was really exciting every time someone came through the door for a trial class. I was nervous about what they were thinking about the place and wondering if it lived up to the grand description of our ambitious project that we had written on the website.

Slowly but steadily, the number of members grew. Thirty. Forty. Fifty.

Despite having a good basic understanding of Jiu Jitsu and MMA myself, I was still struggling to find the best way to pass on my knowledge. My classes must have been confusing, at best, to attend. Running bigger and bigger classes was a difficult balance of coordinating the amount of information to give people, what to tell them, and what to leave for them to figure out themselves.

It was frustrating when people quit. I knew I had a lot of improving to do as a teacher, and every time someone gave up on the training, it annoyed me a lot.

I spent all my waking hours thinking about how I could improve. I researched every bit of information I could find in order to find my own way of teaching. At the same time, I was still just a blue belt, trying to learn Jiu Jitsu myself.

My confidence as a trainer was constantly balancing on the edge of a cliff. I wasn't feeling confident about whether or not I had the skill level yet to be teaching the sport. The other gyms had black belts, so who was I to think I could provide better training than them?

At one point, I considered giving up and joining one of the established teams instead. But it was too late. I had already put myself in a position as a teacher, and stopping there would be like admitting I had been wrong. That I couldn't do, and prove the other guys were right.

There was no turning back. I had to push through, or I could just as well give up and quit training all together.

Carsten proved himself to be an ambitious guy from the moment I met him.

While I was struggling to learn the guard and puzzling my mind about how we could make the shelves with boxing gloves look a little less messy, he was dreaming big. He was already talking about reaching a point where we could quit our jobs and run the gym full time; about finding investors; tearing down walls and moving to a bigger place with room for more mats.

He was ten years older than me, working as an investment banker, and was used to thinking big. Convincing people to go all in on long term visions. Myself, I was only twenty-one and was barely out of high school. Somehow, me being under-ambitious and Carsten being over-ambitious was the perfect match. If only one of us was trying to build a gym, it would go nowhere. But we always seemed to meet somewhere half way, which proved to be exactly the level of ambition that was realistic to make happen.

And so the gym started to take shape. In the beginning, it was like a big chunk of modeling wax we were trying to make something out of. We didn't really know what it was going to end up looking like, but we had a vague idea about it. Eventually, we cut down on the different types of classe, and focused on offering less stuff at a higher quality.

Muay Thai, Brazilian Jiu Jitsu, and Mixed Martial Arts became the recipe.

CHAPTER SEVENTEEN

Japan

Arriving in the airport in Tokyo, I remember standing in line at customs. There weren't many people there, and I thought there was a strange, quiet atmosphere. No one was talking.

I admit, I was a bit nervous when I stood there with passport in my hand—stamp filled, curled in the corners, and with bits of glue from baggage tag stickers on the back—waiting to enter a country that had just been hit by a record size tsunami, earthquake, and nuclear catastrophe.

Had I made the right decision? Was this stupid? Was I being exposed to radiation already?

There was no way around it. I had made the decision to go there, and now I had to go through with it. First task was to find out how to meet up with Ryan.

My phone didn't work on the Japanese network, so I couldn't get in touch with him. I didn't know which bus I should take, and I had no chance with a train map where station names were written in Japanese only.

I was stuck. I didn't know what to do in order to get to Ryan. Signs were in Japanese, and no one I asked spoke English. For about fifteen minutes, I just sat on a bench and felt really lost.

It was a challenge, and I had to get myself together and face it.

I found a small shop where they rented out SIM cards. I have no idea why they didn't just sell them like everywhere else.

With a working phone, I got a hold of Ryan and got the details for which bus I should take to get to town to meet him.

I had shipped my winter jacket home in India, forgotten my old shoes in Manila, and Jonathan was holding on to my hoodie until I got to Los Angeles. I didn't expect to need any of it for the rest of my trip, since I would be traveling to nice and warm places only.

I was wrong.

Tokyo was freezing in the evening, and I only had sandals, shorts, and t-shirts. I had thrown my few socks out somewhere between Singapore and Boracay since they just took up room in my bag.

I texted Ryan and asked him to bring me some warm clothes while I was freezing my ass off at the bus stop.

I was really happy to see him again; not only because he was a good friend that I hadn't seen for many years, but even more because he had brought me socks and a nice, warm sweatshirt.

Now that I had gotten warmer, I was excited to experience Japan and see what was waiting for me there. It was the birthplace of Jiu Jitsu, so it was also, in a way, special for me to go there for training.

We could make it just in time for some sparring if we went straight to the gym, Ryan said. He had always been one of my favorite sparring partners every year when I had gone to New York. I couldn't wait to get back on the mat with him.

The streets of Tokyo were colorful and bright, lit up by thousands of street lights. Most of the lights had been switched off due to the catastrophe at the nuclear power plant, so it was darker, apparently, than normal.

I had almost already forgotten that I had landed in a nation in the middle of an enormous crisis. Everything looked normal. No one was panicking, people strolled down the streets like anywhere else in the world, and life went on. The city showed no signs of damage, not even a small crack in the streets. It was clearly a different picture than the one the media had painted.

There was a certain feeling to the streets. They were peaceful; a strange contrast to the situation of chaos the country was in.

Up north, things were very much different though. The tsunami had destroyed vast areas, and radiation threatened both people and nature. I could see in Ryan's eyes that he was affected by the situation when he told me about it. Him and everyone else in the big city had held their breaths for the six minutes the most powerful earthquake to have ever hit the country had lasted. Now, they only had small, daily aftershocks that could barely be felt.

We took the elevator a few floors up to a Gold's Gym that was housing AACC. It was a big place with impressive facilities. In one side of the room stood a boxing ring, and in the other was a really big wrestling mat.

We arrived late, in the middle of the class. About thirty guys and girls were on the mats, rolling. I recognized a few of the women from MMA but didn't know anyone else.

Ryan introduced me to the trainer—a short, Japanese guy somewhere in his forties called Abe-San.

He spoke little English, but welcomed me and straight away invited me to stay with him in his apartment near the gym.

I had only just arrived from the airport and already, I had two options of where to stay. Ryan had offered for me to sleep on the floor of his place. Since he was moving to another apartment a few days later, Abe-San's offer was a perfect opportunity for me to stay somewhere else in the meantime.

I didn't know him at all, but I gratefully accepted his offer.

We changed and jumped on the mat for thirty minutes of rolling before the class ended. It was mainly blue belts there, and I was much bigger than most of them, but they were very crafty with their guards.

After the last round, everyone sat around in a circle.

"Thank you very much, Christian, for coming to Japan in this difficult time," Abe-San said, then asked me to introduce myself to the class.

I told them a bit about my trip, while another European guy, who was apparently learning Japanese, tried to translate for everyone.

I would be spending the first few nights at Ryan's place. He had a room in a big house for foreigners, who the Japanese call Gaijin. He had Japanese parents and spoke the language, but since he had grown up in New York, he would always be seen by the Japanese as a foreigner.

His room was tiny, barely fitting a mattress and his clothes. I liked the feeling of the house. For some reason, I found the sliding doors to be super awesome and really authentic Japanese.

It was mostly young people living there, who were in Tokyo for studies or work.

I slept on the floor. We didn't have a mattress, so I took out some of my clothes to lie on. Although the hard surface hurt a bit, I didn't mind. It was a part of the experience of my trip to sleep in all sorts of places.

Ryan was off to work in the morning and I had arranged to meet with Aaron in the afternoon. He was an American guy living in Tokyo who was training with Yuki Nakai and had been following my blog.

I was scouting for a non-Asian looking person at the subway station as I saw him waving to me from the other side of the street.

We decided to take a cab to town and spend a few hours there before going to the gym later. The doors of the car opened automatically, freaking me out with its futuristic technology.

I was intrigued by the whole earthquake thing and interested in hearing people tell me about their experience with it. Aaron was finishing his burger and told me about the day it happened. He had been training when the big one hit. The gym was in a basement, and in fear of the building collapsing on top of their heads, everyone had run out on the street, surfing the moving asphalt for six minutes with their gis on. It must been one of the strangest scenes ever.

While the big one had sounded pretty scary, I was still curious to experience one myself.

Paraestra would probably have been impossible to find if I wasn't going there with Aaron, who knew where it was. There were no signs, only a business card sized sticker on a mailbox outside a door that looked like any other apartment front door in the area. Going down the stairs to the basement, a small, wooden shoe rack and a classic gym odor confirmed that it was the right place.

The gym was a total mess. The air was thick with history. And sweat. The walls were covered in old newspaper clips and photos from years and years back.

Yuki Nakai himself was the only person in the room. He was sitting on the mat by the wall and reading some papers. He had become world famous back in the mid-90s, when he participated in a Vale Tudo tournament.

Being the world Shooto champion at that time, he was confident in his skills. In one of the first rounds, he got eye-poked and was permanently blinded in one eye. Despite that, he kept fighting and eventually went on to meet none other than Rickson Gracie. Weighing in at only seventy kilos, he was considerably smaller than Rickson and lost due to a rear naked choke. The tournament was documented in the movie "Choke," and Yuki's fighting spirit and courage captured everyone's hearts.

I had seen the movie when I started training more than ten years earlier. It was one of the first things I ever saw about Brazilian Jiu Jitsu, and it made the choice easy for me: That was the art I was going to learn.

Now, I was in Yuki's own little gym in Tokyo. He greeted us and welcomed me to his gym.

"No, no. Friends no pay for training here," he said to me as he patted me on the shoulder.

He had an elbow injury and couldn't train much himself. His belt was old and so worn out it looked like it could fall apart at any given moment. He cracked his fingers and his neck. A lifetime of fighting had taken its toll on his body.

He was teaching a one-hour technique class from seven till eight, but only I, Aaron, and one other guy had showed up. We were basically having a private lesson with a legend of the sport, and I was eager to get as much information out of him as possible. He showed a sneaky way to escape the lockdown half guard that I have used with success ever since. His understanding of technique and body mechanics was impressive.

After the technique class, there was open mat from eight till midnight. Four hours of rolling where people dropped in whenever they had time. Everyone was working a lot, so it wasn't unusual that someone would come in at eleven and roll for an hour before heading home.

There were lots of high level guys on the mat, and I counted at least eight black belts and six brown belts during the evening. They were good, and I had my hands full with all of them. I spent the whole training practicing my defense. They all had strong guards, and for hours, I tried to figure out how to defend their sweeps and submissions from there. It was funny, since the guard was supposed to be the one position that set Brazilian Jiu Jitsu apart from Japanese. My cardio felt great, and I felt confident with every opponent I had.

The young blue belts tried to kill me. I much preferred rolling with the higher level guys, who would turn it into a graceful chess match instead of a fight for our lives.
One of the black belts was really big for a Japanese guy. He had a good ten kilos on me, and I was seriously struggling with him.

At one point, I set up a single leg from the guard and waited for the right moment to stand up with it. My opponent was standing over me with a solid grip on the back of my gi, waiting for me to make my move.

I didn't get to stand on my feet for more than a split second before I flew through the air in some crazy Judo throw. As I came around and realized what had happened, I quickly decided to just stay on my butt for the rest of the roll.

The atmosphere was really relaxed. People were sitting around on the mat and talking when they weren't rolling. From home, I had always imagined training in Japan to be strict and run with military discipline. Maybe that was the case in other gyms there, but in the ones I had visited so far, it had been the most relaxing training discipline I had found anywhere in the world.

Yuki said my Jiu Jitsu looked good after having watched me roll. I wasn't usually a sucker for compliments, but with him, I was a bit of a fan boy.

Sitting in the metro back to Ryan's place, I felt overly happy. The training had been great, and I had loved to have such a long open mat session where people were just hanging out and rolling. I would definitely have to implement trainings like that in my own schedule at home.

It had gotten late as I caught one of the last trains of the day. Most of the people on board were businessmen in suits on their way home from a long day at the office. One guy had fallen asleep and dropped his head on the shoulder of the person next to him, while occasionally talking in his sleep. It didn't look like they knew each other, but the guy who was awake didn't mind and kept playing some game on his phone.

Most of the people looked drunk, even though it was a regular weekday evening. Ryan had told me that it was common practice to work late and then get hammered with all your colleagues and only sleep for a few hours before going to work again the next morning. This would go on every single day of the week, rendering a scarily large amount of the population alcoholics.

My body was exhausted from training when I stood on the escalator going up from the subway station. The last train of the night rumbled beneath my feet as it left the station. It was a quiet evening, and I really enjoyed walking through the streets to the Ganjin house in the light rain. I just hoped it wasn't radioactive. That would kind of ruin the good mood a little bit.

Ryan and some of the other guys sitting in the shared kitchen immediately asked me, as I entered the door, if I had felt the earthquake. I was confused—I hadn't felt anything. Apparently, there had been a pretty big one fifteen minutes earlier. Then I remembered the feeling of the train rumbling in the station when I stood on the escalator. It hadn't been the train.

I had no idea that it was an earthquake, and I was disappointed that I had missed it. Had it hit a few seconds earlier or later, I wouldn't have been on that escalator and I would definitely have felt it. I really hoped there would be another one before I left for the next destination.

It was nice to finally have time to sit down and talk to Ryan. When we had met in the gym in New York many years before, I had immediately felt a connection with him. We shared many drunken conversations in the local bar there about what we wanted to do with our lives. Ryan talked a lot about how he didn't feel like busy, dirty New York was the right place for him to live his live. Eventually, one day, he sent me an email telling me he was moving to Japan.

I was excited for him and proud that he had the courage to make that big decision. It was like when someone you have trained with for a long time finally gets the next belt.

Back on the wooden floor, I was going through some emails. I still hadn't decided where to go next, but I had to head towards the United States since I was meeting up with my girlfriend in New York less than two weeks later.

Hawaii was right on the way, and I was eagerly looking for an affordable ticket to go there. Robert from Romania had invited me to come for a camping trip with him and his family in Virginia. It seemed very far away, lying on the floor in the little room in Japan, but I had to start thinking about my plans for that area already.

It was hard to decide what route I should head for after New York. I had set my mind on participating in the World Championships in California, but on the other hand, I felt more drawn towards South America than going across the United States.

An old friend from the martial arts community in Denmark, Martin, who was now living in Las Vegas and fighting in the UFC, had written to me on Facebook.

"Hey dude, was just checking out The BJJ Globetrotter. It looks like it is a really cool trip you are on! Hope you are experiencing a lot. The seminar in your gym went well; you have done a great job with that place. It looks really nice and great to see so many members there. Let me know if you are coming by Vegas on your trip. I have a guest room in my house you can stay in, if you want."

-Martin

If I made it to Los Angeles for the competition, I would have to drop by Vegas as well. I still had time to figure that out.

Sleeping on the floor was confusing my brain. During the night, I would often wake up and wonder where I was since I wasn't in a bed.

At one point, I woke up and it was still pitch black. I didn't know if I had turned around or something and used my hand to feel where I was. I was afraid that maybe I had rolled across the floor and was lying next to Ryan. Over my head, I could feel something that immediately gave me the chills.

I couldn't tell if it was an animal or a human, but it was definitely something biological. I worried if it was big, dead rat, but it could also just be Ryan. It was too dark to see what it was, and I couldn't find my phone for light.

I was really afraid and my adrenaline started pumping. I tried to poke it gently. If it was Ryan, I didn't want to wake him up, but on the other hand, I needed to find out what it was. I was not going to sleep with that right over my head if it was a dead rat.

I had to find out what it was. Scared as shit, I gathered the courage to grab it, and pulled it down in front of my face to take a look.

I was shocked when I saw it was a human hand. I was just about to scream when I found out it was my own. The left one. My arm had gotten completely numb from the hard floor, and in my fear and sleepy confusion, I had totally forgotten to check if both my arms were functioning properly.

It took a while before the effects of the adrenaline faded and I could sleep again.

The shower spoke to me in the morning, and the trains played happy, happy music when the doors closed. Bird sounds on the station signaled to blind people where the stairs were—no stress-ful, beeping sounds like I was used to at home. I loved it.

I was moving to Abe-San's place and was meeting him at a train station. There was a little park nearby where I sat down in the sun and waited for him. An old, bald guy with big eyebrows, white as snow, walked by. A woman who had spotted my "Pray for Japan" T-shirt came up to me and had to concentrate on using every single word in her English vocabulary to thank me for coming to Japan despite the disaster.

I was seriously intrigued by Tokyo. There was something very, very different about it. It was like being in a parallel reality, where society's rules, values, and people were so different from what I was used to. I liked different places. I guess that must be quite obvious since I can't keep my ass at home and have to go travel all the time. Japan appealed to me in a way that made me think a lot. Could I see myself living in Japan in the future?

It was safe, clean, and everyone was nice to each other. At least, as far as I could see. The culture was interesting, and the attention to detail amazed me.

Abe-San had a nice apartment right next to his gym. He had a washing machine that could talk and a dog called "Low," named after his favorite technique, the low-kick. I got my own room with a nice mattress on the floor. No more nightmares about dead rats!

He had two backstage passes to a DEEP show the same evening and asked me if I wanted to join him. There was no way I was going to turn down that offer.

It was a small venue, but a fair amount of people had turned up.

MMA was not the same in Japan anymore. Since the UFC bought PRIDE, the popularity had fallen drastically and the shows were much smaller than back in the glory days.

I was introduced to lots of people and taken for a tour of the basement, where the fighters were warming up. Everyone was bowing to each other, and I had a really hard time figuring out what I should do when I met someone. There was a lot of etiquette for me to learn.

A narrow corridor led to the small locker rooms. The place was packed with people, all wearing t-shirts with some sort of fight logos. A guy was sitting on a bench in one of the little rooms with no shirt on, wrapping up his hands. He had a cut over his eyebrow and big cauliflower ears. He looked sweaty and focused. Next to him, a pretty girl with the Japanese mandatory mini skirt and crazy hairstyle sat texting on her phone. She was biting her lip and looked even more nervous. In the corner stood a small, old TV, showing a direct feed from the empty boxing ring.

Another guy sat on a chair with his elbows on his knees and his head between his legs, his face buried in his palms. Abe-San was helping a guy with his hand wraps.

The air was thick with adrenaline. Everyone waited for the show to begin; for the bell to ring.

I found a seat in the hall, right next to where the fighters walked in. The guy with the girl friend was first up. She was shaking as she stood by the entrance and looked at him. The music started playing. He was focused. The palms of her hands were pressed together as if she was praying for him. A tear ran down her chin and she bowed to him as he started walking towards the ring.

Observing her reactions was almost as exciting as watching the fight itself. In the first round, it looked like she kept her breath for five minutes as her boyfriend almost got knocked out. The second round, he came back and won by a rear naked choke.

It was all over, and the relief on her face was immense.

The rest of the show had many good matches. Every one of the fighters acted with class. It was a breath of fresh air to see how these athletes behaved in the ring compared to the in-your-face attitude one would usually see in the American MMA shows. One guy got knocked out and bowed to the audience when he finally got on his feet, receiving a big applause.

I wondered what would happen if a big earthquake hit during a show like that. Once, when we had an evening of amateur MMA matches in my gym at home, some guy in the audience accidentally leaned onto the light switch so the room turned completely dark. It was in the middle of the match and — with all the adrenaline pumping — both fighters thought they had been hit really hard since they couldn't see anything. In the dark, we could hear them go all out, manically trying to knock each other out, while everyone else laughed simultaneously and scrambled towards the door to try and find the light switch.

Abe-San told me that his own student was putting the gloves on the shelf and had asked to fight him for his retirement fight. It was apparently an honorable thing to fight your own teacher in your last match, and it was all set for a show a few months later.

Pretty awesome.

I had looked into visiting other gyms around Tokyo, but it was hard to get in touch with people there and they were all really expensive. Since Japan was already an expensive place to spend my time, I thought that sticking to my offer of free training in AACC and Paraestra wasn't a bad idea.

Sakuraba had a gym just around the corner from Abe-San's apartment that I went to one night. Unfortunately, the mat fee was way over my budget. They offered me a discount, but then I was not allowed to do any sparring with them, just participate in the technique part. Sakuraba wasn't there himself either, and I respectfully declined.

I went to a lot of classes in the two gyms and got tons out of it. No matter what time of day I showed up, there would always be super high level guys to roll with.

The no-gi classes were good. People were focused and worked hard. It was obvious that they were there to improve. There wasn't much socializing, though. Maybe it was just because of the language barrier. Only a few people spoke English and not very well. Megumi Fuji—a famous female MMA fighter—was super friendly and very interested in practicing her language. As we sat on the mat after training and talked, she suddenly stopped me in the middle of a sentence, putting a finger to her lips and sitting all still.

There was another small earthquake, but once again, I didn't feel anything.

In fact, people had been telling me about little ones every day, but I couldn't feel a thing. I just wasn't aware of it, so my brain ignored them, thinking it was just my stomach rumbling or a subway train beneath the street.

I was leaving the next day and felt cheated that I hadn't felt one.

She laughed. So much for the dangers of nature that almost kept me from going to Japan in the first place.

The shower facilities in AACC were pure luxury, and—never knowing when I would have the chance for a real cleaning on the trip—I spent a lot of time in the spa and sauna there every day. Most gyms I had been to didn't even have a shower, so it was a relief to suddenly have facilities like this.

The Japanese guys really liked to shower and, like me, spend a lot of time there after training. The locker room had an area with mirrors where people could sit and dry their hair, clean their ears, and so. One day, when I got out of the shower, a guy was standing completely still in front of the mirror, looking himself in the eyes while drying his—bushy to the extreme, I must add—genitals with the hair dryer on full speed.

I had seen so much weird stuff in Japan that nothing could really surprise me anymore.

Abe-San took me out to eat every day, all around town. I ended up staying with him for almost a week, and he became a special friend to me.

He was one of these Japanese fighters who had fought as an underdog countless times. He had lost most of his fights, but everyone I met had immense respect for him. It was clear to me that this was not only for his courage in the ring. He was a black belt in BJJ, master wrestling coach, legend of catch wrestling, and an experienced kick boxer and MMA fighter. What really stood out, though, when I got to know him better, was his personality, philosophy, and view on life and fighting.

If there was such a thing as a true master of MMA, he would be it.

I had decided to go to Hawaii on my way to New York. I wanted to stay for a while in both Japan and Hawaii, so there would be no time to stop on the United States west coast. I would have to try and somehow get there after New York. The tickets were really expensive, since I would be leaving right in the middle of a Japanese holiday. The Japanese people apparently love going to Hawaii, so all the tickets were sold out, and I ended up paying more than a thousand dollars for a one way flight with a stopover in Korea. It was a rare chance for me to go there, so I took the chance and really hoped it would be worth it. I would try and save some money somewhere else on the trip to make up for it.

CHAPTER EIGHTEEN

Hawaii

I must have looked like the living dead when I walked into the gym. "HMC" was written on the wall. My best guess was "Hawaii Martial Arts Center," but I could've been way off. The reception had one of the first, iconic iMac computers on the desk and white, plastic chairs were placed by the wall. I dropped myself heavily in one of them and stared at the few people training kick boxing on the mat. I must have been sitting there for ten or fifteen minutes without moving at all before someone suddenly approached me.

It was Leandro, the instructor. He was a short, stocky, bald Brazilian with a firm handshake.

He looked a bit suspicious as he asked me where I trained, like he was getting ready to tell me I couldn't train with them if I was from a rival team. I told him about my trip and that I was affiliated with everyone and no one. He lit up in a big smile and welcomed me to his place.

My brain felt numb. I had come straight to the gym from the plane and had only had two hours sleep during the overnight flight, so I made sure he knew that I probably couldn't go very hard.

People had started to show up for the class. Everyone was super friendly, came right over to say hi and to hear where I was from and so on.

The warm-up went ok, but I was really dizzy. Front and back rolls confused my inner gyroscope a lot.

Leandro was teaching a series of guard passing. He was very intense when he explained things.

"You have to fight for this grip... LIKE A DOG!" he almost shouted at the end of the sentence and reminded me that I was about to fall asleep again.

On several occasions, I zoned out for a few minutes, looking at the palm tree tops and green hills that were visible through the little window in the wall.

It is still hard for me to believe how I managed to do five rounds of sparring that day. Fortunately, everyone was nice to me and no one tried to go hard.

My last round was with Leandro. It was one of those humbling experiences where I was reminded that I am still just a little boy, trying to learn Jiu Jitsu. He completely killed my game, doing whatever he wanted with me. His grip was unbelievably strong. When he grabbed my sleeve and pulled it, I could see the little muscles of his wrist flex, looking like they had been doing nothing but gripping gis for an entire lifetime.

It was hard not to laugh every time he swept or submitted me. Everything he did looked so easy and obvious. I, on the other hand, looked like a white belt zombie.

After training, I was sitting around on the mat, talking to the guys from the class. A few of them had been following my blog already and knew about my trip. Neither me, nor they, had expected me to be in that gym that day, though.

When I said goodbye and went back out into the sun, I had five phone numbers, three Facebook adds, an invitation to come watch UFC, and an offer to stay in someone's house. I texted Jonathan to say that I had just arrived in Hawaii and had already been to the first training, keeping up with the pace from Singapore and Manila. He said he would contact a few of his friends who could show me around for training, surfing, and sightseeing.

It took about ten minutes before I had five or six contacts ticking in on my phone.

The magical Jiu Jitsu community would take care of everything. There was no need for me to bother my brain about what to do, where to go, or where to sleep. Everything would be just fine.

Steven was waiting for me at the mall. I had no idea what kind of guy he would be. I had always been talking directly with people I would stay with before I met them. That gave me a chance to get an idea about what type of person they were. This meeting was all set up by Lea, a reader of my blog, so it was a real blind man-date. I hoped we would click so it wouldn't be awkward to stay in his house with his whole family.

He looked Hawaiian: Tanned, in good shape, and wearing fight shorts and an MMA t-shirt. If I had expected something, he was probably exactly that.

The back of his truck was full of puzzle mats and thai pads. His former gym had lost their facilities, so now he drove all the equipment around town to do group classes in a public park and privates in people's own homes. As a professional MMA fighter, he could get just enough students to make a living out of it. It was really interesting to see how someone made training their job through the use of a truck instead of a gym.

Steven lived with his big Hawaiian family in a wooden house, high up on a hill. I opened the double door and walked inside with my backpack on my shoulder. Steven's cousin was sitting alone, eating by the dinner table. The grandparents were on the couch, watching UFC on a small TV in the corner. The typical insecurity of being in someone's home struck me a little again. I said hi to everyone and felt bad about having to go directly to bed. It was only nine in the evening, but I had nothing left in me.

Steven offered me his room that had not much else than a nice, big bed, a massage chair, and a guitar. It was everything I could wish for at that point, though. Before I fell asleep, I wrote a group text message to all the numbers that Jonathan had sent me, hoping that some of them would have time to meet up with me or maybe even offer me a place to stay.

I woke up the next morning with the sun in my face. I had been too tired to close the curtains the night before. Outside, I could hear the sound of birds, dogs, and the wind gently whispering through the palm leaves. The walls were so thin, I could hear every sound from every room.

I got out of the bed. My legs were wobbly as I sneaked my way to the bathroom down the hall. I tried to be quiet and not be seen or heard by anyone.

Once, I got caught in a bathroom in the sports center where my gym is. The men's room was occupied by two boys with Down Syndrome, and I was in a serious hurry so I thought I'd quickly sneak into the ladies' room. As soon as I had locked the door, about twenty women in their sixties entered the room during their afternoon dance class lunch break. I tried to ride it out, but after 10-15 minutes, they started to become nervous that I was feeling sick since the door was locked and no one came out. Directly entering the list of the top five most ridiculous things I have ever done in my life, I faked a female voice for a while to try and convince them not to have someone kick in the door and check on me. Now that they—maybe—thought I was a woman, I couldn't just leave and thereby reveal my true identity. They took forever to finish, and after half an hour, I eventually had to blow my cover.

Their disappointed faces revealed clearly what they were thinking of me.

I looked in the mirror while brushing my teeth in the Hawaiian bathroom. The size of the circles under my eyes had set an all-time record. The clock on the wall behind me showed nine thirty. I had slept for twelve and a half hours straight.

Back in the room, I picked up my phone from the floor where it had been charging. Five new messages.

Twenty four hours earlier, I had landed on the island with no friends, contacts, or ideas of where to train or sleep. Now, I had about ten locals to hang out, train, and surf with. My relaxing vacation in Hawaii had the potential to be yet another of my high paced, busy schedules where I tried to cram as many experiences as possible into a short visit.

I spent a few hours sitting in the sand in Waikiki beach with my shorts and rash guard packed in a little plastic bag before Steven picked me up and took me to the park where he was teaching.

The place was a little concrete pavilion next to a baseball field. Lots of kids were playing in the grass as we laid out the puzzle mats on the hard floor. It was only me, Steven, and two other guys, and we rolled no-gi for an hour in the warm afternoon sun. It was burning hot when the sun hit the exposed skin on my legs, but at least my knee felt fine, and the long night's sleep had done wonders for my energy level.

It was interesting to visit a small group like this one that just trained in a park. Even the most faraway places I had been on the trip, everyone had some sort of gym as a minimum, except of course the interim beach-gym on Boracay. Here, it was just three guys trying to teach and train themselves on dirty blue puzzle mats in the sun.

Victor, a costumer of Jonathan's rip stop kimonos, had invited me to go for a little trip up a hill just outside of town. He said it was about a thousand steps to the top and a really nice walk. He even tempted me with a bowl of Acai afterwards.

I was up for the challenge. A thousand steps didn't sound too bad.

It was.

As we got there, I realized that each step was about half a meter above the prior, so it was basically a thousand lunges to the top. Plus a few hundred more that weren't mentioned in the disclaimer.

It took us a good hour or so to get to the top, which included several stops to rest. My legs were killing me.

Steven had once carried a big heavy bag all the way up there together with Chris Leben and some other fighters. When they got to the top, the chain broke, so they had to carry it down again and go get a new one to do it all over.

Victor was right though, it was worth it. From the top, we had a panoramic view over the entire Honolulu area: Beaches, hills, palm trees, scenic roads snaking their way through the landscape, sky scrapers, and hotels. It was everything I had imagined Hawaii would look like.

We talked a lot about training and life while walking up and down the thousand steps. When we got down again, Victor had to get to work, and I had a surfing date with Steven and his girlfriend.

They were waiting for me at Waikiki beach. It was a beautiful day with a clear blue sky. Lots of tourists walked around the beach promenade as we tried to zig zag our way to the beach with our boards.

Steven had gotten me an enormous eleven-foot longboard. One wrong turn on the sidewalk and I would shovel three or four kids in swimsuits around like a carousel door. His own was no more than five and a half inches. He held it in one hand while laughing at me from trying to navigate my cruise ship between the pedestrians without hitting anyone. I must have looked like the biggest tourist surfer noob of all time.

The water was clear and warm as we walked in. I strapped the cord to my left ankle and positioned the board in front of me, then jumped on. The immediate feeling of floating on it and getting the first little push forward in the water triggered something inside me. It made me happy. I was finally back on a board and eager to catch my first wave in no other place than the famous Waikiki beach of Hawaii. I was like an enthusiastic white belt who had just discovered Jiu Jitsu, thought about it every day since, and now stepped onto the mats of a legendary gym in Brazil. History was in the air and in the water.

We paddled out to our spot and sat on the boards. Hundreds and hundreds of people were in the water, sitting and waiting for the right waves to come in. Surf lessons were going on all around us, and everyone from kids to grandparents seemed to have been bitten by the bug.

"Go, Christian! Turn around and paddle now! Hurry up!"

Steven's experienced eye had called out a slight ripple in the water. Like some mystical Native American chieftain from an old Western movie, his intuition of the wind, star alignment, and nearly-invisible patterns in the wave sets told him exactly when it was time for me to go. Myself, I couldn't see anything, but I turned the board around and started paddling as hard as I could.

He was right. As I looked back, the little ripple had started to rise up behind me, building to become a full sized, beautiful turquoise wave. I tried not to panic, focused on keeping my balance, getting my feet in the right position, and eyes forward.

I couldn't feel the wave yet, but I knew it was right behind the soles of my feet. A roaring sound surrounded me, and I felt nature pushing me forward, quickly accelerating my board.

The wind whistled in my ears, and splashes of water hit me in the face. I wanted to wipe it off but my hands were busy grabbing on to the side of the board, like a push up. It wobbled a little bit, but I managed to stabilize it. My heart pounded and my tunnel vision focused on the nose of the board, making sure there was no one ahead of me I could crash into.

Steven shouted something behind me.

There was no more chaos. The wave that had seemed so brutal and violent had turned gentle and smooth. I had conquered it, and it had accepted me as its friend. Standing up, I got a full view of everyone in the water, the beach, and the beautiful city in front of me. The rays of the sun hit my entire body and warmed me up as I gently rode the board for what seemed like more than a hundred meters almost all the way to the shore. It was by far the longest ride I had ever done in my short career on the waves.

I jumped off and raised my hand with a thumbs up to Steven and his girlfriend, who were just little spots in the water. They waved back at me. I had made it to Hawaii and I was surfing on Waikiki beach, something I had never imagined I would do in my life. It was hard to believe how far Jiu Jitsu had taken me.

In the evening, I fired up my Facebook application on my iPad. Twenty new friend requests from the last 24 hours. Too many messages with invitations and suggestions to reply in one evening. I wished I could visit all of them.

"Been reading about your journeys in Oahu. I have a gym in Honolulu and would love to have you over for some training. Hit me up if you're interested.

Regards, Rylan Lizares"

It seemed like there was a lot of training going on in Honolulu, and I was determined to check out as much of it as possible, so I wrote back to Rylan. He replied right away, and the next morning, he picked me up outside of the house.

Just like Steven, he was a dark-skinned, native Hawaiian, athletic guy with a big smile. His girlfriend was in the front seat with a dog the size of a small cat, and he had already thrown two big surfboards in the back so we could get in the water before class.

I was definitely not going to turn down any offers of surfing in Hawaii, so we went straight for the beach.

Rylan's girlfriend laughed at me as we walked out of the car for bringing my sunscreen lotion towards the water. Apparently, it was a very haole thing to do, but I enjoyed being an uncool tourist with no idea of local etiquette.

The confidence from being in the water the day before was high and I paddled out with a big smile. I breathed heavily from trying to catch up with Rylan, who seemed to have some kind of engine in his board with the speed he was able to shoot through the water.

Dark clouds of a thunderstorm were hanging over the mountain outside of Honolulu. Where we floated around, it was still blue sky and sunshine, but the storm had made the waves bigger, and to be honest, they were a bit intimidating. I just barely managed to go over them as they hit me on the way out. I remembered a story the guys in Taiwan had told about practicing turtle diving for weeks and weeks to become comfortable with padding out in the big waves. I had a feeling that the time had come for me to conquer my fear of going under the waves.

I was right.

As we were almost out, a wave that must have been two or two and a half meters high towered up in front of me. It looked evil and brutal, ready to eat me like a little piece of haole sushi. I paddled hard towards it, hoping that I would be able to get over it before it started crashing.

I quickly realized that I was not going to make it in time.

Rylan had already dived under it and was waiting for me on the other side. I could see his silhouette through the massive wall of water that was coming towards me with thunderous power. I was humbled by the force of nature and the incredible insignificance of my own existence in the universe.

The wave looked like it could kill me, and—even worse—it looked like it was planning on it.

My heart pounded, and the adrenaline rushed through my veins. It was fight or flight. I had no option but to go under. If I didn't, the sea would throw me around like a rag doll, pin me to the bottom, and eat me alive.

"You grab that board by the sides, roll under it, going up-side down, and right before you hit the wave, you kick that motherfucker up with your feet, bro," Gray had said in Taiwan.

There was no way around it. I got ready to fill my lungs with air but was gasping to breathe from being so nervous.

The wave was closing in. It was now or never.

When it was just a few meters ahead of me, I grabbed the board by the edges, holding on to it as hard as I could. I looked up one last time at the wave of my destiny. A huge, blue wall of water, right in front of me. Little white splashes on top of it revealed that it was about to crash right on top of me in a matter of seconds.

Then I took a deep breath, pinched my eyes, and rolled under the board, turning myself upside down. As I could feel the wave coming in, I kicked the tail end up with the toes of my right foot, angling the nose downward in the water.

Then came the rush. Thousands of tons of water raced past me with scary force, like I was being flushed out in a giant toilet. It whistled in my ears, like when you put your head out of the window of a driving car.

I was ready for violence but suddenly, I felt calm. Inside the powerful current under the wave, I felt weightless. Like I was dancing a peaceful ballet in space, floating in a fixed position, holding the board with one foot on the end of it, waiting for the rage of nature above me to pass by.

The ocean lifted me gently to the surface, and I popped my head up. I wiped the water out of my eyes, turned around, and saw my once-was death sentence roaring towards the beach.

"I did it! I fucking did it!"

It felt like I was on drugs as my brain decided to reward me by dumping litres of endorphins into my blood.

I shouted to Rylan in excitement. Twenty meters ahead of me, he sat calmly on his board with a big smile, throwing a hang loose sign to me. To him, the wave had been a small bump on the road. To me, it had been a crossroad in my life.

From that moment on, everything changed. I dived under every big wave and laughed to myself every time I was hanging under them. I had conquered the first big mile stone in the quest that was my fear of the ocean. The chemicals of my brain had changed. Neuron paths had been carved. A new level of confidence was injected into my system.

That wave made me a different person.

After another few hours in the water, battling one big wave after the other like it was the open weight division, we drove to Rylan's gym to train. It was a nice, clean gym.

A small group of blue belts were working on some technique, and I got to roll with Rylan and another black belt. They were extremely tough, and Rylan completely toyed with me. He was strong, fast, and always a step or two ahead. His game was really tight and left no room for me to play the seated wrestling guard I was trying to practice.

We clapped hands when the timer beeped, and I fell down onto my back, soaked in sweat.

After training, we went to a nice restaurant. I was starving after a long day of working out, so I ordered a lot of food while we talked about the usual stuff I talk with people about on the trip, namely traveling and Jiu Jitsu.

One of the guys asked me what route I was planning to take.

I didn't really know yet, at that point. I had a ticket to New York and that was basically it. I was thinking of going across the U.S. to California for the World Championships, and then make my way down through South America until I hit Brazil. I had a few places I really wanted to visit on the way, but nothing was settled. I told them I actually had no idea how the rest of my trip would end up looking.

Another black belt from the gym had been to Brazil for training. He wasn't impressed.

"It's just too dangerous. We couldn't walk on the streets at night. The Jesus statue is nothing but a statue. You walk up some stairs, turn the corner, and there is a statue. Then you go down again," he said.

I found his absolute lack of enthusiasm in describing his travel experiences quite entertaining. He could write the worst guidebook in history.

Brazil was still almost like a mythical destination to me, but it also worried me a bit. I had heard too many stories about how dangerous it was, but I knew there was no way around it. I had to go and check it out myself. It would be months later, though, so there was no need to worry about it yet. I didn't even know what to do in Hawaii yet—that was how little I had planned.

I took a bus up north to visit another of Jonathan's Jiu Jitsu friends, Andrew. He was half Danish and lived in a nice little house near the water.

On the wall, he had a rack full of surfboards and a mountain bike hanging from the ceiling. It was late in the evening as I arrived, and I went straight to bed, sleeping on a big mattress on the living room floor.

An email ticked in from a reader of my blog training at Renzo's academy, who had set me up with a guest card. It seemed like my training in New York was taken care of, and I was excited to finally go train in that legendary gym after visiting the city so many times without doing it.

A thunderstorm had moved in on the island, and the rain was hammering away on the roof. It was one of the most intense storms I had experienced in a long time. Every few seconds, lightning would flash outside the window and light up the living room. I rolled on to my back and closed my eyes, still holding my phone in my hand. I could feel the waves in my body from sitting on the board in the water all day. The rage of nature rumbled right over my head as the little house protected me and kept me safe and calm. The more intense it was, the more peaceful I felt.

Suddenly, a giant lightning struck right outside the house, immediately followed by a loud click sound and a roar that made me think I would go deaf. My body instinctively reacted by moving into fetal position, curling up the sheets underneath me. The phone I had in my hand went flying through the air, hitting the wall. Adrenaline rushed through my veins as nature had just reminded me who was the boss. It took a while for my heart rate to drop to a level where I could fall asleep.

"Did you hear the thunder last night?" Andrew asked in the morning.

"Yeah, it kept me awake a little bit." I laughed.

After a long day of sightseeing on the north shore, my body was really tired. My brain was having none of it, though, and worked hard to stay awake. I started to feel like I had been traveling too slowly; that I had been staying too long in each place. I missed the high pace at the beginning of the trip, where I moved to new places every two days. I had spent a long time in Bali, Taiwan, Tokyo, and Hawaii, and now I was going to be in New York for more than a week. I was eager to step it up a gear and travel fast again. I longed for the high pace change of scenes and the feeling of being overwhelmed with new impressions every day.

I promised myself that after New York, I would go all in and get as many stamps as possible in my passport before my time ran out and I had to head back home.

Surfing in Hawaii had been a great experience for me, and I got up early in the morning of my last day to spend as many hours in the water as I could before I had to leave. It was a sunny day and the waves were nice and calm. I really started to get a feeling for it and caught the longest one I had ridden so far. The view from standing up on the board as it gently pushed me towards the beach was really nice. The palm trees, the people on the beach, the pink hotel from all the movies. Another beginner surfer was struggling to paddle out to the waves and had stopped to watch me ride all the way in.

He shouted to me and gave me a thumbs up as I passed him.

It is somewhat of a cliché that Jiu Jitsu guys also surf, but it had become so obvious for me to see the connection.

Fear. As you confront it on the mat against opponents, you have to confront it in the ocean against the waves. It takes patience, hard work, and failures in order to somehow control that external force for just a split second and get a slight taste of success to just reach it with your fingertips.

And as you think you got it, a bigger wave or a stronger opponent always shows up and beats your ego down once again, proving to you that you will always be a beginner, always have something to improve and something more to learn about yourself. Like Jiu Jitsu humbles you by the defeats of your opponents, so does surfing by the defeats of nature. No one will ever rise above either of them and stay there. It is an eternal struggle that sharpens and strengthens mind and body in the process.

I had fallen in love with surfing and was sad that I lived in a place where it was nearly impossible to practice.

Steven took me to the airport. I was sad to say goodbye to him. He was obviously not a white belt, so I told him to put on a blue instead for the future. He had trained for a long time with no one to promote him and was probably even at a purple belt level, so it made no sense that he was teaching as a white belt.

I was sad to leave Hawaii and even sadder to leave Steven, who he ended up becoming a very special friend to me. We connected in so many ways, and I have rarely met anyone within Jiu Jitsu that is so spiritually similar to me.

As we said goodbye, he gave me the bracelet made of large, brown beads that he had been wearing around his wrist since I met him. It would become my token for good luck during my travels.

I stood in line to check in and was sad to leave. What amazing people I've met and experiences I had in Hawaii—a place that I had even thought of skipping because the ticket was so expensive from Japan. For the lifetime memories it gave me, I would have gladly paid ten times as much.

I wondered if this could go on… If I could keep going to random places and find these great, warm feelings, friends, and experiences again and again.

It was definitely something I intended to put to the test.

CHAPTER NINETEEN

New York

On the plane to New York, I sat next to a man in his seventies. His skin was like leather and his big, rough hands bore witness to a long life of physical labor. His hair was white as snow and he was wearing a checkered shirt.

He asked me what I was going to New York for. We had been flying for an hour or so already, and I had noticed that he seemed a little nervous and anxious. I figured he might be afraid of flying and that talking to him a bit maybe could help. I told him about my trip and that I was excited to see my girlfriend for the first time in two months.

I asked him about his visit to New York.

"I am going there to visit my son. Haven't seen him in fifteen years," he said while staring emptily into the seat in front of him. I could see he had a tear in his eye. There was a lump in my throat and I didn't really know what to say.

There was a silent moment. It was clear that the gentle, old man would potentially break down in tears if I dug any deeper into his story. I was eager to hear more about it, but on the other hand, I didn't want to make him sad.

I told him how I hadn't seen my own father for seven years when I was young, and that when I finally gathered the courage to let him back into my life, it was the best thing that ever happened to me.

I wondered how my own father must have felt when he had been on his way to see me again that day.

When we left the plane, we shook hands and I wished him good luck. His grip was firm.

"Same to you, my boy," he said as he looked at me with slightly red eyes.

It was a strange encounter over time and space, of two very similar destinies and stories going each in their own direction.

I was sitting on a bench in the airport, waiting to hear from my girlfriend. We had arranged our flights to arrive at approximately the same time, me coming from Hawaii and her from Denmark. Across from me sat five Swedish women who just arrived for a week of shopaholic consumer madness. I felt a bit too close to civilization and home, already dreaming myself back to the simpler life on small Asian islands.

I got off the airport train at station number five and there she sat, looking for me with the smile I had been waiting to see for months. It was nice to see her again.

We got in one of those old, local trains that was squeaking its way—metallic sounds on the rusty rails—towards the city. It was evening, and the sun was about to set over the thousands of identical, dark brown, square brick buildings that seemed to make out most of the Brooklyn area we slowly rolled through.

I was, once again, back on the streets of Manhattan. For so many years it had been my favorite destination for training trips, but for every time I had been there it had felt less and less exotic to me. The first time I was there, the high rising skyscrapers and gigantic brick buildings had fascinated me to the point where I just couldn't stop looking up at them. In time, that fascination had faded, and coming back there after having traveled half way around the world, I was sad to realize that it just felt like another boring cityscape to me.

Traveling is like a drug. The more you get of it, the more you want, but the effect of it becomes less powerful.

We were staying with Kyle, a guy who was reading my blog and had offered us a bed for a few nights. He met us on the corner of 1st avenue and 14th street—a big guy in a big hoodie, sharing an apartment with a few friends.

We were both tired from the long flights and equally jet lagged in each of our own time direction.

Kyle had arranged the first training for me, inviting me to come train in a lunch class in his gym, Clockwork Jiu Jitsu.

Lots of people had showed up for an early class like that. I counted at least forty in the little, clean room covered with gray mats. A few guys recognized me from my blog, and I got to talk with two Japanese guys who had trained with Abe-San.

The level was really high, and there were more good guys to roll with than I had time for in one class. The instructor, Josh, was a big guy with a grip that was impossible to break. In the nicest way possible, he absolutely crushed me like an ant.

A brown belt that was a bit bigger than me was having his way with me. I tried my best to defend, but he was just too tall, strong, and clever for me. The way he skillfully combined de La Riva guard, sitting guard, and deep half guard constantly caught me with the weight on the wrong foot and left me one step behind him at all times.

In between my many taps, he invited me to come join a class he was teaching the next day. I would have loved to, but my schedule in the city was going to be busy and I couldn't promise anything.

He pulled himself under me in the deep half guard. Robson, my friend from Sweden at home, is a master of defending the deep half guard with a basic cross choke, and I had experimented with it along the trip with various successes. This time, my grip sunk in just right. The guy swept me, but I still hung on to the collar, throwing my one leg over his back so he couldn't pass my guard.

He was the type of guy who was going pretty high pace and grunting a bit in the process when rolling, so it took a while before I noticed that the sounds he made were not because he was struggling to pass my guard. He was out cold.

His body was completely limp. I let go of my grip right awa, and his head fell forward, hitting the mat. He made a loud snoring sound and was shaking like a chicken that had just had its head cut off.

I panicked as I realized that he was out cold and it seemed like every person on the mat stopped their training to look at me.

I felt horrible about it. Coming into a gym as a guest the first day and choking out one of the guys there.

I lifted his legs and massaged his chest lightly so he woke up again. He was really confused. Last thing he remembered was probably that I was like a grappling dummy to him. I had made a perfect Eddie Bravo vs. Royler Gracie and pulled a submission completely out of my ass in a match I had no chance of winning.

Luckily, he was cool about it, as was everyone else in the room. I was glad that it happened in a place with a good bunch of people and I hoped I wouldn't be pulling off the same stunt in Brazil or somewhere like that.

Central Park was calm and nice as always. In Times Square, religious fanatics were standing all over with signs, claiming that the world was going to end just a few weeks later.

At least I was enjoying my last time on earth.

My girlfriend and I sat for hours on the rooftop of the Rockefeller building, watching the busy urban sprawl below us. People looked tiny as they walked stressfully along the sidewalks, and the long avenues going through town were painted yellow by the roofs of the many taxis. It was a beautiful view of Manhattan, Brooklyn, and New Jersey from there. The constant sound of the horns from the cars below—the ambient sound of the city breathing—seemed so distant as the sun was on its way down and the sky turned orange.

New York was so intense. Being down on the streets, it felt like such a big world, but seeing it from above, it looked small.

So many lives of all kinds were lived on that little island. Short, long, sad, happy, rich, and poor lives. They were all there, crammed into one small piece of land. We could see all of it from where we were sitting.

I think a place like that is really what you make of it. The impressions you can get there are so many and on such a broad scale that it is completely up to you how you end up seeing it.

I guess that is true of any place in the world—any *thing*, really. Perception is a powerful tool that shouldn't be underestimated in its importance of shaping our lives.

If you are about to buy a car, you notice certain cars everywhere on the street that you don't normally pay attention to. If you have set your mind on a new mobile phone, everyone around you suddenly seems to be talking into one. If you pay a lot of money for a meal or bottle of wine, you will enjoy it more. If someone is wearing a black belt, you pay more attention to them than if it was white. If you train for a street fight, you might see potential opponents everywhere. And if you believe the world is a bad place, it is.

It is up to ourselves to choose which version of the world we want to live in. I am only going to live one life here, so I always choose the positive perception.

My mother told me throughout my entire childhood to always smile to the world and then the world would smile back at me. An easily digestible explanation of Karma for kids, I guess.

I had a busy schedule in New York. Besides all the gyms I wanted to visit, I was also trying to be a tourist with my girlfriend. Looking at my plan of the week, it felt a little bit like training was more of a job than it was fun. I was really happy to see my girlfriend again, and the pressure of having to visit all those gyms in only about a week was a little too much. I had about 10-15 invitations to gyms around the area, but I had to cut it down to only a few in order to have time for everything.

Having been to New York about seven times before, I had never succeeded in training at the legendary Renzo Gracie academy. Partly because it was way too expensive and partly because I felt so much at home in the little Ronin Athletics gym.

Now, I had gotten an invitation to train there for free all week, so that was my chance to finally go check it out. I wouldn't mind going there every day for a week, but it just wasn't possible at the time.

I got a text from Jeff, the guy who had invited me. The gym was a bit difficult to find. A guy knocked on the window from the inside of an office as I stood a bit confused by the mat and looked around for Jeff.

"Did you pay?" I could read his lips saying.

I walked in to the office and introduced myself. The guy was very friendly.

He laughed and told me he thought I was someone who tried to sneak in for free training. He had a guest card waiting in his desk drawer for me and told me I could come by as much as I wanted for the week. It was a sterling offer, and I was bummed that I would probably only have time for that one class.

I found Jeff and he showed me around the gym. It was a very impressive place with several floors of training space.

Lots of guys were sitting around on the mats. It was the biggest afternoon class I had seen in my life—there must have been close to a hundred people. No one seemed to talk much. Apparently, they came in from many different places, and it didn't seem like a lot of them knew each other very well. Renzo himself was there and said he was envious of my trip as he laughed and firmly grabbed my shoulder.

I loved his accent and passionate, powerful voice.

John Danaher—the almost mythical BJJ coach—was teaching. I didn't really have a chance to warm up before he started showing a move and people gathered around him on the mat to try and catch every detail of what he was saying. Four different techniques were shown with five minutes in between practicing them and then he set the timer for sparring. Despite being a very large mat, it was hard to do much on it because it was so crowded. There were a ton of super high level guys there that I loved to train with, but it was difficult to really enjoy it since we constantly bumped into other people.

I asked one of the guys if it was normal to have that many people around for a Friday afternoon class. Apparently it wasn't. Renzo was there to promote one of his students to black belt, and I guessed that was why almost a hundred people had shown up that day.

Renzo himself was doing a Q&A session after the class, and I sat around sucking every detail I could get out of him. He ended with a little speech and handed his student a crisp, new black belt.

I wondered when it would be my turn to be in that situation. I had been a brown belt for a year and a half and was in no hurry to get promoted. There were obviously still tons of brown belts around the world who could beat me any day, and I had been thinking about trying my luck with some competitions in the fall when I would be back home.

I was sitting on the stairs outside Penn Station, enjoying the sun and my bottle of water after training. A guy on the sidewalk around my own age had spotted my AACC t-shirt from Japan and asked with excitement in his voice if I trained Jiu Jitsu.

He seemed eager to hear everything about my training; how long I had trained, what my belt was, if I had won any competitions recently—a complete stranger on the street who proved to be a fellow Jiu Jitsu geek. He was training in New Jersey. I knew his type immediately. One of those highly enthusiastic, young competitors who is eager to train as much as possible, watch instructional videos all day, and suck every single piece of knowledge out of your brain. I liked him and we had a good chat on the stairs in the sun. I gave him my card with the URL for my blog. If I didn't have such a tight schedule for my last days in New York, I would have asked if I could come train with him.

A guard had spotted us and, apparently, sitting on stairs in Manhattan is a crime so we were told to leave. In fact, it seemed hard to find many places to sit in that town, other than in parks. I missed Paris, where the whole city seemed to be designed to be used and enjoyed by the people.

My newest friend had to leave for training and we agreed to meet up another time for a roll. It seemed like Jiu Jitsu was all around me.

We had moved to a guy's apartment who trained in Ronin Athletics. He had an old blue belt hanging on the door and a cat with three legs. I was trying to sleep on the couch, but the thoughts of planning were occupying my mind.

I couldn't rest because I worried so much about where I should go next. I just wanted to make a schedule so I could lean back, relax, and enjoy the ride.

Then, finally, everything fell into place. I had emailed something like thirty people from all around the United States and the Caribbean, and suddenly, it looked like something of a plan emerged from the chaos.

The day after my girlfriend flew back to Denmark, I would take a bus down to Washington D.C. and train with Ryan Hall. Then I would catch another bus to Richmond, where Robert and Amanda were camping with their family, and the next day, fly to Orlando and stay with a reader of my blog. One full day there, then on to the British Virgin Islands to visit my old friends on a boat.

What would happen after that, I still had no idea about, but at least I had a week or so covered.

With the plan set, I could finally just relax and try to enjoy New York, the city I knew too well.

When I first got there in 2004, I went to train in Ronin Athletics, since it was the affiliation of the Straight Blast Gym organization I was a part of. It was a small group of people on shared mats in a strange place, where everything from Karate guys to military dressed Sambo weirdos and ninjas trained right next to us.

I made some really good friends there. Amongst others, Adam, whose microscopic apartment I stayed in for a week; Ryan, who eventually moved to Japan; and Christian, who was running the gym as a blue belt.

I felt at home in that gym and returned every year for training. There was something special about sitting, soaked in sweat, on those blue mats after training and listening to the sound of the heavy, Manhattan traffic on the streets below. Jiu Jitsu—the little hobby I was doing at home—had taken me somewhere exciting, made me new friends, and I really took a liking to that.

The kids I had been teaching in Moldova had re-found their interest in training after my visit. Unfortunately, they didn't have many gis or money to do much, but I was determined to help, and so were many of the readers of my blog. Several people had offered to send used gis to them, and a Danish Judo gym managed to ship a box of about fifty gis.

Robert was back in Bucharest but eager to make things happen for the kids. We came up with the idea of doing a fund raiser seminar for them, and Christian from Ronin Athletics was happy to host it.

They had just moved to a new and bigger location, having expanded the gym four times since I got there the first time. The new place was nice, and it was good to see Christian again. I only recognized a few faces on the mat. I guess it was natural that people eventually disappeared over a span of eight years.

A good group of people had showed up for my seminar, and we managed to collect $285. It felt nice to write that to Robert.

He was excited about it and already made plans for setting up a competition in the village and to take some of the kids for a trip to Chisinau. Many of them had never been out of the village, so it would be a big deal for them.

There were many options for training in New York. Too many for the few days I was spending there. Marcelo Garcia's academy was a place I really wanted to go, but the mat fee was $60 and way over my budget for one training session on the trip. I would have to skip it.

A guy from Long Island, who had also donated some gis to the kids in Moldova, had invited me to come train with him and Matt Serra. It was my plan to take him up on that offer right until this email popped up on my phone.

"Hi there Christian,

Bill from BJJ Weekly kindly forwarded us your blog and mentioned that you might be in the city for a few days? Would you be interested in training here with us? I understand that our mat fee is a little out of budget for you, but we'd be happy to waive it. Please stop by, 25 W36st, 6th flr.

Hope to see you soon!
Emily"

There was no way that I could say no to a free training session in Marcelo's gym. There was only one open training slot left in my schedule for the week, so all other plans were trashed and I packed my bag for going to visit Marcelo the next day.

It was on the sixth floor, and I took the elevator up. A few guys with sports bags were in it together with me, and looked like they were going the same place as I was.

When the door opened, the first thing that hit me was the warm air mixed with the smell of wet gis. Literally one step out of the elevator and I was on the mats.

The guy in the reception recognized me right away and said he had followed my other Jiu Jitsu blog for four years. He registered me in the computer and showed me to the changing room at the end of the hall.

I unpacked my little black backpack on the bench and started to put on my gi. Marcelo came in and noticed he had a guest. He said hi and as he shook my hand, he looked at my gi and asked if I knew it was no-gi training that evening.

I had no idea. In fact, I hadn't even thought about whether it would be gi or no-gi training but just packed my gi when I left. I only had the t-shirt I had been wearing to get there to train in. If I would have to go home in the subway bare chested or in my gi-top to be able to train with Marcelo, that was what I would do.

The gym had moved since last time I visited it several years earlier. The new place was clean, spacious, and well lit from the big windows in each end of the matted area. There were lots of room, but it was still very crowded from the many people on the mat for the evening class. I found a corner and stretched a bit before the class started.

One of the things I really liked about Marcelo was that he had a clear passion for teaching. I had been to many place, where the instructor would have someone else do the warm up for him. Marcelo was running the warm up, and he was participating himself, putting more energy into it than anyone else on the mat.

A solidly built guy with a rash guard and big curly hair introduced himself as Josh. He had also followed my trip on the blog and told me that he used to backpack around Eastern Europe to play chess.

Like with all the other guys I had gone rounds with that evening, he was a really tough roll. I had been working on the single legged x-guard myself for a while, but my knowledge of it was not yet deep enough to be able to see it coming against those who were experts of that game. Josh swept me again and again, and every time, he passed my guard and caught me in Marcelo's trademark north south choke.

It was obvious that the guys on that mat were used to having visitors. They all went hard, but there didn't seem to be any ego involved. No one tried to bully the guest. I guess, with all the people they had coming in every day, it would probably be too much of a task to be *that* guy.

Someone called my name across the mat.

I recognized the voice and accent way too well. I had been watching interviews and instructional videos with Marcelo for years and years, studying his game down to every detail. I turned my head around and saw him sitting a few meters away. He was wearing a black, sweaty rash guard, a big smile, and looked straight at me.

He asked me if I wanted to roll with him.

There were lots of people in the class that day and I knew that the chance to go a round with Marcelo was slim to none, but of course I had hoped for the opportunity. I almost stumbled over the words like I was trying to answer before someone else jumped in and took my spot. I crawled across the mat to seize my opportunity.

He was clearly an expert in adjusting his level to his training partner. Not for a second did it feel like I was in the hands of the best guy in the world. It was like he was racing a moped with a top tuned motorbike. He was driving side by side, just for the social aspect of it, and had no reason to go any faster since there was no chance of losing, no matter what.

I couldn't threaten him with my moped-jitsu, and he allowed me to play a little bit. I felt comfortable rolling with him, and in my excitement, I turned up the pace and went a little harder than I would normally do. I even tried a flying triangle over his guard, but he just brushed it off like it was dust on his shoulders and laughed a bit.

As the round ended, he asked me if I did mostly gi or no-gi. I told him my interest was fifty-fifty. Not the position, but fifty percent of each.

He smiled widely and patted my shoulder. It seemed like I had given him the right answer.

I told him I was in town for just a few days more and he said I was welcome to come join any of his classes.

It might have been one of the hardest things in my life to say no to, but my schedule was absolutely packed for the rest of my time in town. I had gone way over my budget and bought expensive tickets to a Broadway show for my girlfriend's birthday the next day. It was impossible to cram in any more training sessions before I was leaving.

I had just said no thanks to training with the best guy in the world. I told him I would be back for my rematch another time. He laughed.

I've always seen Marcelo as a very special Jiu Jitsu practitioner. Not just because he—pound for pound—probably is the best competitor in the world, but also because of his personality and approach to training and teaching. With the closed-door policies of many teams around the world, not allowing their students to train anywhere else in fear of losing their "secret techniques" to the enemy, Marcelo has done the exact opposite. Every single one of his training sessions, techniques, and sparring rounds is filmed and put online for anyone to watch. He rolls with any high level guy who comes to visit in his gym, and that happens daily. His opponents can study every detail of all his moves and tactics, yet no one has found a way to beat him.

It proves clearly that it doesn't make any sense not to train with as many different people as possible.

I had adapted the same policy at home. Telling people they can't go anywhere else to train is like not competing because you are afraid to lose. You have to challenge yourself, both as an athlete and as a teacher. If someone leaves your gym, you know there is a hole in your game as an instructor and you have to fix it.

Josh and I were going the same direction when the training session was over and talked a bit while walking down the avenue. He had written a book himself and we talked about how much work it took. He promised to bring me a copy of it, along with another one about traveling he suggested I should read.

My girlfriend was leaving for the airport in an old metallic-colored shuttle bus the next day. It was parked by Penn Station with the engine running as we arrived.

We hugged for what seemed like eternity. Two months until I was back home was suddenly a long time.

It was hard to say goodbye, but we were both smiling. One last kiss with a tear in my eye, and she got on the bus. I felt that lump in my throat again that I had felt in the airport at home when I left her the first day of the trip.

From the sidewalk on the other side of the street, I observed her through the window of the bus. She was wearing headphones and reading some papers, not knowing that I was still looking at her. She looked sad and beautiful.

"I'll miss you," I said.

She couldn't hear me.

Daniel from Taiwan had just arrived in New York on vacation, and I met up with him in a small bar near Central Park. He was still wearing one of my Jiggy-Jig caps from Bali that I had given him.

I hadn't had much time to hang out with my old buddy Christian from the Ronin gym, so he tagged along for my last night in New York. It was good fun to talk to two of my good friends I had both met on the road.

Christian said—when we talked about how I, on several occasions during the trip, hadn't showered for days—that he didn't know if he could do what I did; if he could cope with becoming so dirty.

Being dirty was one of the least of my concerns while I was on the road. In fact, my entire appearance seemed less and less interesting to worry about. I was wearing nothing but worn out Jiu Jitsu t-shirts I had picked up in gyms along the way, and they'd started to smell a bit. At least I brushed my teeth twice a day, but that was about it. And it wasn't like I was never dirty at home. Like that day when two dogs—independently of each other—were both manically focused on sniffing my crotch on the Copenhagen metro train. Time to wash those jeans.

CHAPTER TWENTY

Fight

I knew that competition was the way to make Jiu Jitsu and MMA grow in our little country. A few MMA-like tournaments were trying their luck with mixed success. My interest was still mostly in the grappling aspect of the sport, and in 2001, I decided to set up the first grappling competition in the country. I'd built a website for the Danish martial arts community, and through the network developed on its discussion forum, we managed to attract the who's who of grapplers in the country.

Most people had signed up for the no-gi competition, but there was also a small interest in gi, and to me, it was only a question of the more the merrier. I had never trained with a gi before, but was eager to get some matches on my record so I bought a cheap one for the occasion. With my mother's sewing machine, I plastered it with patches. I had seen that the Brazilians had tons of patches on their gis, and I wanted to do the same. I didn't have any real ones, so I just cut out some t-shirts with a pair of scissors. I remember having patches from a bungee jump I did in Spain, one with a blue cat, and a flag pole with a Danish flag on the chest. It looked ace.

I felt the adrenaline stiffening my body as it was my turn to step on the mat. It was my first grappling competition ever, and I'd had to arrange it myself to make it happen. The matches were a mess. I had no idea what I was doing. At one point, I had one of the opponent's head and arm between my legs for a triangle choke but couldn't remember any details on the finish. I had only seen it once on one of our VHS tapes a few months earlier and never really practiced it. I got on top of a Norwegian guy and passed his guard with the least technical guard pass I have seen in my life to this date. I found myself in side control and recalled having seen the position somewhere but not remembering what to do from there.

I managed to win a few matches and went straight home to the gym to find out what went wrong so it could be fixed for next time.

It was small steps, but they were on the right path. For every competition, I learned something new, and all the little gyms around the country really began to work hard towards taking home the big trophies I had bought. I didn't win any of them myself. A young, talented guy called Martin—who is now fighting in the UFC—took all of them instead.

After having trained for about four years, I was intrigued by the thought of having an MMA fight. I had played around with the thought of getting a fight in Portland when I was there for training, but it didn't work out. With all the grappling tournaments I had been setting up and competing in, I felt like it was time to push my competitive career to the next level.

Having just been promoted to blue belt was a confidence boost for me. It was like a confirmation that our little gym was going in the right direction and we somehow knew what we were doing. Knowing that competition was a good vehicle for improving and pushing myself, I thought that trying out MMA would be the natural next step. We had been training more striking and clinching than ground fighting at that point, so I was comfortable in my skills.

I started talking to a few of the guys around the country who had ideas of promoting shows. It was a small community and everyone knew each other. One of them offered me a fight with a really experienced guy from the other BJJ gym in town, Nic Osei. He already had a handful MMA fights on his record and was an overall impressive competitor. I knew I wouldn't stand a chance against him, so I told them that I didn't think it was a good match up.

During the time they were working on finding another opponent for me, the show got canceled due to some issues that I don't recall. At the same time, I had signed up for Fight Back, another show that also got canceled.

I kind of postponed the idea of fighting a bit. The nervousness that followed along with just signing up was already hard to bear, so both shows getting canceled was almost a relief. I wanted to fight, but on the other hand, I didn't.

A Shootfighting show was held a few months later, and I was in the spectator seats as always. It was a weird kind of fight with amateur MMA rules, open hand strikes and grappling only when the competitors were on the ground. Guy Mezger was there, since he was doing a seminar in town. I had the occasion to roll with him a little bit and he manhandled me as expected. At the end of the show, he stepped into the ring and announced to the audience that he was going to be fighting in the first ever professional MMA show in Scandinavia. It would be held three months later in Copenhagen and the fights would be in a cage. At that time, events only had boxing rings and the only place I had ever seen a cage was in VHS videos from the early UFC shows.

Psyched up from watching all the matches during the day, I got caught up in the moment. I told my friends from the gym that if it would be in a cage, I would sign up right away. Having said it out loud, I couldn't take it back. I knew that. Somehow, I needed to trick myself into a situation where I couldn't run away and had to step up to the challenge.

The promoter was one of my good friends from the martial arts community, and I found him after the show. I told him—with a lump in my throat—that he could sign me up for December. He would already start finding an opponent for me the next week.

Shit. There was no turning back now. I had to do it. Full contact, professional rules in a cage. Small gloves, no shinpads, no nothing. Just me and my opponent—whoever he would be.

We had just started up the new gym in the Judo place a few months earlier. For the first time, I had facilities whereby I could train every day—all day if I wanted to. Fighting MMA would be a great way to promote the newly opened gym. By stepping in the cage, I wanted to prove to myself and those I trained with that I believed in what I was teaching. With all the debates online about what system and training methods were the best, I would show that at least I wasn't afraid to test out my claims.

The promoters were fast. They already called me the following week and told me they had an opponent for me. It was a guy I already knew pretty well. His name was Sonny and he trained in another town about an hour and a half away from me. We had met and trained on several occasions. I considered him a friend and it was a bit weird to think about fighting him, but the options were few and I didn't want to try and find an excuse to back out. I said yes to the fight, signed the contract, and put it in the mailbox. No time to stop and think about it.

From that day on and every second until I stood in the cage three months later, my thoughts were concentrated on nothing else but the fight. I couldn't get it out of my head. What would happen? Would I lose? Could I die? What would everyone say if I lost? Would people leave the gym?

I wasn't listening when people were talking to me. I didn't pay attention to my girlfriend. I couldn't sleep. When I hit the bag in the gym, I was completely in my own world. Going home from training in the bus, I would suddenly wake up from my thoughts and realize that I had gone two or three stops too far. My mind was taken over by thoughts about the fight. It consumed me.

We had no idea how to go about the training for a fight like this.

My biggest concern was my cardio and my weight. I only had to lose three kilos but knew nothing about cutting weight. Even though there would be a weigh-in the day before, we didn't even think about just cutting the weight there. I decided to diet my way down under 77 so I would weigh that on the day.

Since I had to get lighter, it seemed logical that I shouldn't do any weight lifting or physical training for the fight in case I would add muscle mass. Today, that is a totally stupid idea to me, of course, but we didn't know any better back then really.

One of my training partners who was studying to become a physiotherapist came up with a simple cardio program for me. Instead of running, I would do interval striking on a heavy bag every morning.

With the fresh blue belt around my waist—or actually not, since I didn't train with a gi—I felt really confident in my grappling and thought that I didn't need to train that as much. I was more concerned about not being experienced enough in the striking, since the only standup competition I had done was a single Taekwondo match at the age of eleven. Especially, the thought of getting hit with the small gloves was scary.

Everything in consideration, I decided to do an hour of Muay Thai sparring with the small gloves every morning. My training partner was a heavy guy with a lot of experience, and he basically beat me up for three months to the point where I could eat nothing but yogurt in periods since my jaw was so sore. I didn't really weigh myself but just assumed myself that I would be under 77 by the time of the fight.

Another thing I was worried about was fighting without shin pads. To become accustomed to the pain of potentially getting hit hard on the shin, I would kick the metal pole of the bus stop outside the gym for about fifteen minutes every day while I waited for the bus to get home. Van Damme would have been proud.

In the evenings, I was still teaching classes and didn't get to train much. I felt a bit frustrated that I didn't get the focused training I needed, but on the other hand, I knew that when I stepped into the cage, so many other factors would play a role.

The training itself was only a small part of what would influence the outcome on the day.

After a few months of full on standup sparring with small gloves, cardio workout on a heavy bag, no weight lifting, no grappling, kicking a bus stop, and only eating chicken with vegetables, the time had come. Today, it seems like the strangest preparation for an MMA fight ever, and it probably was. Despite that, it worked. I had come to a point where I had gotten hit in the face so many times that I just didn't care about it anymore. In sparring, I would block strikes with my forehead just to get to an opening on my opponent. I could block the hardest kicks with my shin and ignore the pain. My cardio felt great, and I just kept going forward.

Sonny could hit me as hard as he wanted, and I wouldn't care. I had already won the hardest fight I had signed up for: The fight against my own fear.

At the weigh-in the day before, I stepped on the scale. 74.5 kilos. I had lost almost six kilos and was way below weight. My opponent was 76.5. It was nice to see him in real life again after having had his image in my mind for so long. He was shorter than me, which was somehow a comfort.

My apartment was pretty close to the venue. I had been there in the morning to set up some cameras since I was also in charge of the DVD production of the show. Another thing that seems completely silly, thinking of it now.

The sports hall was still lit up by the sunlight coming through the windows, and standing in the cage didn't seem frightening at all. There was no audience yet, only a few guys walking around, setting up chairs. I tried to look inside myself for nervousness, but there was nothing. I was completely calm and more than anything, felt excited to get in there and get it over with.

The fight card was stacked with big names. Guy Mezger, Travis Lutter, and Martin Kampmann were all there, along with several other stars from the Scandinavian scene. I had the first match, and it suited me well.

As the place was getting darker, people started to show up. I still didn't feel nervous as I walked around the venue and chatted to my friends.

One of the runners told me that they would be starting my match thirty minutes later.

Then it hit me like a freight train. The adrenaline dump was massive. My legs were wobbly and I was shaking heavily.

I asked one of the experienced Norwegian fighters if he was nervous as we stretched out next to each other in the warm up room.

"Always," he replied.

My training partner and the co-owner of the gym, Carsten, held the pads for me and pushed me really hard. He shouted at me to kick harder, to get myself together. I felt horrible. There was no power in my punches or kicks. I couldn't lift my leg. My stomach was turning and I felt like throwing up. I had never been that much under pressure before, and it was mentally the toughest time of my life.

I decided in my head that I was going to go tell the organizers that I had to bail.

Before I knew it, the runner came into the room and called my name.

I looked at Carsten with desperation in my eyes. I couldn't do it. It was too overwhelming. I observed my legs walking through the door to the hall. The announcer called my name, and the spotlight hit my eyes. Everyone stood up in the chairs and started cheering. I had so many friends, training partners, and family members in that hall.

That very second, everything changed. My body stopped shaking and my eyes focused. Five minutes earlier, I had been exposed to the biggest adrenaline shock of my life, but that suddenly felt like the past.

I stopped thinking. My mind was empty and I walked over the floor towards the cage, moving fluidly. I was in complete autopilot mode and the world around me seemed quiet and calm.

I stepped in the cage and high-fived Sonny. He looked nervous and pale.

The referee asked me if I was ready. I didn't notice my mouth moving, but I heard myself replying with a "yes."

Sonny stepped towards me and the only thing I could see was how big his arms looked.

I thought to myself that I didn't feel like getting hit by them, and before I knew it, I had ducked under his jab and taken him down with a double leg.

Despite having trained nothing but striking, I didn't have any game plan for the fight. Now, I had taken him down in the first seconds, and all the morning trainings where I'd gotten hit in the head were suddenly irrelevant.

He felt light. The other guys I usually trained with were almost twenty kilos heavier than him.

I mounted him easily and thought to myself that I'd better finish the fight right there so I wouldn't risk burning out on the cardio later.

Kneeride. Mount.

I started hitting him in the face but it was like a bad dream. Nothing happened. I kept hitting him again and again, aiming for the eyebrows and chin to either cut him or knock him out. He was desperately waving his arms in front of his head, trying to deflect the punches. The crowd went wild. I couldn't believe that the referee didn't step in. I threw the punches as hard as I could, but he was as tough as nails and wouldn't give in.

Then he sat up and reversed me. Everyone got up from their chairs, cheering.

I couldn't believe. It wasn't over.

The desperation hit me for a second as he was lying on top of me in my guard. I could feel something wasn't right in my shoulder. I shook it off and got back in focus. An attempted flower sweep set up a perfect strike to his face. He was starting to swell up badly around both eyes. I was breathing heavily and my shoulder hurt, so I knew I had to finish him.

He grabbed around my neck with his right hand, trying to set up a punch with his left. My Jiu Jitsu instinct took over, and I climbed my leg over his shoulder, then his head. His arm was in the perfect position and I pulled it—probably too hard, but I was desperate. I was in a fight, and it wasn't me.

I didn't feel him tap, but as the audience cheered, I let go.

The referee signaled for us to stop the fight.

A loud, primal scream came out of my mouth from deep within as I clenched my fists and raised my arms over my head. All the thoughts, worries, and frustrations that had built up over three months came out in that scream. I had finished the fight by submission after one minute and thirty seven seconds into the first round.

For myself, I knew right away that it was the end of my MMA career. I wasn't interested in the mental pressure of the preparations. I went in there to prove to myself and everyone I teach that I believe in what I do and that I am not afraid to put it to the test. I completed the challenge, and that was enough for me. I was not, and never will be, a fighter.

Sonny looked horrible, and I felt almost sad for him as he stood there with ice packs on two enormous black eyes. On the other hand, things could only go forward for him from there. He went on to fight more than fifteen times over the following six years and became one of the best guys in Scandinavia with only three losses on his record.

He is a lot tougher than I'll ever be.

CHAPTER TWENTY-ONE

Virginia

It was a four-hour bus drive to Washington DC. I'd looked forward to reading my new books and enjoying the view, but I was hungover badly from the one-night reunion with Christian and Daniel. Whenever I tried to read or look too much out of the window, I got nauseous and had to stop.

Elyse—a reader of my blog, who had offered me a couch for the night—was waiting for me in a Starbucks by the bus stop. She had brought sandwiches for me so I could get some food before training. I felt horrible, so it was nice to have a fellow Jiu Jitsu friend take a little care of me.

I mostly felt like eating and sleeping, but since I was staying only one day in town, I did not want to miss my chance of training with Ryan Hall and his guys. I had to go straight to the gym to make it in time for the class.

The underground stations were enormous concrete structures and must have looked really futuristic in the eighties. Once again, I found myself in an Arnold Schwarzenegger movie from my childhood.

The class had already started when I got to the gym. It was upstairs in a small, isolated commercial building surrounded by a parking lot. Music was playing at a low volume and Ryan was teaching the class as I entered the room. He stopped for a second to raise his hand and welcome me as he saw me arrive.

I'd met Ryan several years back at one of my trips to New York where he had started training in Ronin Athletics with Christian Montes before he moved to D.C. He was on a visit to New York at the same time as me and popped by to have a roll in his old gym. I hadn't been following much of the BJJ competition scene at that time, so I didn't know anything about him other than his name. After tapping me out with spinning triangles from upside down guard a million times in five minutes, I figured I'd better try and learn what he was doing. He was—like myself—still a purple belt at that time, but he manhandled me worse than most black belts I had rolled with up until then.

I had planned to go visit Marcelo Garcia's gym that evening and Ryan had the same thing in mind, so we went there together. I met him a few times at tournaments in the following years but never got the chance to train with him again. Now, I stood in his gym with a horrible hangover and no sleep after a full day of sitting on a bus. I was nowhere near ready for training, but I wouldn't miss it for the world.

Ryan's attention to detail was stunning. He was teaching a pretty basic sweep from when the opponent was standing up in the guard. What was interesting was how he spent a huge amount of time analyzing every single situation that could happen in the scramble that followed. I had seen numerous videos of him compete and pull off moves that seemed impossible to figure out. Observing him teach, it was obvious that the flowcharts he had in his head of every technique had to be huge. He went through every possible outcome of the situation, unfolding the role of each limb, reaction, and possibility. He made people understand the consequences of every counter and counter-counter the opponent could do. He asked the students questions all the time.

What would happen if the left leg touches the ground? What way would your opponent have to turn to make it impossible for you to take the back? Which hand do you need to control to prevent him from standing back up?

My tired brain was overloaded with information, but it was inspiring to see such a deep level of detail and understanding.

The guys looked hungry. The World Championship was just around the corner, and everyone seemed very focused.

Ryan asked me if I wanted to go the first round. There was no way I could say no to rolling with him, no matter how shitty I felt, so I told him that it would be my pleasure.

Pleasure was maybe not the right word. I still felt horrible, and I was not about to get any better in the hands of one of the best in the world.

As we clapped hands, his eyes changed. I saw an immense focus as I looked into them. There was no connection with the outside world—like he put on a mask and went on auto-pilot.

My legs were tired, but even if they were fresh, he would have still passed my guard like he did in only a few seconds.

He put his knee on my chest and I couldn't move. It felt like my lungs were collapsing and my head exploding. Seconds before I was about to give up, he switched to side control. His cross face was one of the strongest I had ever felt. His bicep crushed my face so hard that my ear channel closed up and it felt like I was under water. I think I remembered he was a light weight, but he seemed more like a super heavyweight on top of me.

I had lost a lot of strength on the trip and my muscles felt like jelly. The pressure was insane—I was nowhere near getting out of his control.

I felt like a child in his hands. There was nothing I could do. He mounted me, and the pressure from the position only made it difficult to breathe. I tried to find little pockets of air to suck in, but eventually I had to tap out. And he wasn't even trying to submit me yet.

I looked at the timer. There were still two minutes to go. All I wanted in life at that point was to say stop, but it was my own fault that I felt so bad. I could have chosen not to drink the night before. I could have gone to bed earlier. I could have taken my time to get to Arlington and relax there for a few days instead of going straight from the bus to the gym. Here I was, rolling with one of the toughest players in the world for one night only, and I was about to say "no, thank you?" It was not happening. I had to keep going.

There was no ego. He wasn't trying to prove anything. I sucked and I came in to train during the last preparations for the biggest competition in the world.

Second time around was exactly like the first. It was pure survival from my side. All my focus went on breathing and not throwing up. I gave up the back and Ryan punched his forearm across my face. I tapped out and the timer beeped.

Ryan said thanks for the roll as his eyes and smile went back to normal.

I sat on the mat with my head between my legs. I had a taste of blood in my mouth, a headache, and a big bruise on the top of my head. I had basically just gotten completely beat up.

Despite everything in my body screaming for me to stop, I took a few more rounds of rolling. It was a tough crowd in the gym with lots of seriously good guys. Gianni, a young, strong purple belt, toyed with me for ten minutes. I could only hang on, defend, and try to survive. I had no offense left in me; no timing; no strength. I felt like a white belt in the hands of the hungry, competitive guys who were all in killer shape. I was paying for the way I had tortured my body with alcohol. It was relentlessly punishing me for not being disciplined.

Class was over and people were sitting around on the mats. I couldn't say anything. I wished I could have gone back in time and done things right. I only had one chance to train in this gym and I blew it. I rested my aching head in my hands, holding it up by grabbing my long, messy hair. Ryan was still going at it. He was manhandling a bigger purple belt and not even using his hands. His legs moved like they were a set of arms. It was amazing to watch.

When he was done, I politely asked if he wanted me to pay a mat fee for the class.

"Are you kidding me?" he said, looking almost offended that I assumed he would charge me.

Then he asked if I wanted to meet up the next day around noon and do some more training. I was surprised that he wanted to train more with me after the non-existent amount of resistance I had given him half an hour earlier. I wouldn't have minded a second chance, but I was leaving with the bus the next morning already. Once again, I had to turn down a private training session with one of my idols of the sport. My bad day just got worse.

As I walked out of the gym, bruised, in pain, and on the verge of throwing up, I promised myself to never treat my body like that again the day before training. It was horrible. My year-and-a-half-old, worn out brown belt was wrapped around my gi. I carried it over my shoulder as I stood by the bus stop, waiting for Elyse to pick me up. Despite knowing that I would have done better if I was rested, my confidence had taken a big hit. It felt like I had let myself down. I had lost focus and not taken my job seriously. I still had a long, long way before reaching black belt level.

"Where ya going, son?" the bus driver asked me as I stood there at the station, looking confused with my ticket in hand.

He was excited to hear that I was looking for his bus to Richmond.

Another traveler asked for the bus to New York.

"Neew Yorrk! That's down there, folks! Uuuhum!"

I jumped on the old Greyhound and found a place to sit. I wondered how many times that seat had traveled across the country. It had holes in it and the curtains in my window must have been hanging there for at least a decade or two. The old speaker crackled as the driver turned on the microphone and kindly informed us all that we were now about to hit the road— destination Richmond, Virginia.

Robert called. He would be at the bus station to pick me up twenty minutes later.

As I sat there and waited, I thought about our trip together in Eastern Europe. It almost felt unreal… Like it didn't happen. It was such a different place from where I was at now, and it was hard to recall the feeling of driving small, Soviet busses in the snowy, dark Romanian landscape as anything other than a dream. I thought about how the kids in the village were doing and wondered if I'd ever be able to come back to them again.

As I walked out of the station, the sun was shining and loud music was playing from a stadium across the road.

It was great to see Robert and Amanda again, and they both gave me a big hug. The drive to the campsite took a few hours. It seemed like it was just an endless landscape of fields and forests. Every ten minutes or so, we would pass by a small house. I was pleased that, once again, I had succeeded in finding my way out of the big city to look for adventure. A few days of camping was going to be a nice break from training and definitely something different to cross off the list.

The family had camped by a river in the forest. I shook hands with everyone and they welcomed me to the Redneck Riviera, as they called it.

A few oversized trucks and two enormous campers were parked across from each other on the small patch of grass. One of them displayed an eagle, an American flag, and the text "Big Country" on it. A few tents were already raised, the bonfire was going, and country music came out of the speakers from one of the campers. I was excited to spend a few days in the open air.

I pulled my backpack out of the car and put on a hoodie. It was already getting dark and a bit colder. I gave Robert the envelope with the money from the fundraiser seminar in New York.

It would be interesting to see what the kids in the little village could get out of it.

Everyone in the family was really nice to me, and I felt at home on the little camp site. It was an area big enough to hold some tables and a trailer, and had a roof over it so that when it started drizzling a little bit, we all got under it to stay dry. Cookers were filled with seafood, and everyone was anxious for the dinner to be ready, myself included!

Someone shouted with a singing, southern accent for us to be careful, and poured the steaming hot seafood from the cookers into big, tin containers.

The table fitted all of us, and we sat around it, eating crabs, potatoes, sausages, and mussels with our fingers for what seemed like hours. It looked like there was an unlimited amount of food, and I stuffed myself to the point where I had almost had too much. Robert battled his brother long after the rest of us gave up. The piles of crab shells looked like little volcanoes and filled both their plates to the limit.

When I was done eating, I walked to the bushes by the river to take a leak. It was dark, and the air was damp and fresh from the rain that had just passed. The quiet country music played from the camper on the other side of the campsite, and the re-lit bonfire crackled softly. It was hard not to smile at my own luck, being able to experience something like that on my trip.

We sat in little chairs around the bonfire and talked while making s'mores and marshmallows. Two days earlier, I had been walking around the stressful streets of Manhattan. Looking into the fire was calming and reminded me of my childhood. We had a campfire place in the backyard of our house and during summer, my brother, our friends, and I made bonfires there every time we had the opportunity. In my teens—when we were still too young to go to bars—we often had parties by the campfire in the forest which our small town bordered. More than a few times, the flames got a little too high, and I am still surprised that we never burned that forest down on the dry summer nights.

A few beers went down, and we spent the rest of the evening playing a game with dice and quarters. I didn't have any American change to play with, but my bag was full of coins from around the world that I could throw in the game. A big one from the Philippines became sought after by the players. Anytime someone hit a six with the die, they immediately looked to grab the "Filopian quarter," as it was quickly named.

I shared a tent with Robert and Amanda that we raised in the middle of the night when we were done playing with Filopian and Taiwanasian money. We didn't have any mattresses, but my super light sleeping bag did just fine, even though I was lying directly on the ground in it.

There were crabs and country music for breakfast. The sun had come out and I was enjoying it, sitting in a chair trying to wake up. The crabs tasted as good as the night before, and the eating contest had picked up again.

I was sad to leave life on the Redneck Riviera, but my itinerary was set and I was heading south.

CHAPTER TWENTY-TWO

Florida

A handful of trucks were parked outside the little wooden house by the river.

"Shady Oak," the sign above the door said.

It looked shady.

I entered the old wooden house. It didn't seem like it would be able to withstand a hurricane, but on the other hand, it was so old that it must have done just that several times.

The place was quiet, and there was a smell of beer. It was more of a bar than a restaurant. The walls were filled with old signs, beer posters and registration plates. A few lonely slot machines were standing to my left with flashing lights, waiting for someone to throw in a quarter. Six or seven truckers with flannel shirts and caps were sitting in the bar, each holding their beer in hand. No one was talking to each other and there was no music playing. The juke box looked like it had given up and died years ago. One of the guys in the bar cleared his throat and the bartender bumped two glasses together, but apart from that, the only sound heard was a little buzzing noise coming from a refrigerator. It felt like a place where time stood still.

Derek entered through the door behind me and broke the silence. He had a little grin on his face and said something about getting us a local specialty.

His wife had been worried about letting a stranger stay in their house, but he had assured her that I was just a down to earth Jiu Jitsu guy traveling the world and couldn't possibly be a murderer or something like that. I told him that there was nothing to worry about, since I had put the whole serial killing thing behind me years earlier.

He laughed. And I don't blame him for that, as it really was a quality joke.

We were sitting on a patio over the river with alligators both on our plates and in the water below us. A young couple next to us reminded me of the rednecks from The Simpsons.

Derek said he had come to that place since he was a kid and claimed they made the best alligator tail in the area.

Signs all over indicated that it probably wasn't a good idea to go swimming unless you wanted to end up on some alligator's plate. Growing up in a country with absolutely no mortal threat from wild animals or natural disasters, it was quite interesting to be in a place where you had to be on guard from nature itself.

It was time to head to the gym. As we walked out through the little bar, I stood for a moment in the door and studied the scene one last time. The lack of pace in that place was almost paralyzing. I was reminded to wake up and leave as two of the truckers turned around towards me on their bar chairs and gave me a look that said, "What do you think you are doing here, kid?" like something from a western B-movie, just in the east.

Looking through the storefront windows, Gracie Barra Orlando seemed like a really big place. I had to fill out a waiver in the reception, and there was a $10 mat fee. Before I had a chance to say that I left my money in the car, Derek had whipped out a note and thrown it on the desk, insisting on paying for me.

A few guys in the locker room recognized me and told me they were following my blog. It was a bit weird to suddenly be a "celebrity" in that way, but promoting the trip online was an important vehicle for making all the traveling possible for me.

About thirty or forty people had shown up for the class, and I counted a handful of brown and black belts in between the others. Aside from after my training with Ryan, I no longer had any thoughts in my mind about how I would perform against high level guys; no worries—like I had earlier on the trip—whether I could live up to my belt color or not. At that point, I had rolled with hundreds and hundreds of strangers in gyms along the way, and it didn't bother me a bit anymore. I did pretty well with most other brown belts—they rarely surprised me with any moves that I hadn't been exposed to before—and I had a lot of confidence in the game I played myself.

I partnered up with Derek for the techniques. He was a purple belt and in tremendous shape.

After twenty minutes, we started doing a guard passing round. It felt like some guys went a little hard on me to begin with, and I got swept every single time I was in. It was important for me not to go too hard on people, being a guest in their gym… At least not before I had gotten to know them first. I spent a lot of time standing in line and waiting with all the white belts who got swept like me. I had let people play their guard game in order for me to try and understand what they did. The better I understood my opponent's moves, the better I could handle them later in sparring.

The round ended for me when a guy did a perfect Steven Seagal front kick to my balls. I had forgotten my cup in Montpellier, and now it was most likely lost somewhere in a postal office in Asia, on its way to Borneo. I was probably not allowed to wear it in training anyways and definitely not in a Gracie Barra gym.

After sitting by the wall a little while to give my future kids a rest, I was ready for sparring. In the first round, a guy head-butted me in the balls as he tried to pass my guard.

"What the fuck is up with you guys and my balls?" I laughed as I fell down on my back in pain.

Another round was skipped before I was up for rolling again. No one can ever make me understand that stupid rule about not being allowed to train with a cup.

My game felt much better than my last training session, the hangover catastrophe in Virginia. This time, I had actually rested and hadn't been drinking the night before so that probably helped a bit.

The moves I had decided to practice on the trip had become solid weapons in my arsenal, sharpened to near perfection in gyms halfway across the world. I could hit my arm drag, double leg sweep, and stiff arm side control escapes on almost everyone at that point. Derek asked me to show him how I did it, as I had escaped his side control for the fifth time with the same move.

Another guy I rolled with was a very skilled and tough blue belt. I took his back and sunk in a bow and arrow choke. He didn't intend on tapping, and before I knew it, he went limp. Everyone stopped rolling and looked at me as they realized I had just choked a guy unconscious. It reminded me of the similar, awkward situation in New York.

The guy laughed when he woke up again, realizing what had happened, and said it was his own fault for being so stubborn.

I was happy that I had regained my pace. It had only been a quick visit for less than 48 hours, but I had nothing but good memories to bring along in the backpack.

The feeling of surfing the world was back, and I intended to keep up the pace as much as I could for the time to come. The next day, I was visiting my old friends on their boat in the Virgin Islands, and from there, anything could happen.

CHAPTER TWENTY-THREE

British Virgin Islands

I threw my backpack in the wobbly little rubber dinghy. Dropping it in the water would be a catastrophe with all the electronic equipment I was carrying around the world. It would have been much cooler to do the trip all analogue—notepad, pencils, compass, and a walk man. Mike pulled the throttle and raced the hundred or so meters towards the boat.

It was a beautiful white catamaran. Compared to the other luxury boats that were docked around us, it looked small, but it was big enough for two people to live on full time. Rebecca was pulling some ropes as I got on board. She gave me a big hug and introduced me to Carl, a hitchhiker they had just picked up the same day.

Carl looked very much like a serial killer.

The boat was awesome. It had a little kitchen, a couch with a table, a storage room, and a bedroom. Laptops and books were lying around on the table. I sat down on the couch and listened to the rain on the window above me.

I had never spent a night on a boat and was thrilled to live on one for a few days or however long I ended up staying. It was a great feeling to have made it there. Since I got the idea of going on the trip, visiting Mike and Rebecca was one of the first destinations I put on my wish list. They had both gotten their black belts a few years earlier and owned a thriving gym in Canada, but despite that, they had decided to leave everything behind and permanently move to one of the few places in the world where it was most difficult to train Jiu Jitsu—a boat. It was hard for me to understand, and I am sure it was a very difficult decision to make, but giving up Jiu Jitsu was the price they had paid for turning their lives around and chasing their dreams. It was a big price, but it seemed like it had been worth it to them.

There was a full moon party on one of the neighboring islands that we went to. I had been traveling all day without much to eat, and I hoped there would be some food at the party. There wasn't, but they had plenty of rum! It was a recipe for disaster when combined with my empty stomach and lack of sleep. I don't remember much from the evening other than Mike tapped me out with a flying triangle on the sandy dance floor, and that I won a pull up competition in the bar against the locals.

We took a taxi back over the island to where the dinghy was parked. I insisted on steering the little inflatable boat. Apparently, I was too drunk to change our direction, so I pulled the throttle and we went round and round in circles, full speed. It was a miracle that we made it back to the boat without falling into the water.

I spent my very last drop of energy getting on to the boat and under deck. I fell face forward on the couch with all my clothes on and fell asleep the second my head hit the pillow.

The weather was beautiful as I woke up, and the little waves were gently tapping the side of the boat. I opened one eye and looked up at the window above me. The sky was clear blue, and I could smell the fresh air coming through the cabin.

Something was not right.

As I tried to move, I felt it… the hangover from hell.

I had eaten almost nothing the day before, and I drank rum all night. It was bad. Really bad.

I couldn't move. The waves that initially had seemed so gentle were making me sick. The sunlight hit me, and combined with the warm, humid air, left me feeling overheated and bloated. I couldn't breathe.

Mike was fresh as a seagull and told me to get up and get to work. I tried to answer him, but all I could manage to say was a weird and desperate sound that made both him and Rebecca laugh.

It was one of the worst hangovers I have ever had.

The weather was perfect. Small islands you could walk around in ten minutes were scattered all around the boat. They had green lush hills and perfect, empty beaches, surrounded by turquoise water. The real life Caribbean did in fact look like the Hollywood movies.

I wished I felt better so I could actually enjoy it and promised I would never touch alcohol again.

And by never, I meant the next few days.

A boat near us served as a floating bar and restaurant. It was designed like a little pirate ship, and even though it was early in the afternoon, there was a serious party going on when we got there.

I tried to figure out what time it was, but no one was wearing watches and there was no clock on the wall. Mike explained to me that there was no need for it, since all the days were the same and no one had to be anywhere at certain times. I replied with some highly philosophical remark about how the human invention of weekends and work hours were totally uncool, anyway.

The people on the boat definitely didn't care about what time of day it was. They acted like it could just as well have been in the middle of the night.

Some really voluptuous, black, Caribbean girls, tried to pull me to the dance floor. I still felt horrible and kindly declined the offer. They were having none of it and kept pulling me. Suddenly, one of their huge, dark butts started backing up towards me, rhythmically bouncing up and down. I skillfully dodged the hypnotic effect of it and stiff armed her lower back before she came too close—just like I would escape side control before my opponent had passed the guard and had a chance to settle his position. A local guy grabbed my wrist and tried to pull me to the girls. I was glad that hand fighting drills worked in a real life altercation about life or death as well. Wrestling saved me from drowning between those big, dark butt cheeks.

It reminded me of a similar situation at a full moon party on a beach in Koh Phangan, Thailand, a few years earlier. Yet another thicker girl tried to push me to the dance floor. I kindly tried to explain to her that I wasn't interested, but she would have none of it and kept pushing. Eventually, I gently arm dragged her to get her away, but accidentally—those buckets with vodka and Red Bull were cheap—ended up doing a full Marcelo Garcia-style leg trip. Her not so small body mass moving forward and her state of intoxication made her leap forward into the air as I stepped to the side, Aikido style. She face planted in the sand, getting wet sand all over her face and body, making her look like a sad, drunken sand monster. I felt horrible, but at the same time, it was difficult not to laugh. A quick look at my friend's face assured me that he was thinking the same as I. A little nod, and we quietly agreed that sprinting down the beach was the only right thing to do at that point.

In the dark, there isn't much to do on a boat, so eight in the evening is called "sailor's midnight." My day rhythm couldn't follow theirs just yet, so I was awake much longer than Mike, Rebecca, and anyone else in the boats around us, it seemed.

In front of the catamaran, a trampoline was suspended over the water between the two hulls. It was warm all night, and I lay there with only my shorts on. It was really quiet. A few, small clouds were scattered around the sky, lit up by the nearly full moon. Around them, countless of stars shined, more than I had ever seen in my life. The water was still, and I tried not to think about how many sharks were lurking around right beneath me. The only sound I could hear was the water gently rocking the boat and cicadas from the jungle on the island right ahead of us. Lightning from a thunderstorm far away blinked a few times, lighting up the white sails of the boats in the water around me for a split second. I leaned back and looked up at the stars.

I had to make a decision about whether I should leave or stay on the boat for a little longer. Mike and Rebecca were planning a multi-day sail down to St. Martin, and they had to go when the weather was right for it. I really enjoyed life on the boat and it was tempting to go along, but joining that journey could potentially keep me on the boat for a week more if the weather got us stuck somewhere far away from an airport.

The boat was great, but spending more than a week there, I was afraid I would end up getting bored and restless. And there was no time to waste on boredom on my ultimate, around-the-world adventure.

It was a difficult decision, but I eventually decided to stick with my plan of high-pace travel and leave a few days later. I wanted the memories of my visit there to be the best possible, so I had to move on to the next place and see what awaited me there.

I had an invitation to go to the Dominican Republic, and from a nearby island, I could get a ticket there with a one day stopover in Puerto Rico. I didn't know what to do with that stop over and couldn't get in touch with any Jiu Jitsu guys there, but I was confident that everything would sort itself out along the way. I went downstairs and brushed my teeth in the little bathroom, looking at myself in the mirror. I hadn't showered for four days, and I looked like a homeless guy. In some sense, I was. My hair was longer than it had ever been in my life, and it was curly and dirty from not being washed in anything but salt water since Florida.

Rebecca had unfolded the couch into a bed for me. It had four times the room compared to what I had slept on the night before when I crashed after the full moon party. I lay down and looked up at the starry sky through the window above me. Apart from the roof that sheltered for the rain, the room with the couch was open on one side, so it was almost like sleeping outdoors.

There weren't any waves. The boat would occasionally make a deep, squeaking sound when the water twisted its hull. The mast light of another boat silently moved past the little piece of the night sky, I saw from where I was lying.

It was my first night ever sleeping on a boat, and it felt great. The night before didn't count, since I passed out instead of slept.

The boat lulled me to sleep. I knew Mike was going to wake me up early and put me to work—pulling ropes, setting sails, and what not.

CHAPTER TWENTY-FOUR

Breaking Free

In 2001, at the age of nineteen, I finished high school. My grades were high, and I could pick and choose between most universities. In my last year at school, I'd had a job in a software company as a programmer and graphical designer. I wasn't an expert in either of the fields, but I knew enough of both to become a valuable bridge between the people working on the back- and front end side of our product. I could read and alter codes that the programmers had written and translate it into a graphical interface like the designers wanted it. My lifelong interest in computers had paid off, and it seemed like I had somewhat of talent for it. When I graduated school, they offered me a full time job and a salary that was immensely better than anything else I could go out and get at that point.

Somehow, I slowly accepted that I had this skill to develop, and it could—and would probably be—what I should build the financial foundations for my future upon. It seemed exciting to suddenly make a lot of money out of something that was natural to me after having sat in front of a computer my whole life. Only a year later, I had saved up enough money to buy my own apartment. The feeling of having my own place was thrilling. I had painted the walls myself, sanded the floor, and bought all the furniture. It was a simple little place in a not very exotic part of town, facing a large road with lots of traffic. Despite that, every day when I came home and put the key in the door, I felt more at home than anywhere else I have ever lived. It was my own place. I owned it.

Even though work had been interesting and exciting to begin with, it quickly started to bore me. I began making up ways to get around actually doing something. Most of my time, I spent chatting with my friends or being on martial arts forums, debating with Kung Fu or pressure point masters about training for sport vs. street. I thought less about programming and more about getting to the gym to roll. Jiu Jitsu had taken over my mind, and I was getting frustrated with the outlook of my future.

When I grew up, my father had always emphasized that I should try to create a life for myself, where I was free—where I could move around and not just get stuck in an office.

I had done the exact opposite and was annoyed that I hadn't succeeded in following his advice. Making money and owning an apartment was fun, but I couldn't stop wondering if I was on the right path. There had to be more to life than sitting in an office, getting paid every month, spending most of it on the mortgage and the rest on food and occasionally a night out or a short vacation. Breaking out of it seemed too difficult. I suddenly had bills to pay every month, and looking into the future, I could only see more of them coming.

I thought I owned an apartment but in fact, it owned me. I was already a slave of my life and on a fast track towards getting sucked deeper and deeper into misery.

Luckily, I had my training. Every evening in the gym, I could put on my gi, step onto the mat, and roll for a few hours to forget all about the real world. A world where I lived a life I didn't want. When I was younger, I trained to make my anger towards my father disappear. Now, it was the mortgage, future, and boring life of my colleagues that I needed to ignore for a few hours. Once again, the gym became my sanctuary.

I knew deep inside that I had to do something drastic to change my life. However, nothing happened. I just kept observing myself going to work every day and waiting to get paid at the end of each month. Months of routine life were being washed down the drain, one after the other. Months became years, and I was feeling more and more depressed. I had lots of money to spend, but my job was sucking the life out of me, and I didn't know what I would become down the road if I kept on like that. My colleagues were nice, but they also symbolized everything I didn't want to become. They all had a house in the suburbs, a car or two, and probably a dog and kids. They seemed like they liked their job and lives, but I had a suspicion that that was only because they eventually concluded they had no other choice. They were completely dependent on the cycle of working for, owning, and consuming all they had set up for themselves, and unless they convinced themselves to enjoy it, they would probably go nuts.

There was no room for changing the route or scene of their lives. It was all set, and it was way too late to break out of it.

I saw myself heading straight towards the same destiny. A life I didn't want, working every day with something I was losing interest in. As time passed, my frustration grew bigger and bigger as I realized that I was maybe too scared to do anything about it.

Five years into my so-called career, a short phone call from Carsten, my training- and business partner in the gym, suddenly changed everything, turning my life upside down.

It was an average day at the office. I had lobbied hard for years to get a location by the window with my back against the wall. That way, no one could look over my shoulder and find out that I was actually doing nothing. I had grabbed three discarded flat screen monitors from the stock room, installed them next to each other on my window ledge, and had them play an endless line of triple-monitor-spanning beach scene videos with relaxing ocean sounds. When I got an assignment, I would say that I estimated I could finish it in a week or so. I would be on martial arts forums or look at instructional videos for four and a half days before going full throttle and finish the work in half a day. Everyone was content with that.

After an extended lunch break, I played foosball for an hour with the only other young guy working in the company. I knew it annoyed my boss, but as long as I kept my deadlines, he didn't say anything. Getting fired wouldn't really bother me. Maybe I had been wishing for it to happen so I didn't need the courage to quit myself. I was a horrible employee, really.

Back at my desk, I was reading yet another debate on the efficiency of pressure point strikes in street fights when my phone rang. It was Carsten. The last few weeks, prior to the day, a lot of big decisions were being made around the gym. The national

Judo team, whose room we rented, was about to lose funding due to lack of international results. The sports hall hosting the facilities were deciding whether or not to use the space for one of their many other government funded sports, or to rent it out to a business. The Danish sports federation, who were funding the national teams, should decide whether to keep the room for another year or terminate their contract. They also needed to figure out what to do with all their mats and weight lifting facilities. Another guy from the Judo team had plans of taking over the contract and to make his own gym in the room.

It was a short window of opportunity for us and we had been acting fast, talking to everyone involved, trying to strike a deal and solve the puzzle. Now, we were only waiting for the decisions to be made. It was out of our hands and a complete make or break situation for us. We couldn't afford to buy brand new equipment, and getting another space in the city at the same price was impossible. With the Judo team closing, we needed to stand on our own feet in order for the gym to survive.

Thoughts were flying through my head—maybe he just wanted to say something unimportant. Carsten had a high profile job in an investment bank and disliked his life just as much as I did.

There was a pause that seemed like it lasted forever.

Then he broke the news.

Everything had fallen into place. We had taken over the rental contract and were offered all the mats, weights, and machines at scrap value. Carsten had checked our account and we could just afford it. The gym, and everything in it, was ours. We did it!

I hung up the phone and leaned back in my chair for a second. I took a few slow breaths and looked out the window. The weather seemed to always be gray and boring in the suburban industrial area where I was imprisoned by my lack of initiative and courage to do something drastic about it.

It was time. I knew that very moment would change and define the rest of my life. It only took about sixty seconds from hanging up the phone till I got up and walked steadily to the desk of my boss.

Then I told him that I would like to quit my job as soon as possible.

Cleverly, I had made sure to finish all my current projects and not take up any new ones in case I would get that very call.

I was allowed to leave with only a week's notice and I had literally brought my suitcase to the office on my last day there in order to go straight to the airport and out into the world when the work day had ended.

Less than a day later, I planted my feet in the middle of the Canadian country side, then the bustling city of New York and tropics of Florida. It left me with no doubt. My life with a desk job was over. Quitting that day was the most important decision of my life and I've never looked back.

The confidence in myself and my life had reached a new high. I was eager to go out in the world and learn as much as possible so I could bring it back home. The gyms around the country were all still rushing forward, everyone pushing each other to become the best they could be. It was a race, and I had chosen to sit in the driver's seat of my own car.

Thanks to the Straight Blast Gym organization, I had gotten to know a network of people around the world, especially in the United States. With my prior success traveling to Oregon and New York, I had extended my courage and set a four-destination itinerary in one five-week-long trip, visiting different gyms within the organization. It was ambitious, high paced, and I liked the taste of it.

After a grueling flight to Toronto with stopovers in Amsterdam and New York followed by a four-hour bus ride, I arrived in Kingston, Ontario. I spent a week there with Mike and Rebecca, who were brown and purple belts at the time. We trained every day and went on a trip out of town to hike in the forest. Next stop was Niagara Falls, where a guy called Rich had a small gym. I had a guest room to myself in the basement of his house and rode his mountain bike around town with my camera all day long. I walked the streets of Toronto for a day before flying to my friends at Ronin Athletics in New York. A big hurricane had just hit Florida, but I still went there for the annual Straight Blast Gym training camp. After five days without electricity and people starting to loot, a curfew was being issued for the dark hours.

The camp still went on for six hours a day. I was feeling good on the mats, rolling hard with everyone I could get my hands on. I was an eager beginner, trying to take as much experience and knowledge home with me as I could. Looking back, it is fun to think that I was probably one of those slightly annoying, athletic, 23-year old guys who wanted to test myself against everyone and see just how many colored belts I could beat.

Everyone was sitting around by the walls, and they put me in the middle. I knew what was coming for me. I hadn't even thought about the possibility of getting a purple belt at the camp only a year and a half after becoming blue in Oregon, but now it was kind of obvious what was about to happen.

One tough purple belt at a time went at me, and I took on all of them with everything I had. When I passed the guard of the third guy and submitted him from knee-on-belly with an arm bar, I knew I had passed the test. Matt went the last round with me and pinned me to the mat for fifteen minutes. When he finally let me free, I discovered that he had changed my belt during the roll.

Once again, our little gym at home had proven itself. We had made it to the next level.

Training was really warm and sweaty, and we needed a shower badly. There were no showers or electricity in the gym, so we six guys jumped into the back of a pickup truck and slowly rolled around a residential area in the early evening to look for options.

One of the guys spotted a pool in a house where it looked like no one was home.

We all got out of the truck, jumped the fence to the garden, and got undressed as fast as we could. I jumped into the water and went straight back up again, hurrying to get my clothes back on. We were dead scared that someone would notice us and we would get arrested, naked, for breaking into someone's garden and using their pool during a hurricane curfew.

Up until then, the closest I had ever come in my life to committing a crime would be to put eleven pieces of fruit in the bag in the supermarket when there was a discount for ten. Then stand at the counter—holding my breath, with a pounding heart—as the woman asked if there were ten pieces in the bag, and stumble over the word "yes." What a life on the edge I am living!

Around the same time, I had decided to sell my apartment and move in with my girlfriend. The feeling of having owned it was nice, but letting go of it was even nicer. I felt the load of the monthly mortgage immediately coming off my shoulders. I started to realize that letting go of things I was attached to in one way or another was a really great feeling. It was healthy for my mind and for my life.

The gym was still small, and we could barely afford to pay ourselves any salary at that point. I had basically cut off more than 90% of my income from one day to the other, but with the money from selling the apartment, I could handle the bills for a while. All I had to do was to be sensible about my spending and put everything I had into making the gym a success before I ran out of money. It sounded easy.

Training was going really well, and I felt like our little group was constantly improving. We had hit the first one hundred members, and I had become more confident. My own understanding of the game came through trying to explain it to everyone else every night on the mats. When I looked at a technique or position from the outside and attempted to describe it, I understood it better myself. I was basically teaching myself Jiu Jitsu. Matt had come over for seminars every year, and when he promoted the first blue belts on my team, it was one of the proudest moments of my teaching career.

It all looked like we were going in the right direction in terms of learning Jiu Jitsu. That's when I made a mistake.

CHAPTER TWENTY-FIVE

Dominican Republic

After the shortest possible visit in Puerto Rico, sleeping on a concrete floor in the house of a local surfer, I found myself in the Dominican Republic, trying to figure out how to get to the gym I had gotten in touch with. The bus station was dirty and old. People were waiting on metal benches, watching rugby on a TV hanging on the wall. A small shop sold sodas, snacks, and children's toys. To the left of the entrance was a sales desk. Behind a glass wall, four people sat in old office chairs with old computers, selling tickets. I walked up to one of them to get my ticket.

Each counter had two holes in the window for people to talk through. One of them was above my head, and one in the height of my crotch. I could pick between standing on my toes or bending over, and the girl working behind the glass didn't bother much leaning forward to hear me.

I was inventing entirely new ways to look ridiculous as I stood there and shouted through the holes, switching between standing on my toes and squatting to try and settle on what hole she could hear me best through. I was sure everyone behind me laughed at the stupid tourist trying to order tickets with homemade Spanish words.

Joe, a Canadian guy, picked me up at the last bus stop. First thing in the car, he warned me about trying to buy any form of drugs during my stay as I would probably be sentenced to life in prison on the spot.

The closest I have ever come to being a drug smuggler was in Havana airport in Cuba. I had checked my bag in and was in the line to board the plane as a uniformed guy came running and stopped me. When he confirmed that I was indeed Mr. Graugart, he firmly asked me to come with him.

We walked through corridors that looked like they were taken right out of a horror movie and behind a wooden door with a smoky class window in it, and my bag was put on a table in a small room. Behind it sat a big guy in a uniform, and in the shadow in the corner stood another one. They looked scary as hell and the one, old light bulb over the table didn't add to the coziness of the atmosphere.

The big guy said something in Spanish and pointed at the bag. I tried to explain to him that I didn't understand the language, but with his angry gestures, I understood he wanted me to open my bag.

I was pretty calm until it suddenly struck me. What if someone had put something in my bag?

My heart stopped.

They checked every square inch of it for drugs but luckily, there were none, and my nightmare of spending the rest of my life in a Cuban prison was called off. I missed out on a great chance to learn Spanish, but it was ok.

"Extreme Hotel Cabarete," the sign read as Joe pulled into the parking lot.

Joe and Papo, the two guys running the local Jiu Jitsu club, were managing the place and had set me a up with a room for twenty dollars a night. It was nice and spacious.

There had been a BJJ competition during the day and I arrived right in the middle of the after party. I dropped off my backpack, and walked outside, trying to find Joe again. About a hundred people were having a big party in an outdoor bar.

According to those religious people with the signs in New York, that night was supposed to be the end of the world. At least it would end with a good party it seemed, as the many people in the little bar were having a great time.

I needed a change of clothes after the long day of traveling, so I went back to my room. On the way, I noticed a big hole in the ground next to the bar. It was a skateboard ramp with a metal roof and a wooden fence, covered with palm leaves around it. I looked down and saw that the entire bottom of the ramp was covered with Jiu Jitsu mats.

I remembered seeing some photos on their website back home, planning the trip, but I never really noticed that they were actually training in an outdoor skateboard ramp. I wish I had been there earlier and seen the competition. It had basically been white belts only so there was no one I could compete against anyways, and I had made the decision to spend a day in Puerto Rico instead.

I got myself a drink. Joe and Papo—the only guys I knew at the party—were nowhere to be found.

A very drunk, American guy lived in the room next to me and was sitting outside his door with his laptop as I came by to get some money from my backpack. He introduced himself as Glen and asked if I wanted to go with him and some of the others to a casino.

That was my cue, and before I knew it, we were partying all night like it indeed was the end of the world.

Now, you might think the world ended that night and the book stops here. Think again.

My room was hot like an oven when I woke up. There was supposed to be a seminar at ten, but I had slept till eleven. I put on some shorts and walked out the door. The sunlight was bright, and the air fresh. Especially compared to what I had been sleeping in.

As I walked around the corner of the building, I stopped in amazement.

It had been so dark the night before that I had no idea the bar with the party where I spent several hours was literally right on a beautiful, Caribbean beach with perfect white sand, palm trees, and clear, blue water. The water was full of kite surfers; people were hanging out in couches in the bar; nice music was playing; girls in bikinis were in the swimming pool, and right in the middle of it, about forty people in gis were training Jiu Jitsu in an outdoor, descended skateboard ramp.

The world must indeed have ended the night before, since I obviously woke up in heaven. I looked to see if I could spot Jesus somewhere in the bar, but he was nowhere to be seen.

The place was amazing. They even had CrossFit, Spanish lessons and a fully equipped area for circus training. It was definitely a place where I could spend more than a few days.

Despite being mostly white belts, everyone on the mat looked really good. A seriously large brown belt guy asked me to roll. His name was Abraham. He had a deep voice, a game that was super tight, and he was really technical and moved fluidly for such a big guy. I had nothing on him, and he tapped me out left and right as he felt like it.

I told him about my trip and my plans to go to the World Championships to compete. He was going there as well and expecting to face his nemesis, a Danish guy, in the finals once again. It was Alexander Trans, who trained in another gym in my city, just a kilometer away from mine, who had beaten Abraham several times.

My new, tall friend was a nice guy, and he invited me to come stay and train with him in Santo Domingo, the capital in the south.

I had dinner with Papo. He was a charismatic guy with a worn out brown belt and a clear purpose. He wanted to help the young, local boys to have some opportunities in life, and he did it through Jiu Jitsu. Now and then, a few tourists from the hotel joined in on the training, but the majority of the people training there were locals in their teens.

Here, society was completely divided between rich and poor. There were some very, very rich people and some very, very poor. It was an easy place to get into trouble with drugs, gangs, and stuff like that, Papo told me. The kids there needed an alternative in career opportunities.

He seemed to know everyone on the island and had a deep reach into the local communities. A friend of his was selling fried chicken in one of the poorest areas of town. Knowing every boy running around on the streets, he acted like a talent scout for the Jiu Jitsu team, convincing the young, wild ones to take up training instead of getting into trouble. Trouble, in that place, would very likely lead to a bullet in the head one day down the road.

None of the kids could afford to pay for training, but if they stayed away from drugs and alcohol and showed up to every class, they would be allowed to train for free. Some of them worked as spear fishers or in the fields, and they paid with fish or vegetables instead of money. The more privileged guys on the team paid for training, well aware that they were sponsoring their team mates, viewing it as a donation to benefit their local community.

I hadn't had a chance to train with the local guys yet, as there had been so many visitors from out of town for the tournament and seminar. Papo assured me that I would get my chance the next evening when all the guests had left.

I spent most of my days in the little beach hotel, just relaxing. I had gotten used to the slow paced days on the boat and already felt exhausted from the short trip to Cabarete through Puerto Rico. It was nice to do nothing for a while and just hang out on the beach and by the pool.

I took motorcycle taxis to town to get water bottles and basic food supplies for my room. There were a few more tourists there, but it was still a pretty undeveloped place.

I had quickly gotten some friends at the hostel and enjoyed talking to people there. I wouldn't mind hanging out in a place like that for a little while.

Joe asked me how long I was planning to stay as we sat in the little bar by the beach and had a juice. I had no idea. I'd better start figuring it out.

I didn't want to worry about it but just relax and enjoy the beautiful little place I had found.

It was late evening. Wet season had just begun, and the heavy rain was pouring down hard. The open air skateboarding half pipe was kept dry by the tin roof and the wind was blocked by palm tree leaves weaved into the wooden railing that surrounded the ramp.

About twenty boys in their late teens were sitting in a half circle on the mat, listening intensely to Papo, eagerly absorbing every experienced word of wisdom that he spoke. A single light bulb in the ceiling provided the light and cast long shadows of young, ambitious boys onto the mats and the curved skateboard ramp around us. No one said a word. I could see in their eyes—steadily fixed on their instructor—that they looked up to him. His words inspired and shaped them.

The rain was drumming on the roof and soaking the beach, but no one seemed to notice it. Just like no one took notice of whether the person sitting next to them was from a different part of society than themselves.

In everyday life, those people never met, but on the mats, everyone was together. The rich and poor. There was even a Haitian guy—and there is notoriously always bad blood between the Dominicans and Haitians, Papo had told me.

Nobody cared. Jiu Jitsu was all that mattered.

It was dark outside the ramp, and the palm trees around us were moving in the heavy wind. Papo was giving a long speech, complimenting the boys on their effort in the competition. They had taken most of the gold medals, and he was visibly proud. I couldn't understand the Spanish, but it was clear to me what he was talking about.

The energy and enthusiasm coming from these young boys was so dense in the air that I expected lightening to strike from the storm above us at any moment. A lot of them didn't have many opportunities in life, but this was definitely one. Jiu Jitsu could create a path for them, just like it had done for me, in a very different place on earth.

Rolling with them was as intense as I had imagined. They were very tough and I was amazed by their strength. Manual labor or a life of kite surfing had made its mark on their bodies, and I had my hands full trying to handle both their physical and mental strength. It wasn't every day they had a visitor coming to train with them, and everyone wanted to have a go at me to see if they could tap me out. Luckily for me, the humid weather made everyone sweat a lot, which vastly aided my guillotine grip.

A local police officer had joined the training for the first time that evening. It was a very big thing—a milestone—for Papo's social project. I am sure that on numerous occasions, him and some of the very boys he got to roll with must have been in conflicts on the poor streets of town, staring at each other with adrenaline-pumped eyes for long heartbeat-stopping seconds, anticipating hell to break lose any moment.

That night, they met on neutral ground and learned to respect each other through Jiu Jitsu. He became an equal.

At the end of the training, everyone lined up. Papo asked the police officer to come forward, and all the boys showed their respect for his courage to show up with a synchronized bow and a loud "OSSSS!"

I asked Papo to tell these guys they were the toughest group of white belts I had met on my entire trip. It was true. They were the toughest. I hoped that they would stick with it; then it would only be a matter of time before they would see some really big results.

I think that many of the gyms I have been to in tourist areas are too focused on catering to expats and tourists, also known as those who have money. This place was different. Papo seemed very aware how he could have a positive influence on the split society around him.

The people from the rich and poor parts of town never interacted in daily life. But in that skateboard ramp by the beach, they came together as a team. All were equal, all fighting under the same flag. Boys from the richest neighborhoods trained, competed, and drilled techniques together with boys from the poorest. Strong, unlikely friendships were being forged through sweat, blood, and bruises.

I thought about how my own gym at home was a social tool as well, albeit on a different scale and in a completely different society.

It was only a week and a half before the World Championships, and I had to decide where to go on my way there. California was far away and in the opposite direction to Brazil, where I was planning to head. I was tempted by the thought of skipping the competition and using the time and money to travel around the Caribbean and South America instead, but it was almost like a pilgrimage thing to do and had been on my wish list since I planned the trip at home.

I was lying in my bed all morning, trying to get myself together to decide whether to go or not. I eventually decided to go for it and cram in as many destinations as possible on the way, getting as much out of the detour as I could.

I was becoming a master of finding cheap plane tickets and crazy routes. Within an hour, I had cross checked all the travel sites, flight times, airport transfers, and emails with invitations to come visit. The route was set... and it was ambitious.

In ten days, I would go to Costa Rica, then to Oakland to visit my old friend Søren, on to Las Vegas to train with Martin Kampmann. and finally to Los Angeles for the competition. My old friend, Chris, had just emailed me and confirmed that I could stay with him there.

I thought to myself how tired I would be when I was going to step on those mats. It was a crazy schedule that would honor the hectic pace I had been traveling at since New York.

My credit card was red hot when I was finished with all the flight bookings. It was nice to be able to relax in my head without having to worry about when to leave and where to go.

While having lost some weight on the trip, I still had a bit to go if I wanted to reach light weight, which was under 76 kilos with the gi. I decided that with all the traveling I was going to do leading up to the competition, it would be way too difficult and stressful to cut weight. I signed up for middle weight, went straight to the beach bar, and ordered a large burger.

Later, I knocked on the door of my neighbor, Glen, to check if he wanted to go with me to the beach and check out the waves.

He had an old, green moped that looked like something the Germans would drive during the second world war. I squeezed my butt onto the edge of the seat behind him, and he warned me to not let my sandal get caught in the chain as we got on the road towards the water.

The weather was perfect, and the waves looked gentle for beginners like us. Little wooden houses on the beach rented out surfboards, and we got us some ace looking ones.

There was something special about the feeling of getting onto that board in the water for the first time. I hadn't surfed since Hawaii and really missed it. I had even dreamed about it at night. It felt great to be in the water again, and I was comfortable with the waves, catching many of them during the day. The last one was perfect and took me all the way to the shore.

We were in the water for hours before the waves started to die out a bit and we decided to head back. I jumped on the back of the moped and Glen said he knew a shortcut through a little jungle road.

The old little machine did it's best to carry us through the narrow, sandy road.

Glen was a kite-surfing instructor at the hotel and had been in the Dominican Republic for five months. His original plan had been to keep traveling, but once he got there, he never left.

The moped was struggling to carry us up a little hill, so I had to jump off and walk. Glen was pulling the throttle and giving it all it had in first gear while pushing along on the ground with his feet in order to get to the top.

"I can't stop now!" he shouted, "get on, get on!"

I couldn't stop laughing at the whole scene, and it didn't help when he finally picked up speed and I was running behind him with my legs spread out, trying to jump onto the little seat. We were surrounded by beautiful palm trees, birds singing, and gentle waves pushing against a small, deserted beach. A horse stood next to the road and looked at us, probably thinking that we looked like two complete idiots.

I smiled. It felt fucking great that I wasn't sitting in front of a computer in an office at home.

After a cruel, six-hour long bus trip, I made it to Santo Domingo to stay with Abraham for a day. I felt at home on the couch in his girlfriend's apartment as they cooked dinner and I enjoyed the warm, breeze of fresh air coming from the window, mixed with the smell of food from the kitchen. Steak, salad, and water—a feast for athletes. That would be Abraham; I was more of a drunk, homeless bum who just happened to have signed up for the world's biggest Jiu Jitsu competition.

There were a few black belts on the mat in the gym that evening. I felt confident when we sparred. The relaxing pace of Cabarete had been good for my body. I'd gotten lots of sleep and there had been no stress from moving around too much.

One of the big black belts totally crushed me, but I didn't mind. I found myself feeling very calm under pressure, something that I had definitely improved during the trip. Being stuck in mount or side control bottom didn't worry me. At some point, I would either tap or escape, and then everything would be comfortable again.

I rolled with a handful of other guys and felt really good. The loop choke I had been working on for a long time started to solidify as one of my strongest moves.

It was Abraham's last training session at home before going to the competition in California. He knew that he was most likely going to meet his Danish rival again and that it would be a tough challenge to beat him. I could see in his eyes that his focus was on that one match. All the other opponents would not be a problem; he only had one person to beat to become the world champion—Alexander Trans.

By the end of the evening, he was rolling nonstop against all the high level belts. As he got more and more tired, his game fell apart. He was being pushed to his absolute limit for one last time before the most important tournament of his career so far. I jumped in a few rounds and gave him all I got.

I shouted at him to not give up as he tried to escape my side control. He burst out his last energy in a loud scream, but he still couldn't escape. The gentle giant was all out of energy. The time ran out and he didn't get up but just lay there on his stomach—face down, nothing left. Everyone tapped his back and wished him good luck. I really hoped for him that he would succeed this time, and I couldn't wait to compete alongside him in California a week later. Oh yeah, the competition. It seemed like there was so much else going on first.

While Abraham would be resting and training in California, I would be visiting Costa Rica, San Francisco, and Las Vegas before finally going to Long Beach for the World Championships. It was a tight schedule, especially before such a big competition, but I had many people to visit and wanted to get moving down to South America as soon as possible instead of staying too long in the United States.

The next day, I would be sitting on a plane towards Costa Rica and ten days of extreme-paced travel. I wouldn't have a second to think about the competition before I actually stood on the mat, clapping hands with my opponent and looking for that first, initial grip.

CHAPTER TWENTY-SIX

Costa Rica

A girl who was visiting the gym, had just had her camera stolen in the hostel the day before. I was paranoid about losing something. If my camera, phone, or iPad got stolen, it would be pretty bad. I should take a backup of my photos somehow, I thought to myself.

My budget was getting tight, but I decided to take the private room instead of a dorm bed. I really needed to get some sleep and relax after that flight.

The hostel was an interesting place. The guests were mostly middle-aged Americans who had come to Costa Rica for dental work. They lived there for weeks and weeks, and I don't think they ever left the house except for when they were going to the dentist. A guy in his fifties was watching "Gladiator" with the volume turned up high on a small analogue television, and I caught him crying at the end scene when I got back from a short walk to the supermarket. He quickly got up from the couch and hid in the kitchen, not having time to turn off the TV, so the loud end credit music from the movie filled the common room coming from small, crackling speakers.

Juanito sent me a text message saying that there would be training at 6:30 in the evening.

I was determined to learn some Spanish and apart from downloading lots of podcasts with lessons, I had found a great translation app for my phone that was reading out loud prefixed sentences when I clicked them. I tried it out on my way to the gym. It even had a section with romantic sentences.

Walking to the gym, I was concentrating on the application and forgot the world around me.

"You have a beautiful smile," it said loudly in Spanish from my phone's speaker as I realized I was walking right behind another guy on an otherwise empty side street.

I desperately tried to find a stop button, but it was too late. He turned around and gave me a weird look, then started walking noticeably faster.

Out of the blue, it suddenly started raining. Hard. People had told me about the afternoon showers, but it was way more intense than I had imagined.

I had bought a small umbrella at the hostel for a few dollars and quickly unfolded it. The heavy wind pretty much rendered it useless. It kind of kept my face dry but everything else got wet. A bus passed and splashed water on me. I jumped away from it but realized that no matter how hard I tried, I would probably be soaked by the time I got to the gym, no matter what.

I didn't mind the rain. I had some new music on my phone, and with my earphones plugged in, I was walking quickly on the sidewalk, wearing a big smile. My body was exhausted from the hard training in Santo Domingo the night before, but I was really excited about being in a new place and to see how the training would be there.

I was alone, far away from home with no friends yet, and still I knew it was going to be awesome. My travel mojo was strong, and I felt like I was on the top of the world.

The rain was insane by the time I finally made it to the gym. I was early, but a few guys were already on the mat, rolling lightly.

I stumbled over the words as I tried my best Spanish to introduce myself to one of the guys, but he just replied in perfect English and welcomed me to the gym.

Juanito was teaching the class, running a warm up routine of fifty jumping jacks, a hundred crunches, and a hundred push-ups. My tired body didn't think it was the greatest way to warm up, but I was the guest and went through it anyway.

There wasn't much energy in me for rolling, but I went a few rounds all the same. The level of the guys in the gym was seriously good, and I didn't have much on the core group of high level guys there. I was impressed by the intensity of which everyone seemed to roll and witnessed some all-out ten-minute wars that I would never have survived myself.

We were sitting around on the mats after training and chatting. Some of the guys were heading to a beach for the weekend of surfing and training and asked me if I wanted to join them. I was only staying in Costa Rica for four days and wouldn't mind seeing something else than just the city.

As I walked back to the hostel, the rain had passed and it was only drizzling a little bit. I had just landed that same morning, and already I had trained, made new friends, and planned what to do for the rest of my stay. I knew Jiu Jitsu wouldn't let me down.

I was getting really good at this and felt confident that I could go anywhere in the world with zero planning and things would work themselves out.

My body felt over-trained the next day as I opened my eyes and tried to get out of the bed. It was only a week till the World Championships and I had to be careful not to push myself too hard before that.

There wasn't much for me to do during the daytime, so I decided to go for a walk through the town with my camera. Photographing cities always provides a real challenge in finding the interesting details between a constant bombardment of images. There is no beautiful landscape presenting itself with a panoramic sky and lots of interesting colors and details, ready to be captured in the first attempt—a city demands one's full concentration and patience.

It usually also involves a good amount of footwork to find the right shots, which is why I normally like to do city photography on a bicycle. That day, I had to make do with my sandals.

I walked for four hours around town. Probably not the best idea when I was so sore, but I got some good shots out of it. I walked down all the little side streets, not entirely sure if it was safe for me or not. Simple shops were set up in little, wooden town houses, and I practiced my Spanish, trying to understand the handwritten signs on them.

It was a challenge for me to be in South America. I enjoyed pushing myself to learn a new language and involve myself in situations where I didn't know what to do; to have to ask strangers for directions and maybe make a fool out of myself. I felt like I grew way more from traveling to places like that compared to places where everything was easy.

I packed my backpack in the evening and walked to the gym.

The training was just something I tried to survive. There was no energy left inside me to go hard in sparring, and I tried to do as little as possible to try and recover before the competition.

After training, me and three guys threw our bags in the trunk of a little car and drove off towards the beach.

"I suck the big fat gringo cock of capitalism every da, so I can make money to live my rasta life. I don't give a shit about anything but rolling," one of them told me.

Leo was waiting for us as we pulled in at the small parking lot in front of the hotel about three hours' drive later. It was a narrow, concrete building with a big surf school sign by the road.

I was tired from training and the long drive, but Leo was full of energy. He showed us to our small room. It had a tiny kitchen and simple beds for four people. His family was running the hostel that was right on the beach. Leo taught the surfing lessons and had some puzzle mats to put out in the sand for Jiu Jitsu training. Every other weekend, the guys from the town would drive out there to surf, party, and relax. Roger and Igor Gracie had just been there on vacation.

In the morning, we packed Leo's little black truck with as many surfboards on the roof as it could possibly fit. Then we stuffed the seats with as many guys it could possibly fit. I was crammed into the back seat and hoped it wouldn't be too long of a drive.

It was a beautiful day. The sun was shining in a clear, blue sky. A gentle wind was blowing through the palm trees along the road as we drove to a nearby beach.

We laid the boards out in the sand. Some girls from the hostel were taking surf lessons and got the two biggest ones.

I couldn't wait to get in the water. Eager as a little kid, I quickly grabbed a beautiful eight footer, and strapped the leash around my ankle. The other guys seemed a little slow getting in the water, but I couldn't wait. I walked out and immediately noticed how warm it was. It felt nice around my legs as I stood in the shallow water and brushed the black sand off the board.

My shoulders, neck and back had gotten more accustomed to the paddling, and it wasn't as tiresome to get out through the waves as it had felt in Taiwan or Hawaii.

The water was shallow—I could touch the bottom hundreds of meters out. There were no rocks, just soft sand under my feet. No reefs or sea urchins to worry about. It was the perfect beach for me to surf that day.

The other guys came to the outside of the break a little after me. We only sat there for a minute talking before I noticed a ripple in the water, turned my board, and started paddling. It grew bigger and bigger behind me and with a roar, it pushed me forward. The white foamy water chaotically surrounded me, accelerating me from almost standing still—when I was paddling in front of the wave and it pulled me backwards—to full speed with the wind blowing in my ears and water splashing in my face. I put my front foot on the board, then the rear foot, and stood up. The adrenaline kicked in and I held my breath for the first few seconds as I felt the wave smoothly taking me for a beautiful ride. I took my eyes off the board for a moment to look up. The scenery was amazingly beautiful. Lush hills surrounded the bay. The green palm trees on the beach stood in stark contrast to the black volcanic sand.

"Globetrotter! Put your knees more together! Woohooo globetrotter!!"

Leo was teaching the girls how to paddle and stopped to cheer for me, as I rushed by them on a smooth, crystal-clear wave. It took me all the way to the beach, so I had to jump off in order to not hit the sand with the fins. I turned the board around and looked at the guys, sitting all the way out where I caught the wave. The thrill and sheer happiness I got from catching a wave like that is hard to describe. It was like pulling off that perfect move in competition. I loved it.

It was a great day of surfing. The waves kept coming, and I was riding more of them than I could count. I tried not to think about how much I was going to miss it when I got home to the flat waters of Denmark.

It was a short visit to the little beach town, and the bus came right on time at six o'clock in the morning. I must have looked pretty sleepy as I stood there by the dirty side of the little road, waiting for it.

"Aeroporte?" I asked the driver.

He said something in Spanish, and I was too tired to try and ask more. I found a seat and rested my head on the window. The bus was packed with people, and I was the only gringo on board. I crossed my fingers that I was going the right way.

After a few hours of driving, we stopped in a small city. I was the only passenger left. Everyone else had gotten off along the way. I sat and waited for a few minutes, then the bus driver realized I was still there and signaled to me that we had reached the last stop.

I was nowhere near an airport.

I tried to talk to the driver about it, but he just mumbled something and quickly disappeared around the corner of the little building in his hurry to get to his coffee break.

It was eight in the morning on a Sunday, and I stood in the burning sun on a little, empty street in the middle of a random town. I had no idea where I was or how to get to the airport. I had taken the wrong bus, and time was running out for me in terms of making it to the airport in time.

It didn't look like a place where many people would speak English, and even if they did, everyone was sleeping. I put on my backpack and started walking in desperate search of anyone to ask for help. It was a like a total ghost town. No one was outside that morning. I made it down to a harbor before I finally saw a guy around my age walk towards me on the opposite side of the road. I crossed the street and had to use every single "learn-Spanish" podcast lesson I had heard to try and ask him how I could get to the airport. He was really helpful and drew a little map for me with directions to the bus station.

"Muchos gracias, señor!" I shouted and smiled to him, as I ran down the street.

The bus station looked like somewhere drug dealers would meet in a movie set in a small Mexican town. Tickets were sold by a fat, sweaty guy sitting behind a small window in the wall. He was wearing a dirty white shirt and had a disgusting mustache. It was obvious that he hated both his life and stupid, backpacking gringos like me.

I knew how to ask for a ticket because I once had a henna tattoo on my arm in Mexico saying "Two Tickets to the Gun Show." When I said it out loud—trying to sound all serious and realizing that I was basically reading the line from my stupid tattoo and just switching out "Gun Show" with "Aeroporte"—it was hard not to laugh a little bit at the weird connection of events in my life.

The guy behind the window wasn't laughing at all. Without even looking at me, he mumbled something that was completely impossible to understand, probably even for the locals as well. I figured he meant that the bus was about to leave.

I ran to the other end of the bus station and was just about to take off my backpack as another guy with a dirty white shirt and a disgusting mustache put his arm out in front of me. The bus was full. Or so he claimed, at least.

I had to wait for the next one. It was serious gringo fail.

Finally on a bus, we raced over the deathtrap roads along the mountains. I sat by the window and opened it all the way up, leaning my head towards it, and closed my eyes. The sun was shining and the air was fresh. Some men were cutting the grass by the side of the road, and the smell of it reminded me of being in a summerhouse as a kid. That memory was so far away in both time and space, and yet, for a second, I felt that I was right there.

It was a victory to get to the airport that was full of tanned Americans with bright, white teeth on their way home to show them off. I was there right on time and spent the wait at the gate writing an article for a Jiu Jitsu magazine about my trip.

"It has been quite a ride for me, since I wrote the article for the previous issue, two months ago," it started.

CHAPTER TWENTY-SEVEN

California

"So when do you ever work?" the customs officer asked with a laugh after I explained to him how I got all those stamps in my new passport.

Søren was in the airport to pick me up. Being two meters tall, he was always easy to pick out in a crowd. It was good to see him again. We had been in school together, and when it finished, he was one of just two guys I had kept in touch with. We had traveled a lot together. The year after having gone to Boracay in the Philippines, we went on a trip to Niagara Falls and New York for a few weeks. My friend Adam from Ronin Athletics in New York managed a bar where we were hanging out almost every night: King's Head Tavern. One night, I stood in the door talking to Adam as a girl handed me her ID. She assumed I was a bouncer and I took advantage of the situation, pretending that I thought she had a fake ID.

The joke didn't really work, but half an hour later, she was talking to Søren in the bar and before I knew it, they were married. Søren had left Denmark to move to Oakland with her, and they were expecting their first baby. Visiting my best friend from school in his home in California—basically on the other side of the planet—and seeing his wife Kristin pregnant was like coming to see the end result of a crazy butterfly effect caused by thousands of micro-decisions we had made together years earlier.

It didn't feel like me and Søren had been away from each other for long. I couldn't even remember when I had seen him last time, but it seemed like time was warped for me in a weird way recently. I felt at home in his and Kristin's company. It was the most natural thing in the world for me to stay there.

Sitting on the couch with the TV on, high speed wireless Internet on my iPad, and a big fridge full of food, I could feel how I was back in the civilized world again. It was easy. Too easy. It didn't feel like I belonged there. Being sucked into western civilization and staying there for too long would be a big mistake. I had to remind myself that it was only a quick visit in the real world—I actually couldn't really tell what the "real" world was at that point—before heading back to the deep water in unexplored South America. It was like that one cheat day, where you go home for a nice, warm shower and a shave during a muddy music festival rather than sleeping in a tent, eating bad food, and not washing. Been there.

When I woke up, Søren and Kristin had left for work, and I was home alone. "BJJ Weekly" called me on Skype for an interview. They asked me about my preparation for the World

Championships where I would be competing only a few days later. I still hadn't had time to think much about it, but I definitely had the best preparation of all the guys in my division, maybe even the whole tournament. While they had been working out hard in dirty gyms and only eaten chicken and vegetables every day for months, I had been surfing, partying, sailing the Caribbean, chilling on the beach, riding motorbikes around Asia, and making hundreds of new friends. No one could beat my preparation that year, was my reply.

I was only going to stay in Oakland for two days, and I felt mostly like just resting before the tournament. However, I didn't want to visit a place without training, and even though my body was exhausted after the long trip from Costa Rica, I decided to look into it a little bit. In my head, I had almost already made up my mind to skip training, but in case anything interesting popped up, I didn't want to miss it.

Searching through my inbox, I had lots of invitations for training in the Bay Area. I had no idea which one to choose or how to get there. Instead of trying to pick one, I decided to do a small post on my blog, asking if anyone could help me out. I didn't expect much of it really, but it couldn't hurt to try.

I had gotten about twenty replies in a few hours. Most of them seemed too far away and I was about to conclude that I would just stay at home and rest until I saw this one.

"Hi,

I hope you don't mind but I noticed you were working on your BJJ blog on the plane. My wife and I were sitting on your row.

I train out of One World Martial Arts in Union City CA. You are more than welcome to stop in and train with us. We have classes daily at 6:30pm.

-Tom"

It was the perfect, spontaneous opportunity and I had to grab it. I replied to him right away, and he told me to meet him at Union City station later that evening. Tired as a dog, I packed my gi and asked Søren to take me to the train station.

I enjoyed my little breather in the civilized world. The train station was clean. The map on the wall was easy to read. Buying tickets needed no language training or courage to approach strangers and ask for help. The air was clean that evening as I sat on the bench, waiting for the train. I was excited to meet Tom. Having been sitting next to so many people in planes already on the trip, I didn't remember anything of him or his wife.

The story of bumping into a stranger like that and possibly becoming friends through training was really interesting on so many levels. I remembered Chris and the group of Brits whom I had shared taxis with in Perhentian Island in Malaysia who had become friends out of the blue. That experience definitely played a part in my reaction to Tom's invitation. Anyone right next to you at any given time can potentially be a new friend and change your life. Talking to and meeting strangers was something I wanted to do more of after what happened in Malaysia. This was a great chance for that, and I was chasing it up right away.

It was a wonderful train ride along a big, open landscape. Trees and houses filled the flat area between the train tracks and a long hill. They were typical American cookie cutter houses, as I remembered them from my many earlier trips to the states. I thought of how Derek and the family in Florida were doing and wondered if they would really come visit me for Christmas, as they had been talking about. Being back home for Christmas seemed like an eternity away. I still had half a globe to travel first.

The seat was spacious and comfortable. The sun had almost set, and the valley was covered in long shadows. A big sign saying "Sunshine Biscuits" reached high enough to be hit by the day's last rays of sunlight. A woman next to me was reading a book on a Kindle. I was wondering if some day, someone would be sitting there reading my book about sitting in that same train. The project of writing a book was exciting, but it also seemed like an overwhelming amount of work.

I used the last credit on my phone to text Tom, letting him know that the stranger from the plane was almost there. I couldn't see anyone on the parking lot outside of the station and was just about to take out my phone to check if I had any battery left before I saw a guy waving at me.

"Nice to meet you again," I said as we shook hands and both laughed.

He had seen the BJJ Globetrotter logo on my iPad on the plane and thought he recognized it from somewhere but didn't remember where. It wasn't till he got home and looked it up that he realized he had read one of my posts on the Sherdog forum a year before I left for the trip. Some of his training partners were already following my blog, so he decided to invite me to come train in his gym.

It looked like a big warehouse, and I immediately noticed the sign over the entrance.

"One World Martial Arts."

I liked it.

I changed into my gi and sat on the mat, starting to stretch. It was a small class run by a friendly black belt who introduced himself as Mike.

Class started and I did warm up drills with one of the guys. He asked me about what weight category I would be competing in, guessing that I was under seventy kilos. I must have gotten really skinny at that point if he guessed twelve kilos under my division.

I wasn't really paying attention to the class. My mind was somewhere else, thinking about what I would find in South America. I just had to get to Las Vegas, get the World Championships over with, and then I would be back on the road. I felt tired, but it was good to get some work done so I shouldn't move on to the next destination without having been to at least one gym first.

I went really light with the rolls. There was no need to use up too much energy before the competition. My timing wasn't right, but it didn't really bother me. A few good purple belts had really good game, and I had to find my focus and pick up the pace a bit to keep up with them.

Tom gave me a ride to the train station, and we said goodbye. We were still laughing at how random our meeting had been and what had come out of it.

The train had just left, so I had to wait twenty minutes for the next one. My knee injury was itching strangely. It was never a good time for it to hurt, but with the biggest competition in the world coming up a few days later, it was very bad timing if something were to happen.

Finally, I was on the train where a guy sitting a few rows in front of me was smoking something from a piece of tin foil and another one was having a very intense conversation with an imaginary friend. I just wanted to get to bed and get some sleep before flying to Vegas the next morning.

I found a seat and sat down to look out the window. I was dead tired but glad that Tom had contacted me and that I had taken him up on his offer. Apparently, Jiu Jitsu was everywhere. I wondered how many strangers I had passed on the street that could have become friends or training partners.

CHAPTER TWENTY-EIGHT

Nevada

"Does anybody feel like going to Veeeeeegaaaaaas todaaay?? Wooohooo!"

The steward in the flight from Oakland was pretty excited about his job that morning. The plane was full of bachelor party groups and couples probably on their way to get married. I had just paid twenty five dollars for checking in my backpack, so I wasn't in as great a mood as most of my co-passengers.

I texted Martin that I had landed when I waited for my backpack at the luggage belt. I walked through the arrival hall—which of course was full of slot machines—and sat on a little bench outside. It was warm and the air was really dry.

Martin pulled up in a black car. He had just been to my gym back home to do a seminar, but I had been in India that day so I couldn't attend. Now, he was on his way to Robert Drysdale's gym for the first training of the day. Even though it had been a short flight, I was still pretty tired from it. The lack of sleep didn't help either, but with my short stay in Vegas, it would be my only chance of training in that gym, and I wasn't going to pass on it. I hoped I had a pair of shorts somewhere in my backpack that were clean.

Martin said I looked skinnier than he had ever seen me. It was difficult to see myself since I was looking in the mirror every day. Gaining and keeping weight was always a problem for me, and without a steady rhythm for my diet and weight training, I had probably lost around five kilos on the trip at that point.

Drysdale's gym looked nice and clean inside with a big matted area and a small front desk.

I had been studying the guillotine choke for about half a year at that point, and it was one of the techniques I had on my list for the trip, so I was pleased to hear that it was the subject of the day, especially since Robert is one of its absolute masters.

The class was great, and we went through the guillotine game from quarters with a depth of detail I'd never seen before.

Some of the guys looked really serious when I rolled with them. I didn't blame them. They were prepared to train, where as I was merely focusing on trying to find the mental and physical energy to get up in pace and be able to match them in sparring.

"Beautiful sweep, Christian!" Robert shouted across the room.

Forrest Griffin had showed up and was going hard with all the heavy guys. A young kid with crazy strength—he seemed like he could keep going forever. I had literally just landed in Las Vegas and was already running out of energy.

When I had visited Martin back in 2007, he had just gotten into the UFC and lived in a small room in a house he shared with five other guys. A lot of water had been running under the bridge since, and with a growing success in the cage, a lot had changed. He had bought a beautiful house, gotten married to his Danish girlfriend, and their first child was just around the corner.

His mother was visiting to help out in the house while his wife was pregnant. She had made a nice salad for us as we got back from training. With all the traveling and time spent in airports and planes, it was difficult to get good, healthy food all the time. My body needed it, and living with a professional fighter for a few days who had a lot of focus on rest and nutrition would definitely help with that.

I had always admired his work ethic. He was one of the smartest, hardest working fighters I knew.

When I started training Jeet Kune Do in 1999, he already had lots of Muay Thai and amateur MMA matches. We were the same age with only a few days between us. I remember talking about him with the guys in the gym back then. I wished it was me who had competed that much. I knew it was the right path to follow if I wanted to get really good, but I didn't have the balls to do it.

When I arranged tournaments back in Denmark, he always showed up and won all of them. I fought him once in a grappling match. He dumped me on the head in a double overhook, belly-to-belly suplex, then triangled me from inverted kneeride. I had no idea what hit me.

He was way ahead of everyone else, even back then.

Martin was training again in the evening, and I tagged along. My body felt really tired, and I could feel the soreness coming.

I wanted to train in the Xtreme Couture gym, but I had to listen to my body, especially since the World Championships were only three days away. I told Martin I would bail on the evening training and roll with him in the morning instead.

I hated to skip a training, but I would still have done three different gyms in three days, which wasn't too bad... except when I thought about the competition.

I was looking forward to going there. Søren had said he would come down and hang out for the weekend, and Jonathan from Kauai Kimonos would be there too. I had arranged to stay with Chris Haueter, an old school black belt whose VHS tapes were the first Jiu Jitsu material I ever saw. Robson, my friend from Sweden, was competing as well, and it was nice to have someone from home in my corner.

Randy Couture walked past me in the reception. Martin had gotten changed and was warming up on the mat. Xtreme Couture was an enormous place. Since I had been there last time in 2007, it had doubled in size. It was the biggest and most impressive MMA gym I'd ever seen. There were boxing rings, two cages, a weight lifting area, and two big mats surrounded by cage walls. At my own gym at home, we had struggled to afford a small cage wall. Here, they used it as decoration behind the spectator seats.

The only thing missing were showers. I have never understood why so many American gyms don't have showers.

Only a small group of people had shown up for the pro class.

I was glad I decided to skip. My body felt very warm, a sure sign of over training. I sat by the mat and watched the guys go through a hard wrestling class. Both for my body and my knee, it was probably a good idea I hadn't joined in.

It was nine in the morning when Martin woke me up. We were leaving for training half an hour later.

My body was sore and every muscle hurt. I wanted so badly to just stay in bed and sleep for as long as I could. That's what I would do at home if I was tired from training, but now I tried to live the life of a professional fighter, so I decided to get up and join him for the morning training.

The gym was busy already. Randy had just finished his training, and Tyson Griffin was wrapping his hands, getting ready for a boxing session. His brother, Kyle, was warming up on the mat, waiting for me and Martin to show up.

We did positional sparring for two hours. I felt weak and tired, but as I got warmer, things started to go more smoothly. Kyle and Martin were in great shape and much stronger than me. There was a big difference between being a hobby Jiu Jitsu guy like myself and full time professional athletes like them. Technically, I could hang, but physically, I was light years behind them.

Food and sleep; that was the only thing happening during the day between the training sessions. It suited me just fine.

In the evening, fans were sitting outside the gym, waiting for fighters to come by to take photos with them. It was strange to see Martin like that, but I admired how far he had come since the sport first started to pop up, back in Denmark.

I stayed out on the stairs in the sun while Martin went inside to train. The air was dry and birds were singing. It was quiet in the desert. There were a lot of unanswered emails in my inbox— invitations to train, questions about the trip, and an offer from Pakistan to buy 8,500 bath towels in assorted colors. I tried to get through some of them.

I still hadn't decided where to go after the World Championships. South America seemed so immensely big. The options were too many for my mind to comprehend at that moment. Should it be Mexico? Panama? Or should I go straight to Brazil and stay there for a month? I had almost no contacts in the whole of South America, so it would be a lot of work to travel around there.

I talked to my girlfriend over Skype for forty minutes. What I wouldn't give to lie down and rest on our bed at home for a few hours before moving on; to feel the familiar feeling of the sheets, my blanket, and my own pillow; the summer breeze coming in through the window, and the sound of people coming home from work, parking their bicycles in the back yard; to be able to close my own door.

I missed home. Was I getting tired of traveling or was it just the over training that took my enthusiasm away?

I was having a serious down moment sitting on those stairs in the evening sun. I felt depressed. I didn't want to continue. I didn't want to put any more effort into the trip. Everything in my body ached. How could I possibly be ready to compete at the World Championships in only two days?

Had I gone too far? Had I pushed myself too much?

The thoughts raced through my head. I was paying the price for the insane pace I had set for my travels since New York. I checked my blog and counted.

Eleven destinations in eighteen days.

Just hearing myself say that made me exhausted. It had been less than a day and a half per destination going on for almost three weeks.

I couldn't decide what to do. I had promised myself to travel fast and then relax when I got home, but maybe it was time to slow down a little bit and stay in one place for a while without having to be in an airport every second day.

I was also running out of money. My South America adventure was going to be on a tight budget, especially with that one flight from Brazil to Europe that looked really expensive.

I had to get the stress out of my head, so I decided to post on my blog and ask people what they thought I should do. That way, the decision wasn't in my own hands anymore, and I could try and clear my mind a little bit.

In the evening, I had gotten lots of comments on my post.

"Quality over quantity is my advice. Best to enjoy one place in depth and comfortably, rather than to zip through several."

"Definitely slow it down. If it were me I'd honestly just go straight to Brazil after the Mundials. -Derek"

"Although a lot of people might be tired from Worlds, I'm sure you can make some nice social friends who would be willing to drive down and tour some of the many famous schools in San Diego with you. -Spencer Yeh"

"A month in Brazil (or San Diego, where all the great bjj academies are)… ie slow down… -Kris"

I couldn't believe people were so unadventurous. I couldn't possibly be the only one who thought racing through South America would be a great idea? Some people even suggested I should stay in the United States and travel around there instead of going south.

It annoyed me that no one understood me, but in a way, it was the kick in the butt I needed to pick myself up. I had to prove to myself and everyone else that adventure is out there in the unknown. There was no way I was going to stay in the United States and play safe.

"Fuck this," I thought to myself.

I would somehow find the energy to keep pushing forward. I had to tap out South America. How hard could it be?

I realized that it was my hundredth day on the road. Looking back, it was weird to think that I had traveled for so long. In a way, it felt like it had been a short trip, but in another way, I felt like I had been going for years.

Martin was taking an afternoon nap, and I lay on my bed, thinking of my accomplishments so far.

One hundred days on the road.

It sounded sweet. I had beaten the system and escaped the boring life of my office job. In a hundred days, I had visited 35 different places and met a ridiculous amount of fantastic people. There was still a month to go, and it had already way exceeded my expectations. How could I possibly allow myself to be tired of traveling?

It was Thursday evening. Next morning, I was flying to Los Angeles and had planned a full day of rest there before the big competition at the weekend. I couldn't wait to get it over with so I could move on to my big South American adventure.

CHAPTER TWENTY-NINE

Back on Track

For a long time after my belt promotion in Florida, I didn't compete in more than a few tournaments.

Looking back, it is obvious to me—albeit still difficult to admit—that I was afraid. The race to become "the best" as fast as possible was fully on between the different little gyms around the country. With my shiny and rare purple belt, and as head of one of the few teams, expectations for my performance were high. At least inside my head.

I competed once as a purple belt, and while decisively winning five matches by kimura, I lost one to the same technique. That loss haunted me, and I stumbled under the pressure.

I knew the right thing would be to keep stepping onto the mat, win or lose, and grow from the experiences. But I didn't do it, and there was no one to push me away from the easy decision to just say no. I lost the interest in competing, but deep inside myself, I knew that I had always liked it. I have never had a competitive fire inside of me or an urge to win, but I like the feeling of making things from training work against an opponent; of pulling off that take down or submission and feeling the rush that comes along with it.

It had all stopped at one point.

There were a lot of eyes on me. Was I really good enough to run my own gym? If I had just been a regular student under some instructor, it would probably have been different. Then the responsibility would not have been on my own shoulders and name but on someone else's.

Most likely, it was all just inside my own head and not real.

I had gotten a herniated disc in my back from a heavy deadlift, and it kept me from doing weight training and rolling too hard. I used it as a reason to stop competing. It was pretty legitimate, since I really couldn't train as hard as I wanted to prepare for competitions. Cardio training was completely out of the question. On top of that, I just didn't feel like a competitor. But in reality, I would have gotten a lot better if I just jumped onto the mat anyways and did the best with what I had. No one is ever 100% when they compete anyways.

I admired competitors and still do. Those who put everything on the line, live out all their emotions on the mats, face their fears and conquer them. I presumed I didn't have it in me to become one of those. What I didn't see at that point was that I missed out on a lot of opportunities to do exactly that; to grow and push myself. I might have dodged a lot of losses but I also missed out on a lot of wins. The experience—no matter the result—is worth way more than giving in to your natural fear of failing.

I should have done it.

I broke up with the Straight Blast Gym after some financial issues with Matt. I was nervous about standing on my own two feet without an organization of people behind me to help me anymore. I had learned a lot of good and bad lessons about life and training from them. Where would I get my inspiration now?

Luckily, I quickly realized that as one door closes, a hundred new ones open. That saying had never been more true and relevant than in my life. Before the break up, my realm of training pretty much existed inside a semi-closed bubble of that one organization. Not that they didn't allow me to train anywhere else. It just felt natural not to do it. As I suddenly stood on my own two feet, I realized there was a whole world outside of it. I got in touch with tons of people who were just as passionate about training as me—people I would otherwise have been unlikely to meet. I traveled around the United States and backpacked in Thailand, and everywhere I went, I found cool people to train with in cool gyms. I collected little bits of inspiration or ideas from people I met that shaped me into the athlete, teacher, and person I wanted to become. I took note of the good things from the good guys and the bad things from the bad guys.

The Jiu Jitsu community seemed like an endless resource of friendships and experiences, and I had only just scratched the surface.

It made no sense to limit myself to only training with a certain team or group of people when everyone everywhere could potentially be my new favorite training partner. That's when I decided that I would stay unaffiliated for the rest of my training life.

While being a free spirit and training with everyone was nice, I still somewhat lacked a source of inspiration; some one person, who could guide me and show me and give me some direction. In many senses, I just trained a little bit here and there and worked a little bit on everything. No one pushed me, no one told me what might be a good idea or not.

A young Brazilian black belt, Robson, had moved to a city in Sweden about an hour away from Copenhagen. He was always a referee at the many competitions I took my kids to, and he saw the development in the little team over the years. We got along really well, and eventually, I invited him to come and teach a bit in my gym.

His game was quite different than mine. I always had a heavy emphasis on conceptually understanding the core mechanics of the game, whereas Robson had a more traditional technique-based approach. He was always smiling and having fun during training and got along really well with the kids in my gym. He was also an extremely passionate competitor, signing up for every single competition and putting everything on the line.

I wasn't interested in becoming an affiliate with all the politics, gi-patches, and business that followed along with it. In my opinion, affiliations—in most cases—come down to business. Small gyms will affiliate themselves with some big team in order to have a perception of legitimacy of their training. That comes through external validation, which is embodied in our sport as colored belts. Would there be any affiliations if belts didn't exist? I am not sure there would. Imagine the same system of affiliations, teams, and rankings for, let's say, tennis or swimming. It makes no sense.

The really evil side of affiliation, though, is the fear that drives someone to tell their students where they are allowed to train. Someone I know traveled around South America for months to train and was told by his teacher when he got home that he was never allowed to do that again. Only training within the organization's own academies was allowed.

At the end of the day, we are all just grownups who like to wrestle. Why should we not be allowed to do that with anyone we want? Especially when we pay to do it, not the other way around.

Robson was different to most of the guys who had offered me affiliation. There was no money involved, no contracts, no obligations, and no rules about not training with certain people. In my opinion, friendship and training is the only affiliation that makes sense to me, and that was exactly what I found with Robson.

It was a big class I arrived at on a dark, December evening in 2009. The mat was packed to the limit. Robson had given out four new purple belts to the guys, and I couldn't be more proud of what they had all achieved. We were lined up by the wall, waiting for his command to finish the class, as he took out a brown belt from his bag.

Everyone started cheering and clapping as he gave me hug and changed my belt.

It had been more than four years since I got my purple belt in Florida, and at some points along the way, I had wondered if I would ever get to the next belt level because no one seemed to have the same view on training affiliations as I did. I was never going to sell my soul just to get a promotion.

Robson had become the friend and inspiration that I had been looking for.

I felt in a hurry to start competing again. I had postponed it for way too long, and now was the time to get going. The black belt was visible, somewhere far away on the horizon, and I didn't want to be one of those guys who stopped competing at blue belt and never tested himself again.

I told some of the guys on the team that I'd decided to compete throughout my brown belt. I could already feel a knot tie in my stomach. I knew that the only way to get rid of it was to jump straight into the deep water and get going. Just like with surfing, my fear of the ocean would only grow bigger if I stayed on land. I had to break free of the vicious circle before it was too late.

I signed up for the first competition I could find: A sixteen-man submission wrestling tournament in Germany. I was nervous and tried to find my routine of warming up and getting in the right mood. It worked out pretty well, and I won five matches by heel hook, taking home a big trophy.

It took a few competitions and losses before I really felt comfortable about being back on the mat. I had pulled myself together, and the snowball had started to roll.

I had mostly done no-gi competitions, and my first win with the gi came almost a year after getting my brown belt. I felt the pressure, but I was not nervous as I walked in onto the mat. Thirty or so of my students were watching, half of them from my kids team.

I pulled guard. Swept. Passed. Passed again. Mounted. Cross choke. He tapped.

The feeling of winning in my belt division was nice. It took a lot of pressure off me. I had just proved to myself that all the thoughts I had produced in my head about not being able to handle myself at a high level were just crap. I did fine and from there on, there was only one way to get even better: Keep going.

The confidence coming from constantly challenging myself in competition was incomparable. Facing your fears and ego are such healthy things and I regretted now that I hadn't kept doing it. A few knee problems kept me away at times, but I still had fourteen matches in my first year as a brown belt, and it made a world of difference to my Jiu Jitsu.

For the first time, I started to believe that I could one day be at genuine black belt level. Not just someone who trained for more than ten years and had been teaching a lot, but someone who had the performance level in sparring and competition to match it.

I was still looking inside myself to try and find a will to win, to accomplish. It wasn't there. I had no urge to win. For a long time, I had concluded that in order to compete, I had to be a competitor. I had to feel like a competitor inside, to have that personality. That's what everyone else who competed seemed to have anyways.

I was different. I only had an interest in using competition as an analytical tool to fuel my training and teaching. In time, I finally concluded that it was a perfectly fine approach to competition.

When I let go of that expectation of being a competitive guy in order to compete, everything got much easier. I never felt much joy or sadness when I won or lost a match but would immediately go home and analyze the result. It was a tool to become the best possible athlete and teacher I could be.

There really is no secret to becoming a good competitor. You just need to do it, and do it a lot. It's that simple.

I finally felt like I was on the right track. I had a clear direction that I was heading towards for myself, my gym, and my students. To a large extent, Robson had given me the push I needed to really start testing myself in competition on a regular basis and understand the importance of doing it as a coach and role model.

I had made a decision to stop teaching my weekly MMA class and focus purely on Jiu Jitsu. Carsten did the opposite, quitting his Jiu Jitsu classes and quickly developing into a high level, professional MMA coach. We had been running around in little circles for a while, but now each set our directions and were both racing down the road, full speed.

The gym was growing and growing. We were always looking into the horizon at the point, somewhere in the future, where we could finally put a stamp on the project, determining that it was a real "success." I'd arranged lots of grappling competitions and even had my take on the big MMA shows with four successful events. Down the road, I decided to stop all of that and focus my energy on making my gym a success instead.

The definition of success was difficult. Our first goal was to be able to make a full time living out of martial arts. That succeeded for me in 2005, and Carsten the year after. Quitting our regular jobs were milestones in the gym's development, as we could then dedicate all of our time to training and expanding the gym.

The business can always grow bigger and have a bigger profit, but making more money is not necessarily what makes it a success. I realized that it was like chasing a carrot on a stick. The goal was right there in front of my nose.

Running a successful gym is made up of so many other things than just making a living from it. Lifelong friendships are made; love is found; we are able to give people jobs, good experiences, help them lose weight, live a healthy lifestyle; and the list goes on.

Creating jobs for other people is a huge thing to be able to do. One thing is to make money for myself, but I also want to make money and opportunities for others. People have walked through the door with no prior experience and years later, teaching and training is all they do and care about. I had the opportunity to give a thirteen year old boy from my junior team his first job, and it was one of the proudest accomplishments of my life.

How could I, for one second, wonder whether the gym was a success or not?

CHAPTER THIRTY

The World Championships

Waking up, it felt like any other day. My body was still notice-ably over trained, but it had gotten a bit better. I took a shower in the little bathroom installed in Chris' garage gym, packed my bag, and we drove off to the pyramid shaped building of Long Beach University. We arrived just 45 minutes before my division was scheduled to start, and I was in a bit of a hurry to get changed and warm up.

It was a grand venue for a Jiu Jitsu competition. Twelve mats took up most of the floor space. Matches with grunting, sweaty, and heavy breathing guys and girls were on. Some raised their arms in victory, others sat there with their faces in the palm of their hands, crying from defeat and broken dreams. The span of emotions that were there on those mats was fascinating. It was surreal to think that I would be in there—a part of the spectacle and theater—in only a matter of minutes. I didn't feel like I belonged. Everyone seemed so focused. They all wanted to become world champions. I was just there, passing by, just making another step on my journey.

There were thousands of spectators—many crammed into the lowest rows of seats, trying to get close to the mats. One guy right next to me shouted as loud as he could to his friend on the mat. It was chaotic, and I tried to find a place that was a little more peaceful for my warm up while at the same time, still being close enough to make sure I could hear when my name got called.

Søren had flown down from San Francisco for the weekend just to see me compete. It was nice to have him there with me. I asked him to help me get some fruit and water while changing into the gi I had borrowed from Chris. My own lightweight gis would not be permitted for the competition because of the fabric, except for the white pants that were made of cotton.

"UNAFFILIATED."

Chris had made a stencil over the back of his gi top. The message fit me perfectly. The training I had done up to this competition was with everyone everywhere in the world. I represented no one and everyone.

I put on my hoodie over the gi top and plugged my earphones in. I didn't have much music on my phone, but what I had reminded me of all the things I had experienced on my trip. I was going to try and put all of them together and boil them down to eight minutes of intense rolling.

I tried to break a sweat, but every few minutes, someone recognized me from the blog. Two of them were Africans who had traveled all the way from Angola for the competition. It sounded like a long way, but on the other hand, I probably took the prize for the longest trip to get to the event that day.

I wish I had included Africa in my itinerary, but apart from Angola and Morocco, it had been too hard to find enough places to train there. I'll do an African Jiu Jitsu safari another time.

My division was delayed, and I realized that I had been seeded to the second round. I hadn't looked at the brackets, and I had no idea who my opponent was. There had been no research on Google to figure out his game plan. I didn't care who he was or what he was trying to do. I was just going to try and play my own game, no matter what.

And the game was simple. Low on energy and with the cardio and endurance of an overweight, World of Warcraft-obsessed teenager, I decided that my best bet would be to pull guard and turn the match into a slow pace, tactical chess game.

A half bald guy with a number seven on his shirt called me up.

I started to warm up and asked Søren to hold my stuff while I was on the mat. I weighed in at 80.3 kilos with the stomach full of food and water, way under the limit for my division. Basically, the only things I had to bring to the table were my technique and experience. Everything else was at an all-time low.

The guy with the IBJJF shirt on told me to take a patch off my pants or change them. I had a Kauai Kimonos patch that I had superglued and sewed on the bottom of my pants. There was no chance I could rip it off and he only gave me three minutes to find another pair. I didn't have any.

I had taken the longest detour ever back to the United States from Costa Rica to compete that day, and I was about to be disqualified for a patch on my pants.

Half an hour earlier, I had talked with fifty different people I knew. Now, I couldn't find any of them as I ran around the stairs in panic, looking for someone who could lend me a pair of white pants.

Robson spotted me from far away and came running with his. He is about a head and a half shorter than me, and his pants resembled mostly shorts on me. It was my only chance, though. I pulled them down as low as I possibly could and ran back to the check point.

The guy, who was stressed out checking all the people going through, didn't even look at my new shorts as he told me to hurry to mat number seven for my match.

I couldn't believe I just made it through and gave Robson a thumbs up. He was laughing at me as I tried to make my walk look natural going around the mats in the super tight and short pants. If that guy at the check point had taken one look at those pants, I would have been disqualified on the spot.

The runner was waiting for me at the mat. I was up next.

My opponent was already there. His eyes were fixed on the mat.

I shook his hand. He didn't say anything. The side of his mouth lifted a little bit into what could have resembled a slight smile, but it was hard to tell.

He looked concentrated and no parts of his face seemed to be moving after the smile attempt. He was shorter than me but looked to be about double as wide and wearing a Mongolian flag and a big Ralph Gracie patch on his gi.

He looked like any other guy I might run into in a gym next week somewhere in the world, I thought to myself.

Søren, Robson, and Jonathan were at the sideline right next to me. They looked nervous. I, on the other hand, probably looked like some karate guy who had walked in and signed up for something he didn't know what was.

I bowed before I walked onto the mat. I wasn't really big on the bowing stuff, but I knew that little things like that can make a big difference in competition Jiu Jitsu, and making a good impression on the referee usually goes a long way.

As it always is with these matches, they seem to start much sooner than expected. There is no talking from the referee like in MMA, no backing up to your corner and getting ready. As soon as both guys are on the mat, the referee—usually a lazy and tired Brazilian guy—signals the match to begin right away.

"Here we go."

I tried to find a tiny bit of will to win inside of me.

The Mongolian guy looked strong and focused. I looked like I was on my way to the beach.

As soon as the first grip landed, I sat down and started to work my spider guard. I was relaxed and felt comfortable, hanging on to the sleeves of the aggressive giant that was trying to rip my legs off.

I took my time and concentrated on my breathing. I knew that my cardio would be the biggest problem in an eight minute round, so I focused all I had on not gassing while looking for the sweep.

In a split second, my feet were in the right position and I broke his balance perfectly with a tripod sweep. He was like a cat that couldn't land on its back and spun around, powerfully scrambling back on top. Back in my guard.

"Judo," I thought to myself as I looked up and saw the referee give me an advantage point.

God damn it. I didn't have energy to scramble against that shit.

His grip was strong, and every time I grabbed his collar, he broke mine with fury. My fingers snapped as he ripped his own gi out of my hand. I could see his chest muscles flex under the gi whenever he tried to throw my feet to the side and pass my guard.

I had to be patient. Every time I tried to sweep, he was steady like a rock. Eventually, the referee gave him a warning point for being stuck in my guard.

My game plan worked, and he got more and more frustrated. At one point, he almost passed my guard, but my stiff arm side control escape saved me in the last second. I was glad I had practiced it so much on the trip.

The referee raised my hand, declaring me the winner. The only thing I could think about was that I was way too exhausted for one more match.

I hurried back to the warm up area and was lying on my back on the floor of the warm up area, soaked in sweat, looking up into the ceiling. My body was so warm; it felt like I was on fire. Søren and Robson were massaging my forearms. I could feel the exhaustion in all my muscles, and I was trying to catch my breath. I had never been that tired before after a match. I was paying the price for all the traveling, over training, and Cuba Libres.

I only had a ten minute break before that number seven guy called me up again. I was exhausted. The plan of switching out my usual training of tire flips and stair sprints with drinks and surfing had done nothing good for my endurance.

My next opponent was smaller than the Mongolian powerhouse who had just molested me for eight minutes. He was pale, bald, and looked even more focused.

My legs were shaking as I walked onto the mat.

"Combate!" the referee said, and before I knew it, the little, energetic chipmunk in front of me had pulled guard with lightning speed.

I immediately knew that I didn't have energy to keep up with his pace as I tried to step away from his legs, defending myself with the fury of a beginner tango class. I wanted to get him in my guard, but we pulled guard at the same time and before I knew it, he had jumped up, passed, and locked in a tight side control.

I tried to catch his bicep in order to do my escape, but he was too strong and too fast. It was too late to move anywhere, and I had to wait for him to make the next move.

His arm crushed my face as I looked up in the ceiling and wondered what the architect had thought when he designed it. I listened to my breath and my heart beating. I was completely inside my own world, a place where time didn't seem to exist.

I couldn't believe how much I had learned and grown from the trip. I felt vibrant, and the world seemed so colorful. I had never been happier inside than I was at that moment.

Snapping back to reality, I found myself in half guard with the opportunity to sweep. I got on top, but he was all over me, and before I knew it, he had tapped me out with a bow and arrow choke from the back.

I couldn't care less. It seemed so infinitely unimportant, whether I had won or lost that match.

I wished my opponent good luck. He hadn't broken a sweat. His bald head was completely dry. I was tired in all my muscles and glad it was over. I high-fived Søren, Robson and Jonathan.

That was it. It was over, and I was ready for the next adventure.

We hung around for a few hours to see some of the matches.

Gianni was in an 82-man purple belt division and won the gold for the third time. He got promoted to brown belt, which made me feel a little better after he had been tearing me apart that evening in Ryan Hall's gym.

Rylan from Hawaii had drawn Marcelo Garcia in his first match and did a great job against him. I was excited to one day be a black belt and have the chance to compete against my own idols like that.

Abraham, the gentle giant from the Dominican Republic, was competing at the opposite side of the bracket, as was his new arch enemy, Alexander Trans from Denmark. They fought on two mats next to each other, each winning one match at a time. A pattern was showing. They didn't look at each other across the mats, knowing what was coming. They would be meeting again in the final. Alexander eventually won 2-0 by advantages, and Abraham was devastated. He had misread the score card and thought he was ahead, just waiting for the time to run out.

I wrapped my belt around my gi and walked to the car in the parking lot with Søren. The tournament was over, and everyone was leaving. All the other competitors had had their adventure for the weekend and were going back to their gyms and jobs the next day. I was going to Panama.

Competing at the World Championships was officially crossed off the list. It felt good to have fulfilled the goal I had set for myself at home before the trip.

We were back in the garage gym in Chris' back yard by the evening. A handful of his friends and students who had competed at the tournament came by, and everyone sat around on the mat and chatted. Music was on the stereo, and there was a great vibe. Everyone was tired but happy.

A handful of guys started rolling and Chris was joking around, still playing with Jiu Jitsu after all these years like a kid who had just opened up the Christmas present he had wished for all year. The walls were oozing with history, filled with artifacts that could compete with any mad archaeologist's secret basement. He was an old school Jiu Jitsu guy, having started training in Rorion's garage back in 1988 and becoming only the fifth American to receive a black belt.

Sitting there, feeling the atmosphere and type of athletes that Chris had spawned from his own personality, I realized just how much he had inspired me in my own journey of Jiu Jitsu. I hadn't really thought about it up until that point, but in my early years of training and watching his VHS tapes, I had adopted huge chunks of his philosophy on training, teaching and life. The little garage gym looked exactly how I would imagine I would build one myself. In fact, it looked a lot like a smaller version of my gym at home.

Without consciously knowing it, I had been thinking the same way as him. His ideas had become a part of me, and coming to his place so many years later, I saw how I had come full circle. I was in the very birthplace of my own Jiu Jitsu. Chris was my teacher, but neither of us ever really knew it.

I was unimaginably tired from the long day of competition, but the vibe in the little garage gym was great, and I hadn't rolled with Chris for many years. Last time was when I was a blue belt fan boy on one of my first trips alone in the big world. I borrowed one of the many gis hanging by the wall and clapped hands with him.

His game was still really good and his grip felt seasoned as he grabbed my pants by the knees and passed my guard. It was great to roll with him. People were laughing, joking, going hard and easy rounds, and singing along to the music. It felt like home, and I somehow found the energy to train for about forty five minutes the evening after competing in the World Championships.

That guy would never know just how much influence he'd had on my life and everyone I trained at home.

I was sleeping like a prince in the middle of the mat as the garage door opened with a loud noise. The sunshine hit me right in the face, and about ten people wearing gis, walked in, loudly talking and laughing. It was about 9 a.m. and apparently, there was a morning class about to begin.

I tried to hide in my sleeping bag in the corner, but when the music started playing and people began rolling, I realized, I might just as well wake up.

Chris asked if I wanted to join in. I was totally wasted from the day before. At least three of my fingers were badly sprained from the Mongolian Judo guy breaking my grips on his collar for eight minutes. I would skip.

Søren and I took Chris' low rider bicycles for a ride along the beach in the beautiful weather. I wouldn't see him again until he would come to Denmark to spend Christmas with his family. It was a beautiful day. People were tanning on the beach, and surfers were in the water. Strolling next to girls in hot pants on roller skates along the little concrete trail on the bicycles, it was the perfect American beach scene.

I was sitting on a plastic chair in the garden that evening. There was no one home. The sun was just about to set, and I had put on my hoodie to keep warm as the temperature slowly started to drop. It was quiet. There were no sounds of cars, just the wind in the trees of the little gardens around me. The air was fresh and clean.

My body was sore. Every muscle and every joint hurt. My eyelids were heavy, and I tried not to fall asleep. It would only be an hour before Chris came back to take me to the airport. A few hours later, I would be sitting in the plane on my way to Panama.

I was going back to South America; back to visit places I didn't know anything about; trying to communicate with people in a language I didn't speak. It seemed like too much for me. I couldn't find the energy to pick myself up and go on another adventure off the beaten path. That moment, all I felt like doing was going into the house, getting some food from the fridge, throwing myself on the couch, and watching some stupid TV show. Learning another language, navigating through South American cities and airports, putting myself in difficult situations, and having to approach strangers that probably didn't speak English was the last thing I wanted to do.

Once again, it scared me how fast I had become accustomed to the easy, comfortable life in the United States. Only a week away from adventure and it seemed too much. Of course, I was dead tired at that point, so everything seemed like it was too much.

There was no way around it, though. I decided that I had to pull myself together and stick to my promise of actively searching out the difficult and unknown. I could not allow myself to get too comfortable… not before I got back home to Denmark, anyway.

I went into the garage and packed my backpack. The next day would be a new day for me in a new place with new friends.

Chris drove me to the airport. He talked about his book project; some kind of a Brazilian Jiu Jitsu science fiction book set in a post-apocalyptic future, where different species were fighting each other, just like the Jiu Jitsu teams are fighting each other today. He was doing the art work and was planning to have some of the big stars do some instructional material in it as well.

It sounded like the craziest book I had ever heard of. But on the other hand, it wasn't really a surprise as Chris was definitely the craziest Jiu Jitsu guy I had ever known. He was like a mad scientist, often a bit confusing to try and understand, but now and then coming up with something completely amazing that blows everyone's minds.

He told me stories about surfing with Rickson in Hawaii and getting lost in the streets of Copenhagen in the rock-and-roll eighties. There was no doubt that he had a lot of interesting stuff to put in that book.

CHAPTER THIRTY-ONE

Panama

When I was back at home, planning my trip, amongst the first invitations I got was one from Panama. The only things I knew about the place were random facts about the canal. I often like to watch documentaries on Discovery Channel before I fall asleep, so I know quite a lot about sharks, tall buildings, Hitler, and survival in the wilderness. The Panama Canal documentaries are classics for falling asleep.

Miguel had picked me up in the airport. He was on crutches from a knee surgery and had trouble driving his car.

He lived in his family's apartment high up in a tall building, and my room had a panoramic view over the city. The air was extremely humid. If I turned off the air conditioning for just five minutes, it felt like I couldn't breathe. It was nice to have my own room with a large bed and a shower. My body was seriously over trained from the intense week in San Francisco, Las

Vegas, and California. Every muscle felt sore, and I was warm as if I had a fever.

I crossed my fingers, hoping I would recover enough to be able to do some training there before I left.

Miguel took me to his gym.

Puzzle mats were lain out around the floor, and two big fans in the wall were running at full power to suck out the heavy, humid air from the little room.

About twenty or so guys were sitting around on the mat. I had promised to teach a class, though I really didn't feel like it. My body was screaming for rest, but a promise is a promise. Fortunately, the heat and humid air was great for my sore body, and I felt my muscles relax and get warm after a short warm up. In the Danish winter, warming up takes some serious effort, but in Panama, I just needed to do a few minutes of rotating my wrists and I was all set.

Despite feeling better, I decided only to roll a little bit. Martin, a tall, strong black belt in a thick Judo gi, gave me a very good technical round along with a suggestion of going to visit his friends in Venezuela and Ecuador. I hadn't planned anything for South America other than knowing I wanted to end in Brazil, so I made some mental notes of his suggestions.

It was gym number forty one since I left home in late February. I felt a little tired of everything, and it seemed like my adventurous spirit and excitement of visiting all these gyms was a little bit lost.

I was in a gym in Panama full of nice people and good training. Everyone was eager to talk to me, and they could all potentially be my new best friends.

If this was the beginning of the trip, I would be thrilled with excitement. Where had it gone? Had I become too accustomed to walking into strange gyms that there was nothing special about it anymore?

I had to pull myself together. Of course that place was as amazing as everywhere else. I was just heavily over trained, over traveled, and in need of rest. I had pushed myself way too hard. Since I decided to travel at high pace after I left New York, I had been running from one place to the next with no stopping. It had all been happening so quickly that there was no time to sit down and consider if it was too much. My brain was overloaded with experiences, and I needed to slow down a little bit so I wouldn't burn out.

I zoned back to reality, realizing I had been sitting by the wall in the gym for forty minutes and done nothing but stare at the sparring with an empty look in my eyes. I was soaked in sweat and couldn't move.

"Man, you look really, really tired."

Miguel was poking me and woke me up from my open-eyed sleep. My eyes were saggy and despite having built up quite a tan over the months, I was as pale as the white wall behind me.

Training was over long ago, but people were still sitting on the mat and talking. Miguel told me how they put a lot of emphasis on the social aspect of the gym, often resulting in people hanging around for hours after training.

It was just like my gym at home. We even had a note on the wall that encouraged people to sit around after training and chat.

My knee hurt a little bit after the few rolls. I had been trying to lure people into shooting for low singles from their guard so I could do a one-legged sprawl, BJ Penn-style, and go for a guillotine. The tactic was great for tapping people out but not so good for my knee injury.

Back in the apartment, I was going through my emails. Since I wrote on my blog that I had arrived in Panama, I had already gotten invitations to visit three more gyms. I was only staying for three days and was in serious need of rest, so I knew it would be a challenge to discipline myself and not just visit everyone. I couldn't keep telling myself that I'd just rest the next place I would go.

My blog was really reaching far. Every time I wrote something on it, thousands of people within the Jiu Jitsu community would read it, and I would get immediate response. It had become a huge machine, almost living a life of its own. I was confident in going anywhere in the world and being able to get help for training and accommodation just by posting on the blog.

Just two days later, I was going to Medellin in Colombia. My contact there, Carlos, had written me a long email with a packed itinerary for the visit. It looked like I wasn't going to rest anything there, either.

It was too much for me at that point. My brain was overflowing with thoughts on planning, buying tickets, training, teaching, and people.

"Just one month left," I heard myself say, as I turned off my iPad and sat on the edge of the bed with my face buried in the palm of my hands.

I quickly shook off the thought. How could I think like that?

I brushed my teeth, getting ready for a long sleep. Standing by the window, I had a great view over the city from the ninth floor. With the string to the curtains in my hand, I stood there for a moment and observed where I was. It was beautiful. Dark, menacing thunderclouds roared across the sky. The day before, I was riding a bicycle around Hermosa Beach in sunny Los Angeles, a few days earlier I was training with UFC stars in Las Vegas and before that, I stood by the Golden Gate Bridge. Now, I was in my own room in a giant apartment in Panama City.

I pulled the string, and the curtains rolled down.

"Good night, Panama. I want to be your friend, but it will have to wait until tomorrow," I thought, and before I knew it, I had slept for twelve hours straight.

In the morning, I pulled the curtains away again, revealing a city bathed in sunlight. Green hills, mountains in the distance, big trees, and old buildings mixed with modern skyscrapers. I felt a hundred times better than the night before.

Miguel was asking how I'd slept as I stumbled downstairs. I told him I was sorry I was so tired and not up for anything. He just laughed and said that Panama would be the place on the trip where I could just relax.

It sounded like a good plan for me, although a handful of training sessions were already lined up for me, so it wouldn't be all rest.

Gio—a guy, who had emailed me the day before—picked me up to take me to his gym.

My body may have felt better, but I had gotten a new injury, which was probably the most stupid one I could imagine. Cashew nuts were pretty cheap in Panama, so I ate lots of them. During the day, I threw a handful of them into my mouth and accidentally hit myself in the jaw with a palm strike. It hurt.

I managed to roll a few rounds with an enormous Brazilian guy whose knee-on-belly position kindly reminded me that I had eaten way too many bananas before training.

On my last day in Panama, we had planned to go to the beach but I was still very much in need of sleep, and over the two o'clock breakfast, we decided it was a bit too late to get there in time. I was bummed to miss out on the beach and surfing, but on the other hand, I had a lot of sleeping to catch up with.

Everything else would have to wait.

CHAPTER THIRTY-TWO

Colombia

Garry, a British guy with a big beard and big curly hair was waiting in the lobby of the hostel for me. He was living in Brazil, training Jiu Jitsu, but was tired of the rainy season so had come up to Colombia to stay in Medellin for a while and learn Spanish. Carlos took us around the city for sightseeing. He told us how the city was known for one thing in particular. When girls are in their teens, instead of traveling, they spend all their money on plastic surgery, giving the city its nickname as "the Silicon Valley."

Looking around, I could tell he was right. Even the grandmothers dressed like they were nineteen and single.

A cable car with panoramic windows was running all the way up the hillside around the city. All the poor areas were located high up on the steep hills, and it was almost surreal to slowly fly right over the little streets. We were only a few meters above the roofs of the houses and could see everything that went on beneath us in the vast favelas. Boys were fighting over a basketball game, school kids were riding bicycles, women were cooking and washing clothes, and men were hanging out on the street corners.

As we got higher, we could feel the pressure in our ears. The view of the city drenched in sunlight was breath taking. Carlos said it was his first time in a cable car too, and he felt like a gringo being on a sightseeing tour.

Back at a train station down in the city, we stood on the platform and waited for the train. Three American girls all had big, expensive cameras hanging around their necks. We all agreed that there was about a ninety percent chance that they were getting robbed before the day was over. I took my phone from my pocket to write a note about it for the book, thinking to myself that I wasn't much better, showing off my own phone like that.

Two minutes later, as we stood on the train, I realized that my phone was gone.

A few moments of confusion and disappointment were replaced with a kind of strange calmness. Before I left for the trip, I thought a lot about what things would inevitably happen to me: Food poisoning, injuries, getting sick, skin infections, theft, and probably getting into a fight. It was all things I imagined would come my way sooner or later, during the trip.

The food poisoning had already hit me in Borneo, so that was off the list. I hoped. Now someone had stolen something from me.

I was waiting for it to happen to me, so when it did, it was no surprise. There was nothing I could do about it but accept it right on the spot. It was a part of my experience. A necessary lesson in life, to learn how to conquer and handle the emotions that come along with it.

Someone was going to be happy with their new phone... someone who probably needed it more than me.

I lost a few notes for the book but remembered most of it later. Other than that, I only lost the usual naked photos of myself taken in the bathroom mirror. They might be available online one day for a small monthly fee.

We dropped by the hostel to pick up my gi and then drove to the gym.

It was a small place, where Carlos' wife was teaching dance lessons. Upstairs, a mix of different types of grappling mats were laid out over the floor. A cork board on the wall had a few notes posted alongside a handful of medals. About fifteen guys were sitting around on the mats, warming up and waiting for the class to start. Carlos introduced me to a few of them. He had originally trained in Panama and then moved to Colombia to try and start Jiu Jitsu up there. Before he came, there was no training in the country. Now, he was riding busses all around the place to teach in multiple training groups he had set up.

For a small gym that had almost just begun training, the level was high. Carlos was a brown belt, and there were a few blue belts on the mat too who had good game. Garry was a strong blue belt with a really powerful game that took a lot of concentration for me to handle. My skinny body had little strength left, so I was relying more and more on my a-game moves that I was practicing on the trip. To have a very deep understanding of a few moves like that is really helpful in sparring with stronger or better guys.

Outside the gym, a small place that looked like a bar, cafe, restaurant, and convenience store combination had set up a big screen on the sidewalk, playing music videos from YouTube in really bad quality. The low bit rate sound was blasting out through a small set of laptop speakers, and people seemed to be getting in the mood for Saturday night.

Medellin was a party town, and I was staying in a party hostel. The common room in the lobby was full of people in the evenings, buzzing around the pool table and small bar. I really enjoyed hanging out with fellow travelers for a change. They were all eager to socialize, and it was nice to talk about traveling and share stories with people coming from so many places around the world.

I had a crazy night out that Saturday. A tube of super glue I had used to fix basically everything on my trip had been in my pocket when Garry and I left the hostel together with a group of other guests. In the beginning of the evening, it was annoying to carry around, but as the evening unfolded, it suddenly seemed like the greatest thing ever to have with us. We had a long night of combined rum and super glue adventure until I finally hit my bed early morning around seven.

It was only about three hours later, at ten in the morning, that I woke up to the sound of someone playing guitar in the room next door. The song sounded really good the first five times it was repeated. At twenty, it drove me nuts, and I had to get out.

Sitting up in the bed, I felt my head spinning. As I attempted to position myself to get down from the bunk, I realized that bringing the super glue out the night before might not have been such a good idea anyways. Chunks of glue, hard as concrete, were all over my arm. A few round spots on my left arm had hair missing and four or five coins still well-stuck in the same area. On my right shoulder, a shot glass and a straw had survived the night. I couldn't find the mental energy to try and rip it off at that point. All I could think about was to brush my teeth and get outside for some fresh air. The room smelled funky, and despite three other people sleeping there, it was probably mostly my manly odor that dominated the air.

Stumbling to the rooftop to sit in the pool, my roommates—a New Yorker guy and the two Danish girls—had beaten me to it. They laughed at me as I came up the stairs, looking filthier than ever. Just three hours of sleep hadn't done anything good for my looks that morning. I couldn't even answer them as they said good morning but walked directly into the pool and cut straight to the chase, desperately commanding that one of the girls should go get us all pizza and mandarin juice.

The girls were traveling on a tight budget, driving busses around South America for four months. I knew they would never say no to free pizza, and I totally took advantage of it. I had spent a bit too much money myself, but at that point, my urge for fast food and mandarin juice was at extreme levels compared to my urge of calculating my budget.

Laura was on the mission right away with a handful of my curled notes in her pocket.

The pizza and juice was a very short fix for my hangover and only made me feel better for about ten minutes. I needed to get some more sleep and was about to go downstairs and look for my earplugs as Garry called. He sounded surprisingly fresh and wanted to know both whether I was coming with him to a pool party on the top of a hotel and also, if I knew why he had coins and a drinks menu super glued to his shoulder.

I told him he had to be absolutely mad. There was no way I was going to go anywhere that day.

He laughed and hung up.

I battled with my second slice of pizza. Melted cheese had seemed like such a good idea but now, when I finally sat with it in my hand and the hot sun was hitting my buzzing head, it wasn't everything I dreamed of. Instead, I just felt slightly dirtied by it.

The phone rang again. It was Garry.

He said he didn't care how tired I was, I had to come to the party, trying to convince me that I didn't want to miss out on it.

There was nothing in the world I could think of that I wanted less than party and melted cheese, at that point. I had only slept for three hours and could barely keep my eyes open. I wasn't going anywhere.

Garry insisted and refused to hang up before I had promised him to come.

In any other situation than this—where I was traveling the world and had promised myself to pursue every single opportunity for adventure—there was no chance I would let him convince me. I knew it was crazy to say yes, but I had to. I had no plans the next day, no work responsibilities, no training I had to do, no classes to teach, no competitions to prepare for. I was responsible for myself and no one else, and I was free to make any decision I wanted; including going to a party after just three hours of sleep. I had become too old and sensible.

When else would I do something like that in my life?

Apparently, we had dropped into some super fancy party for the young, beautiful, rich, and famous. With my circled eyes, wife beater, and dirty Jiggy Jig hat, I definitely didn't live up to the dress code and had really no idea why they would let me in.

Garry was sitting in a chair by the pool, waving at me with a big smile and a bottle of rum in his hand as I came out the elevator on the rooftop of the skyscraper hotel.

It was a really cool place in three open floors. The lower floor had a long bar and a glass wall to the pool on the middle floor. All floors had panoramic views over the whole city through big glass walls. A DJ played on the top floor, and even though it was only around noon, the place was full of people in their most fancy swim suits and expensive sunglasses.

Garry had picked up right where he'd left when he went to bed only a few hours earlier. The amount of times in my life where I had woken up with a hangover and then went straight to the next party could be counted on very, very few fingers. But I was on the vacation of my life, so I thought to myself, why not?

Within a very short time, we had all forgotten about the hangovers and lack of sleep. The organizers gave everyone multi-colored shutter shades, foam cans, and water cannons. Combined with the sunshine, music, and people throwing each other in the pool, it was one of the funniest parties I have ever been to.

A guy dressed in all white who looked like a classy Cuban golfer, invited us to come visit his family's house in the countryside. I was leaving the next day, but it would have been cool to see somewhere other than the city.

Garry shouted to me through the crowd to go get another bottle of rum. Wearing plastic sandals, it was really slippery by the bar because of the water that had splashed onto the floor from the pool. As I walked past it, I paid more attention to the girls in bikinis swimming behind the glass wall than my feet, resulting in an epic slip where my feet went straight into the air and I landed with my tailbone right on the hard, tile floor. It was a beautiful self-throw that must have scored a lot of points in most wrestling rule sets.

Over the course of a few hours, several guys from the hostel had shared bottles of rum with us at a table, and the mood was high. Suddenly, everything seemed to change from one moment to another.

As I stood by the bar, a really angry guy approached me along with a waiter, claiming that I had broken his bottle of vodka and that I owed him a hundred dollars for it. The waiter seemed a bit pissed off too, demanding that I would pay the bill for our table as well, probably thinking that we were trying to run away from it.

He looked at me with very firm eyes, staring right at me and not blinking at all. The guy was furious.

In a matter of seconds, I felt very sober again. I had no idea if I had broken a bottle or not. I could have. More likely did it seem that he was just looking for someone to blame, and really standing out from the crowd, I was an easy target.

Apart from my early experiment of putting myself inside of a cage in front of a crowd, I had only been in one fight in my entire life, and it wasn't even a real one. It was more of a late evening clinch and knee-on-belly demonstration on a drunken guy in a supermarket who attacked the teenage girls working there. I had no interest in getting a second flight on my unofficial record, and especially not that far away from home.

I suddenly felt very unwelcome at the party. The waiter called over the security guys, and I could understand he told them that I was not allowed to leave before I had paid. A few of the angry guy's friends had also showed up, and they had all cornered me with my back up against the bar.

I told them that I didn't notice breaking anything, but I also didn't want any kind of trouble, so I'd just pay for it.

I only had about fifty dollars in my pocket, so there was no way I could pay everything myself. The waiter presented me with the bill for our table and had added an expensive bottle of vodka to it. I knew they were setting me up, but there was nothing I could do about it.

I had to get to the other guys, so we could all pay it together, I told the waiter. It was obvious that they wouldn't let me go anywhere, not even to the pool to look for my friends.

Mike, one of the guys from the hostel walked by and noticed that something didn't look quite right. I told him about my slightly uncomfortable situation and he told me he'd go get everyone right away to get things sorted. It felt like he was gone forever as the guys got more and more angry. I tried to just smile and be friendly, telling them that there was nothing I could do before I found the other guys.

He came back with none of the other guys. They had all disappeared and we stood there alone with the bill. He tried to pay with his credit card, but it didn't work for some reason, and that didn't make my newly found friends any happier. They wouldn't even let me go to the bathroom anymore.

It was a long wait at the bar, trying to fence off the angry guys and waiters, while Mike ran off to get some money. The funniest party had just turned into a nightmare, and I all I wanted was to get away.

I wrote a text message to Carlos, telling him that I was maybe in some sort of trouble and I might be in need of his help.

Mike was breathing heavily and excused himself for taking so long, as he finally came back out of the elevator.

He had run all the way to the hostel to get money and had to go by a bank first to exchange it. It was a relief when he paid the bill. I tried to shake the hand of the guy whose bottle he said I broke, but he wasn't interested.

Mike and I agreed that it was probably for the best that we called it a night and left the party at that point. We stumbled over the slippery floor to the elevator to escape before anything happened. I was planning to leave the next day and preferred it to be in an airplane instead of a coffin.

We all laughed as we came out of the hotel, still with our hearts pumping all the way up in our throats. Down on the street, Carlos parked his car like in the end of an action-movie car chase and jumped out with desperation in his eyes.

He dropped everything when I texted him and raced through the city to come help. Needless to say, he was confused as I strolled down the streets with Mike, laughing at the whole situation. I told him the story and he said he was glad to hear that I made it out of there.

Apart from having things stolen, getting picked for a fight would probably be hard to avoid, partying everywhere in the world, often standing out in the crowd. Fortunately, it wasn't that day. I could cross that experience off my list, and I was pleased to find out that in case anything happened, friends around me were ready to help out right away.

At least some of them.

I still hadn't found Garry or any of the other guys from the party who were supposed to share that bill with me. It annoyed me that they were nowhere to be found when it was time to pay up, but I would talk to them about it the next day… especially Garry, who had seemed like a real friend. He had totally disappeared and was of no help when I was in trouble.

The next morning, I was looking at plane tickets and trying to figure out where to go. I wanted to leave the same day, but the flights around South America were all really expensive and I was running low on money. I considered going to Argentina, Peru, or Chile before Brazil, but I couldn't find the right tickets. I even thought of doing a trip down to the Antarctic, as I realized that—after I had gotten to South America—it was the only continent in the world I hadn't put my foot on yet.

I flicked through my emails, trying to find some ideas of where to go next. One guy had invited me to Ecuador. I had never thought of visiting that place, but he sold it really well. I looked through the travel sites and within minutes, I had found a reasonably priced ticket the same day to Guayaquil in Ecuador, and from there, on to Rio de Janeiro a week later.

Argentina was another option, but it was too cold at that time of year it seemed. I'd had big plans of traveling around South America, but it was just too expensive for my budget at that time. At least I would get to see Ecuador before spending two weeks in Brazil.

I got a confirmation email of my booking. I was leaving the same evening and would stay there for a week. I remembered that a few days earlier, I had gotten another email from a guy called Juan Miguel in Guayaquil. I emailed him right away and he replied after just a few minutes, saying that I could stay with him and he would pick me up at the airport.

And so it was determined that I would go to Ecuador. I was excited to explore another unknown place and spent the rest of the morning researching what to do there.

One of the guys in the hammock next to me woke up and grunted a bit. I didn't pay attention to him. There were so many disgustingly hungover people in the hostel that day—myself included. He was moving around a little bit before suddenly, he jumped out of the hammock and stood up. I turned my head and realized that it was Garry. He had been sleeping right next to me in the hammock for two hours, and I hadn't noticed at all. During that time, I had called him several times and been annoyed that he didn't pick up.

"Christian! Holy shit, what happened? I woke up in some gay guy's house! And what the fuck am I doing here in your hostel???" Garry shouted, with the most desperate and confused look I'd ever seen on someone's face in my life.

He gasped for air and looked like absolute trash as he stood there. The hammock had pressed into his face, leaving behind a checkered pattern all over his chin and forehead. His white tank top had stains of rum and burger sauce on it. He could barely stand on his feet and had no memory of what happened after I lost him at the party. The only thing he remembered was that he woke up in a bed in an apartment he had never been in before. Confused, he got up and realized that the only other person in the place was a very gay guy, who apparently lived there. In desperation, he ran out of the place, leaving his phone behind. Somehow, he ended up passing out in a hammock in my hostel, instead of his own apartment right around the corner.

He told the story with such desperation in his eyes, and I almost fell down my chair laughing. It was the craziest hangover wake up I had ever witnessed and the perfect ending to my flash visit in Colombia.

CHAPTER THIRTY-THREE

Ecuador

Juan asked me whether I wanted him to wake me up for the 6.30 or 9.00 class in the morning—people would be there who were looking forward to meet me.

I had just arrived late in the evening and was as tired as a dog from traveling, not to mention all the partying in Colombia. I needed as much rest as possible, so the 6:30 class was out of the question. I wouldn't mind sleeping in and just training in the evening, but since everyone had gathered to meet me, I wouldn't let them down.

When I woke up in the morning, I could have used a handful more hours of sleep, but I decided to hit the gym anyways and rest later. Juan picked me up and we got in the car. It was a busy and dirty city, just like the other South American cities I had been in.

The car broke down half way to the gym due to the heat, and despite many attempts to get it going, we had to give up. We got in a taxi to Juan's wife's workplace, and then switched to her car. In the early morning, Latin American city setting, switching cars like that felt like playing Grand Theft Auto. I was just waiting for us to get on BMX bikes with Uzis next.

The academy was in a university's gym hall. It was a big building with one big room and several meters to the ceiling. The guys trained in a boxing ring surrounded by lots of weight lifting machines. The owner, Juan's father, was a former body-builder. His three sons had basically grown up there and were now all doing BJJ full time, running gyms around town. Judging from the many medals and trophies on the wall, they had been doing really well in competitions.

We changed and I tried to warm my tired body up. There were five black belts on the small mat already. The coach was Brazilian and spoke Spanish very loudly with a heavy Brazilian accent.

I warmed up my knee while the guys went the first round. I was amazed at the intensity they put into it, especially since it was the first round in the morning. They gave it everything they had and rolled really competitively, like the guys in Costa Rica but even harder. I was really not in the mood for it, but I was the guest, so I would follow whatever way my hosts trained.

My first round was with Juan's little brother, Sinistro. He had just gotten his brown belt after winning the Worlds as both blue and purple. I tried to signal by my pace that I was all about going slow, but he was in a different mood. I couldn't pick myself up to follow the pace and even just try to give him a fair match, so I just followed along as he swept me left and right and submitted me every ten seconds.

My cardio sucked, and I was really tired after just three rounds. My body had taken a hard hit from the four days of drinking and lack of sleep in Medellin. The humidity was making it even more difficult to breath. The party injury on my tailbone from the pool party hurt a lot when I was playing guard, and with these guys, I was on my back all the time. My knee was complaining and my fingers were sprained from the competition. I wished I could come back another time, fresher, so I could get something out of the training with these high level guys.

That day, I was worth nothing.

I was searching for surf spots in Ecuador, as I realized that the Galapagos Islands were the number one reason tourists would fly to Guayaquil. I didn't know much about them other than history lessons in school and documentaries on TV. In fact, before that day, I didn't even really know where they were. Geography is usually a strong subject of mine, but not South American. The islands being so unimaginably far away from my home, I have never considered going, but now I suddenly realized that I was right next door.

That was it; I was targeting the Galapagos Islands next for my adventure. Now, I just had to figure out how to get there and where to stay. Juan told me that Soluco had a student who ran a small group there and promised to get me his phone number.

I was excited. It was really a different destination, hard to get to and even better, there seemed to be Jiu Jitsu as well. I was eager to talk to the guy there and see where it would take me. Little did I yet know that it would be one of the destinations on the trip that would make the biggest impression on me.

Juan and his brothers each trained in their own gym around town. His was only a few minutes from where he lived, and he was teaching two classes there that night.

The owner of the gym was a big fan of MMA and had de-signed it like one big cage with UFC posters, flags, and other merchandise on every square centimeter of the walls. My own gym is pretty decorated, but nothing compared to that one. Juan agreed that it was a little over-the-top.

He used to be a long-haired heavy metal guitar player pur-suing a career in the music business before finally settling on Jiu Jitsu instead. I couldn't imagine him as a hardcore heavy musician; he seemed much more like a laid back Jiu Jitsu guy.

He introduced me to the class and a young, strong purple belt asked me to roll. He had a really nice guard and I had my hands full just practicing to defend his sweeps and keeping my base. Suddenly, I felt a pain in my knee injury.

It was the worst I had felt since Cyprus, and I had to stop training immediately. So many thoughts went through my head. Had I been going too hard in the morning when I was tired and not properly warmed up?

I didn't want to be injured when I was so close to Brazil. What would a Brazilian Jiu Jitsu trip around the world be with-out training in Brazil?

Those few minutes were the only training I managed to do in Juan's gym that evening. The rest of the time I was just sitting by the wall with an ice pack on my knee, depressed.

Juan and four of his Jiu Jitsu students had opened an Irish pub just upstairs from the gym. He had been falling in love with the pub culture during his trips to Europe in his musical days. He had opened the only Irish pub in Ecuador as a hobby project. Business-wise, it hadn't become a big success yet, but it served as a social meeting point for everyone training in the gym, and that evening after class was no exception.

The pub only served Budweiser, a few local beers, and two German ones. It didn't look exactly like pubs back in Europe, but the idea was there. It was a little strange to be in an Ecuadorian Irish pub in which an Irish person probably never had set his foot and where you couldn't get a pint of Guinness, but I enjoyed it.

I met one of Juan's female friends and tried to say hi by shaking her hand. I could immediately see that it was the wrong thing to do. It was awkward—I'd done it wrong again. I had never expected that the culture of greetings would be one of the big challenges on my trip, but it was.

Every place has their own way to greet each other. Some places have a regular handshake. Some places they do a reverse handshake and a chest bump. In Hawaii, it was a reverse handshake, a chest bump, and then back into a regular handshake. In some places, Jiu Jitsu guys do a hand slap to a fist bump—some places everyone does that, and in other places everyone just do fist bumps. In Japan, some people bow, while others shake hands. In Moldova, I had to shake every guy in the room's hand or they considered me totally strange.

Imagine the awkward situations when trying to figure this out in every new place I went. Not to mention that greeting women, of course, is totally different than greeting men.

It was a real challenge to figure out.

In Ecuador, most of the Jiu Jitsu guys did the hand slap to fist bump. In Colombia, where I just came from, most people shook hands. Several times, I would instinctively grab the hand of someone who was trying to do a hand slap. They always managed to pull it back a little bit for the fist bump before I clenched on to it, resulting in a really weird and awkward handshake, where I was just holding on to the end of their fingers and shaking them.

Thinking about it, the culture of greeting in Denmark is not easy to figure out either. It is an intricate system of handshakes and hugs that is almost too complicated to explain. I'll leave it to the visitors to figure out and amuse myself watching them fail, as I did myself so many times on my trip.

Juan had gotten the phone number to Mario, the guy in the Galapagos, and called him up for me. His English was simple and I had to speak slowly for him to understand me over the crackling phone connection. I asked him if I could come visit him two days later, and his voice sounded full of excitement when he told me that his house was always open for anyone, especially Jiu Jitsu people.

I told him I would send him the link to my blog so he could check it out, but he didn't have any Internet connection. No Internet and he hadn't seen my blog. I was excited about that. I liked the idea of visiting someone far away who had no idea about who I was or what trip I was on. And even better, someone who didn't know that I was writing about it in my blog and a book.

I hung up the phone and felt a rush of excitement mixed with the alcohol in my blood. I had just found another remote place to explore through Jiu Jitsu. It was on the same level as Moldova. I couldn't wait.

When I woke up the next day, my body was still tired, despite having slept for more than eleven hours. I had obviously pushed myself too hard, so I relaxed all day while looking for a ticket from Brazil to Estonia. In order to get into Brazil, I would need to present a ticket out of the country.

Getting to Europe from Brazil was expensive. It was right at the height of the European summer holidays, and no matter how much I tried, I couldn't seem to find a ticket at a reasonable price. I still had some time to buy it, so I would wait and see if the prices changed. It was tempting to just stay in Brazil and spend the money there instead, but I had a deadline. I had to be in Estonia by the first of July to meet up with Daniel from Taiwan and my friends from the gym at home who were there for a Jiu Jitsu summer camp.

After a quick visit to another gym in town that evening, I was back at Juan's gym. Class had just ended, and everyone was gathered in the Irish pub. It was a Wednesday evening, but the place was packed. Somehow, I got involved in a contest about drinking the most shots on fire and finishing the largest glass of beer I have ever seen in my life. The next morning, I was leaving for Galapagos, and everyone was eager to buy me shots to say goodbye.

The amount of planning I had done for my trip to the islands was at an absolute minimum. I had called Mario from Juan's phone and told him when the plane would land. I got a text back with the directions to his place.

Take a bus to the little ferry, then cross the water and get a taxi to La Casa Rosa, the only pink house in town, and Mario would meet me there.

There was no address. Apparently, the roads didn't really have names. My phone didn't work, so if I didn't find that pink house or something else went wrong, I would be lost on an island in the Pacific Ocean. Since I had my iPhone stolen, I had become really accustomed to using my camera instead for saving notes, contacts, reminders, or anything else. I took a photo of the text message on Juan's phone and strapped up my backpack.

The flight to the islands was relatively short. Candid camera was on the TV screens, and everyone on the plane laughed at one stupid scene after the other. It was pretty funny, but I found it hard to concentrate on anything other than my knee. It felt warm and itchy, and there was a sharp pain right under the knee cap. I crossed my fingers that it wouldn't be anything serious this time. Training in the Galapagos would be a cool thing to be able to cross off the list, not to mention that I was going to Brazil just five days later and didn't want to miss out on training there either.

The islands and landscapes, shaped by lava, reminded me of Iceland. The water was crystal clear and the sky was blue. Aside from a tiny airport, the island we landed on looked barren and empty.

Going through customs, the locals stood in a line to the left and the tourists in a line to the right. It was a simple little building with basically nothing but a metal frame and a plastic roof. The desks looked like old tables from school classrooms just put on the bare ground. When I got to the counter, I presented my passport and a little receipt for a $10 natural preservation fee I had paid in the airport in Guayaquil.

The guy didn't bother to look at me when he said there was an entrance fee to the islands of a hundred dollars. It would have been nice to know in advance, but there was nothing to do about it at that point. I found my wallet in the backpack and looked through it. I only had sixty dollars in cash.

He kindly let me know that they did not take credit cards and there was no ATM nearby either.

The airport was basically a tent in the middle of a desert. Of course there was no ATM there. I asked him what he suggested I should do then. He didn't say anything for a good five or six very slow seconds before he looked up at me with a facial expression that showed he couldn't possibly care less. It was my problem, not his, he said, shrugging his shoulders slightly, then looking at me with an empty stare and slightly raised eyebrows.

I didn't buy into his scare tactics. I couldn't possibly be the first person to stand in that situation, not knowing that I needed to bring a hundred dollars in cash.

He sighed deeply. Then he rolled his old desk chair back a little bit and leaned down to open one of the wooden drawers in his little desk. He took out a piece of paper and slammed it on the desk, then scribbled down a few hard to read numbers. My passport went down in one of his drawers. Then he said I could go to the office at the national park to pay the fee and collect my passport. The opening hours were Monday to Thursday, eleven to one.

He shoved the piece of paper at me while he was already waving the next unknowing tourist in line to come to him.

I didn't like the feeling of not having my passport on me. Especially not when I was on an island in the middle of nowhere without a working phone or any idea of where—or with whom—I was staying. It was Thursday morning and I was leaving again Sunday, which meant that a two-hour window that one day would be my only chance to get my passport back. It was not going to help anything to worry about it, so I just accepted the situation and focused on getting to Mario.

Flicking through the images on my camera, I found the one of Mario's phone number. The directions he had given me were too confusing now I was there, and I wanted to let him know I was on my way and he could expect me soon.

I saw a guy with a mobile phone, and asked him if he spoke English. Of course he didn't. I had to stretch my shortly learned Spanish skills to the absolute limit, in order to ask him if I could borrow his phone to call my friend real quick. Something with *"telephono," "amigo," "mucho rapido,"* and several other homemade words. Approaching strangers has never been difficult to me, but doing it while knowing that I don't speak their language is something else. It worked. He understood me.

I called Mario and told him I had landed and was leaving the airport.

Bus. Boat. Everything seemed so simple and straight forward when I finally did it. I hated myself for not just trying without having to call Mario first. I caught a taxi from the little ferry dock and asked him to take me to the pink house. He knew exactly where I meant.

The first twenty minutes of the trip were on a deserted road that ran in a straight line through a massive landscape of solidified lava. There was nothing else to be seen but that one road and it looked like it just went on forever. It was a bit bumpy, and going straight forward with no other traffic, the driver found no reason to not go as fast as he could. The seat belts didn't work (they were for display only). Spanish music was on the radio, and once again, I noticed how often the words *"corazón"* and *"amor"* were being used. I had to learn some more so those songs wouldn't drive me crazy.

At the end of the road, it began to look more populated. We passed some small houses with smoke coming up the chimneys, people working in fields, and dogs taking naps in the middle of the streets. It looked very Caribbean and it felt nice to be out of the big city again.

The taxi driver stopped the car on a quiet, dusty road. A short, bare chested guy was sitting outside a pink house, playing guitar. He was unshaved, his hair was messy, and he was wearing board shorts and sandals. The light from the morning sun reflected on his guitar. As I opened the door, he stopped playing and looked up. When he caught my eyes, a big smile came across his face.

It was Mario. He didn't know when I would arrive, so he had just been sitting there for hours, slowly playing his guitar while enjoying the day. There was no hurry or stress.

He was half Ecuadorian and half Brazilian. Having gotten tired of the busy capital on the mainland, Quito, he had decided to move to the Galapagos and start teaching Capoeira and Jiu Jitsu there. It was difficult, but he could just make it work.

It was a small apartment. Mario shared it with a young Brazilian couple who were working as tourist guides while studying the turtles. They were friendly but didn't speak much English. I threw my backpack into the corner and jumped in the hammock hanging between the living room walls, right next to an open balcony door. It was so quiet outside. Birds were singing, and I could see far away over the roof tops of the small town. Silhouettes of palm trees and a mountain were on the horizon. I put my hands behind my head and closed my eyes. The tropical air coming from the door was humid and fresh, dancing past my nostrils along with the whiff of a joint being lit on the sofa. The sound of birds singing mixed with the sound of Mario chatting with his roommates in Portuguese. The trouble with my passport, the hangovers, and the pain in my knee didn't seem to exist.

Mario said—while concentrating on holding the smoke from the joint in his lungs—that he would call his friend so we could get some surfboards for the next day.

I had just arrived in paradise.

It was hard to keep my eyes open, but I couldn't allow myself to fall asleep in the hammock. I needed to go pick up my passport before it was too late.

It was still a few hours before the office in the national park would open. Mario was meeting up with his band to practice for a small reggae bossa nova concert they were doing a few days later in a bar.

One of the band members suggested I could take a boat to the other side of the harbor, where there should be a nice walking path to check out. It was a long walk along a small track in a beautiful volcanic landscape of lakes, lizards, and strange trees. I could see why people described their visits on the islands as if they had been to another planet.

That feeling quickly vanished as I got to the end of the path and found a school class of about thirty teenage kids swimming around in a big cave filled with water. So much for pretending to be alone on an unexplored planet.

I didn't wear a watch and hadn't brought my phone, so it wasn't until I got to the cave that I could ask someone for the time. One of the school teachers told me that it was a quarter past noon.

Fuck. I had to pick up my passport within 45 minutes, and it took me way more than an hour to get there. I panicked a little bit. I didn't know exactly where to go, I hadn't gotten any cash from an ATM yet, and my stomach suddenly felt really, really weird, rumbling and threatening to explode any minute. Wearing only sandals and with my butt cheeks tightly squeezed together, I stumbled my way back through the alien landscape to the boat in record time.

It was like setting foot on another planet as the first human ever, and the only thing I could think of was that I really had to take a shit. The taxi boat wasn't there, so I asked a local to take me over the water to the harbor for a few dollars.

It took me quite an effort to explain to the taxi driver that I needed to go to an ATM first, then to the national park. He didn't understand any English, and neither did he understand my amazing Spanish.

I had expected some sort of entrance with an information desk or someone that I could talk to. There was nothing of that. It was basically just a walkway into the jungle. A map of the area revealed a huge network of paths and lots of buildings scattered around the area, none of them looking like they were an information office of any kind. It was almost one o'clock and time was running out, both for my passport and for my ass.

I asked someone who was walking by wearing a polo shirt with the national park logo on if he knew where the office for picking up passports was. He just looked at me like I was an alien just landed from outer space. Maybe I was on another planet.

After much detective work, studying of the map, asking people, and running around on my heels with straight legs—trying to hold everything in—I finally found a small building with a very small window where I could get my passport back.

The woman behind the window laughed and said I was lucky to get there at the last minute. I didn't even have time to tell her how stupid their system was and ran right back to the toilets I had spotted on the map to reach the second catastrophic deadline of the day.

I have no idea what the 100 dollars entrance fee for the islands are being used for, but it is definitely not for the public restrooms. There was no toilet paper, no soap, no water, and no seats on the toilets. I was so desperate and had no choice but to unleash my upside down volcano anyways and all hell broke loose in that little white restroom in the middle of the national park.

Up until then, I hadn't had time to worry about the lack of toilet paper. Now, it was suddenly an urgent problem. I needed it. Badly.

There was no way around it; I had to sneak out and steal some leafs from the bushes around the corner.

"What the fuck would Charles Darwin have done?" I thought to myself, as I scouted over the bushes to see if anyone could see me standing there with my pants halfway down, gathering the biggest leafs I could find.

I had seen lots of signs in the park, warning people about disturbing the animals and the plants, so I was really nervous about getting caught and arrested.

Luckily, everything worked out and I could relax again. I wanted to check out the rest of the park, but it would have to wait for another day. I preferred to be near toilet paper for the rest of the day.

I walked back to the city. The weather was nice, and it was a beautiful little town, full of small houses, souvenir shops, and tour companies. I had heard about nature's beauty on the islands, but my biggest interest was in meeting Mario and seeing how Jiu Jitsu training was in a remote place like this.

Guys were walking around the street with surfboards under their arms. I couldn't wait to get back in the water. I hadn't managed to send any postcards since New York, so I spent 50 dollars on a bunch of them. It was a lot of money but also an important thing for me to do. I sat on a bench by the water and wrote all of them. For the last one, I only had a big pile of $0.25 stamps left that filled out the entire postcard that was en route to one of my hosts in New York.

"Hey Kyle! -Christian," was the only thing I could find room to write on it.

Mario was waiting for me back in the apartment, ready to go to training. He had wrapped his gi up in his purple belt. It was old and worn out. Marks on the black tip witnessed about four stripes that had used to sit there. There was a lot of pride in his voice when he told me about his recent promotion, inheriting his professor's old belt.

We walked to the gym through the dusty streets of the little town. All the tourists lived by the main street at the harbor, and the locals were hidden away in the backstreets. It was a really small place and everyone seemed to know each other.

Every two minutes, we stopped for Mario to talk to friends he bumped into.

He had only been in the Galapagos for a short time and could barely make a living out of teaching Jiu Jitsu and Capoeira. There were a small handful of dedicated students in his gym, but on a remote, isolated island with a low population and no competitions to train for, it was hard work up hill for the little Brazilian with the big heart.

They trained in a little community building about the size of an average garage for a small car. There wasn't much light; only two small lamps that didn't have much power in them. Five by five old puzzle mats were spread out on the floor. In the corner stood a little wooden table and a chair which doubled as a dressing room. On the wall, a handful of old photos of a local football team were hung up.

"Galapagos FC 2009-2010."

The last time I played football was with ten of the guys from the gym in a park in Riga, Latvia, on a beautiful summer day. At one point, the ball rolled away from us towards two girls who were sleeping in bikinis on a blanket. One of the guys sprinted to get the ball before it hit them, but instead of the ace move he had planned to stop it with, he accidentally stepped on it and ended up doing a full speed sliding tackle, going under the blanket and under the girls, waking them up in horror, screaming at the complete maniac who had violently crept in under them!

Five people showed up for training: one girl and four guys. With their white gis and white belts, they looked really excited that someone came to visit them for Jiu Jitsu. The only people who ever came by were tourists coming to see the scenery. I must have been the first Jiu Jitsu tourist there… ever.

I had no idea about their level and tried teaching the side control escape I had been working on for the entire trip. I had only been showing it to higher level guys, so it was a challenge to explain every detail of it to beginners and make them understand how it worked. They were working hard and really wanted to learn it, and it seemed like they got it down by the end of the class.

My knee was still sore from the hard training in Guayaquil, but I decided to roll a little bit anyways. The eager white belts went really hard on me, and I tried to relax as much as possible and be careful about using my left knee.

Mario was short, strong, and rolled in a high, grinding pace, like a steam locomotive constantly going forward, looking for holes to exploit in his opponent's game. To slow down the match a bit, I locked him up in my spider guard, with my legs hanging heavy on his arms and a tight grip on his sleeves. His feet aligned just right for me to go for one of my favorite sweeps—the tripod—and in the blink of an eye, my legs had moved in position and outbalanced him, making him fall backwards.

Since Mario had moved to the island, he had only been able to roll with white belt beginners, and was rarely—or ever—caught by surprise in sparring. It was probably the first time he was swept clean in a long time, and his body wasn't accustomed to it so it reacted wrongly. He posted his arm behind him, and as he fell, landed on it with all his weight, dislocating his elbows.

Mario was screaming in pain—his arm was bent 90 degrees in the wrong direction. From all the stickers on the glass doors of stores around the Spanish speaking countries, I knew that the word "haje" he was screaming, meant pull.

I asked him nervously if we shouldn't call someone instead, not wanting to push or pull anything that was dislocated like that, and on the other hand, wondering if there were ambulances on the island at all.

He insisted. I wasn't sure it was the right thing to do, but I grabbed his wrist and elbow with my hands, slowly pulling it. Mario screamed as I could feel everything slip into place in his elbow. He instantly looked better and his face was less pale, thanking me for the help.

I felt really bad about having dislocated his elbow like that, but both of us, being experienced Jiu Jitsu practitioners, knew that nothing was to blame but bad luck.

Mario went on to teach a Capoeira class with only one arm. The guy was unstoppable.

Back in the house, we made gigantic tuna steaks. It tasted too good for me to worry about my stomach. Mario had bought a whole fish for ten dollars, and it had lasted a full week.

He had an inflatable mattress I could use for the night, but I had fallen in love with the hammock in the living room by the balcony door. I decided to give it a shot and grabbed a pillow for my head. It was perfect, and I slept in it for eleven hours straight, wondering why I had never thought of doing that before.

People came to the islands to do week-long sightseeing trips, but the only thing I managed to do was a short walk to the national park area right outside town to see the giant turtles. They were seriously gigantic and looked almost fake. Most people—myself included—stood there and waited for them to move to confirm that they weren't just made out of plastic.

The place was full of tourist groups with guides, fanny packs, hats to block the sun, and "Save the turtles" t-shirts. I walked by one of them, as the guide was explaining something, getting a little freebie fact for my own little walk.

"These trees and bushes are very rare local species that are almost extinct, so that's why we have them here in the national park."

It was the exact same bushes I had stolen leaves from the day before to wipe my ass with! It was difficult not to laugh as the group of American turtle-lovers observed the tree with an "Ooooh! Wooow! That is sooo interesting!"

Mario's concert was the same evening, and he was supposed to play the drums. With his arm seriously damaged, it was probably a very bad idea, but with his passionate live-by-the-moment spirit, I was certain that he would do it anyways. I was right.

As I got to the little outdoor bar, he was singing from the bottom of his lungs and pounding the drum like nothing had ever happened to his arm. Only a small, white bandage bore witness to the fact that it had been completely dislocated just hours earlier.

I sat in the bar and felt a little lonely while eating a burger with yet another giant tuna steak in. Mario was the only person I knew on the whole island, and he seemed like he could play those drums all night. Traveling to Jiu Jitsu gyms had been easy because someone always just came up to me to talk about my trip or training or something. When I was alone, I had to kick myself in the butt to do something about meeting people. There was no one to share a taxi with here, so I just jumped into it and broke into a few conversations with random people. I was pushing the social boundaries, but it paid off.

One guy had been traveling for years, and we exchanged stories from around the world. Someone overheard us and asked us both where our favorite place on earth was. We looked at each other and laughed. If there was one question that I had gotten most times during the four months on the road that was it. My new friend seemed to have experienced the same.

"Everybody asks me where I like the most. I like the world, man! I was in the desert in Morocco, lying in the sand, watching the million stars and thinking; man, this world is awesome!"

I couldn't agree more. People had asked me so many times, and I always gave them the same answer. Planet earth is my favorite place: not a country, not a city, not a place. The whole entire world is the best place I know.

A guy came up to me and shook my hand. I struggled to recognize who he was. Could he be from training? No, then I would remember him, surely?

While I chatted with him a little, I discreetly checked my camera in the pocket. I found the group shot from training, zoomed in on the faces, and recognized the guy.

It hadn't even been twenty four hours, and I had already forgotten him. Remembering names had been really difficult on the trip, but apparently, I was also running out of faces at that point. It was in some way embarrassing, but on the other hand, I shook the hands of between twenty and fifty guys every three days when I moved location. My brain must have been running out of storage space for new faces, and I still had lots of people to meet in Brazil and Estonia on the rest of the trip.

Even with an elbow swollen to double the size from drumming all night, I couldn't convince Mario to skip surfing the next day.

A German girl with dreadlocks opened the door of her old house in the other end of town, offering for us to pick any board on her wall we liked.

We chatted a bit about the beach we were going to. She said it was full of animals, especially turtles and sharks. Every time she went surfing, baby sharks would circle around her feet in the water as she sat and waited for the waves.

I was just about to worry about the parents of those sharks, but she assured me not to, since they didn't come out to eat till after five o'clock in the evening. I wasn't exactly sure what to think about this. How on earth do the sharks know what time it is? I thought I'd better be out of the water by four already, just to be absolutely certain.

It was a long walk to the beach, and I was glad I had gotten a smaller board than usual since I had to carry it for an hour on a small path going through a dense forest. I spent the whole walk listening to Mario telling stories about his life.

He had traveled around Europe for months alone, learning languages, and walked barefoot around Ecuador for half a year without touching money. His uncle had been a hitman in Brazil, killing people in the favelas to steal their drugs and kids to steal their organs.

Compared to my own quiet upbringing in a suburb by the forest, Mario's life in Brazil sounded like a high paced action thriller.

He went on with the stories for the whole walk, and somehow, an hour walking through the jungle in sandals didn't seem that bad with him.

Occasionally, I would wonder about the beach we were headed to. As a beginner surfer, I was anxious about visiting a new beach, just like a beginner Jiu Jitsu traveler would be anxious about visiting a new gym. Instead of worrying about douchebag guys going hard, injuries, or not living up to a belt color, I thought about if there would be any big waves, dangerous currents, or reefs. It was the exact same feeling, although I had gotten rid of it with Jiu Jitsu and now re-lived it through surfing.

I had faced hundreds of unknown sparring partners on my trip and no one could make me nervous anymore, so why shouldn't the same be possible for the ocean? I knew from traveling and competing that the only way to conquer fears is to take them on head first. And so I did.

The beach was wide and beautiful. A big group of iguanas had claimed an area of volcanic rocks as theirs, and strange birds the size of refrigerators were scouting the waters for prey.

The waves looked big, and the frequency of them was high. There was only one other guy on the beach apart from me, Mario, and the many animals. At least one person had survived the sharks out there, I thought to myself, wondering if the beach was so empty because everyone else had been eaten.

He was sitting in the sand by a wooden surfboard rack, observing the waves and pointing out to me where to paddle and what to look for. He had curly, dark hair to his shoulders and a tan that witnessed he spent a lot of time in the water with his small board.

He told me in Danish that his name was Jofre and he had lived Denmark. Apparently, he used to have a girlfriend from there, and he went there one summer for three months, remembering a single sentence of the language. He had brought his surfboard all the way from Ecuador to Denmark, just to find out that there were no waves there at all. Even on remote islands—as far away from home as I could be—I was still being reminded that the world is a very, very small place.

The water felt warm around my feet as I stepped in. The board I had borrowed was much smaller than I had tried before, and paddling on it was a lot of work. It was frustrating to try and get out through the waves. Every time I felt like I had worked as hard as I could and dived under five or six waves, I would look up and realize that the current had pushed me back to the same position again and I hadn't moved more than a few meters.

Catching the waves was even harder on the small board. I tried for hours but only managed to stand up once and keep my balance for a few seconds before it wobbled and threw me off and for the hundredth time, introduced me to its old friend, the shallow, sandy bottom.

I came to a point where I just gave up. I was still far away from the shore, so I sat on the board to relax and gather my energy before trying to paddle back in. I was exhausted and felt demoralized from the lack of success. I had been so looking forward to surfing again, and it annoyed me that I hadn't been able to stand up. I was frustrated and didn't enjoy it.

Then I looked up and observed the scenery around me, realizing where I was.

I was sitting in the warm waters of no other place than the Galapagos Islands. I was traveling around the world with no obligations. I was not in an office, like most of my friends probably were at that time, and I didn't have to work in one when I got home. I could go whereever I wanted on the globe and do whatever I felt like. The life I had created for myself was basically the most amazing one I could possibly imagine at that very moment. How could I be in a bad mood about not catching any waves?

I had to look at surfing just like I looked at Jiu Jitsu. There, the submission or the win were never important to me. Through years of confronting my ego and standing face to face with raw emotions of failure and success on the mat, I had learned that it was always about enjoying the process and the life it brought me.

I was still a white belt in the water.

Jofre had been out of the water for a while, and I walked by him to say goodbye before we left. He worked in a bar on the main street and offered for us to swing by in the evening.

The walk from the beach back home took several hours. It was a long walk and getting through town was impossible without having to stop and chat with friends of Mario every five hundred meters. One of them was sitting at a small basketball court where the local kids played.

He couldn't believe I was only visiting for a few days and looked genuinely sad about it—to the point where he could almost cry. He was puzzled as to why I didn't stay longer so I could see more of the wonderful things there.

At that point, I had been asked that question everywhere I went for four months and was too tired to give him the long explanation. However, this time, it did start some thoughts in my head that I couldn't get rid of. Why didn't I have any particular interest in staying to see the scenery there?

We took Jofre up on his offer to come to his bar, and it ended up being a long night there. Mario knew everyone on the island it seemed, and thereby, I ended up doing the same.

I had built up a pretty heavy tab by the end of the night, but as they were closing and I tried to pay, my card didn't work. I tried both my credit cards, both in the bar and the ATM, but with no luck. I was leaving early the next morning, so I couldn't even call my bank and try to fix it the next day.

Jofre said I didn't have to pay then. I would just owe him a drink when he would come visit me in Denmark one day. I couldn't believe the hospitality from strangers like that. I felt horrible about not being able to pay the bill, but there was nothing I could do about it at that point really. All I had left was a few dollars in coins in my pocket that I had planned to use for a taxi home. I emptied my pockets on the bar desk and decided to walk home instead.

I thanked him and told him to come surf in Denmark any day. I was in big-time debt to karma.

Mario had brought about ten people back to the apartment for an after party. Having walked and surfed all day, I was dead tired, and there was no chance I could stay awake. He offered me the use of his bed in the other room so I didn't have to listen to the noise.

Not hearing anything he said, I walked straight from the door to the hammock and lay down in it. People were sitting in the sofa and chairs around the living room table, drinking vodka, playing cards, smoking, and talking loudly. The hammock was hanging right above the table with me in it.

Mario was poking me, saying I should go use his bed instead, but I was already fast asleep. Next thing I remember is Mario's friend laughing at me from the couch when I opened my eyes. I had slept like a rock, snoring loudly while everyone had a big party around me for hours.

Getting to the airport on the other island was a bit of a trip. I was late and hadn't even packed yet. With eyes almost closed from being so tired, I stumbled out of the hammock, scraped all my things together from the living room floor, and stuffed it in my backpack.

Mario stood at the top of the little staircase to his apartment with his arm raised, a clenched fist, and a determined face.

"My friend! See you in Dinamarca!"

Visiting him had been really interesting. He had no Internet and no knowledge about my blog, my trip, or book project. In a sense, it was a relief. I don't really think anyone else I had visited had behaved differently because they knew I was going to write about them later on, but it was sometimes difficult to see through it for me. It was difficult to ignore the thought that someone *might* have been acting differently towards me than if I were an unknown white belt backpacker.

You will only see people's true self when they don't need anything from you. I have found that to be true more than once in my life.

I wanted to meet people as they were. The uncensored version of them. There was no doubt in my mind that Mario was being himself. He didn't have a single reason not to be.

Sitting in the taxi to the airport, I still couldn't stop thinking about that guy at the basketball court. Every single place I had gone, people said I should have stayed longer. The nature of my trip was short, intense visits. Anything more than a few days, and I would quickly get bored. I was a junkie that needed my fix with a new destination more and more often.

In a way, I already knew the answer. It was just one of those things I had to think out loud to fully understand. It was like a technique in Jiu Jitsu you have been doing for years to perfection but realize you have no idea about how works until you have really tried to explain it to someone.

I wish I could stay longer in the places I went, but then I would have to skip other destinations with adventure and people to meet. Galapagos is an extremely unique and historical place far, far away from my home with a lot of wildlife and nature to see; a place I could easily have spent weeks traveling around to explore. However, that didn't really appeal to me. I was in one of the most amazing and beautiful places on earth, and I didn't care about seeing it but only wanted to train and hang out with people there.

I didn't go on any boat trips around the islands, looking at birds and iguanas with hundreds of tourists wearing hats, practical backpacks, binoculars, and Darwin t-shirts. I am sure they saw some beautiful things, but what I saw, was—in my opinion—much more interesting and valuable.

I stayed in a small apartment with three locals, many blocks from the main road with all the souvenir shops and day tour organizers. An area where the people of the island live and which the average tourists never get to see or experience. I got to know the real locals, experienced a little bit of their everyday lives, and met many people who inspired me, who changed me a little bit, and who I can now call my friends.

This is what happened to me everywhere I went. It was just so obvious in the Galapagos, since I had all this highly sought after tourist stuff right around the corner and I didn't bother to go see it. I would check out the BBC documentary in full HD when I got home instead.

Having to leave beautiful places or giant turtles didn't bother me a bit. However, having to leave new friends who I didn't know when—or if—I would see again, was difficult.

Those feelings inside made it very obvious to me that experiencing people and their lives was the real value of traveling. No place or visual impression could ever match that.

Juan picked me up in the airport in Guayaquil. Coming back to his apartment was like coming home.

Two of the postcards from Galapagos were to Japan. I didn't have enough stamps, so I asked Juan to send them one day. It could take a week or a year, but that didn't matter. One of the fascinating things about postcards is that they are non-instant in a very instant world. People are used to emails, instant messages, phone calls, SMS—all right in their hand. Postcards remind us not to hurry; to make other people happy, not in the instant moment, but sometime in the future.

I hoped my friends in Japan would receive them much later and they would be really happy and surprised that they came. It is like buying a ticket to make someone happy at a random time in the future you don't know when will be. I forget too that I sent them, and one day, they will thank me for a postcard they just received. Being a very digitally connected person in my normal life at home, I really enjoyed this simple, analogue gesture.

I was leaving for Brazil already the next day and still hadn't bought the ticket to get out of there again. I needed it for the customs to enter the country, and it was my last chance to get one. They were expensive. Very.

I looked through every travel site I knew, but my cheapest option was $1,700. Both my credit cards were still blocked, so I called the bank back home. I had reached the maximum withdrawal limit for the month, the lady in the phone said, and offered to reset it for me.

After my phone got stolen in Colombia, I hadn't been too strict about looking at my budget on a daily basis. She told me that I had just around $2,000 left. After buying the ticket that left me with $300 and a 500 euro bill I had hidden somewhere in my backpack for an emergency. I would have to be on a serious budget in Brazil. My plans of traveling around that country were not realistic anymore, and I would probably just have to stay in Rio. I knew it was an expensive place, but fortunately, my friends in Connection Rio had offered me a free bed as long as no one else came around and booked it. It was a tremendous help, and I don't really know what I would have done at that point if I didn't have that option.

I sat and looked at the confirmation button for the $1,700 one-way ticket from Brazil to Estonia. I could travel around the nearby countries for weeks on that money.

I eventually admitted that I had no choice but to do it. It was the single most expensive thing I had bought on the whole trip, and it hurt really badly. But now it was done, and there was no turning back.

I was finally going to Brazil.

CHAPTER THIRTY-FOUR

Brazil

Hywel said he was going up the hill behind the house and asked if I wanted to join.

I was really tired from the long flight from Ecuador, but I was also excited to meet the people in the house and get to know them a little, so I jumped on the opportunity for a bit of fresh air.

He said it should take us about an hour and a half to the top. It didn't sound that bad, and I got ready for a stroll. It turned out to be much more than that. The way to the top took a good hour more than expected and included a steep climb on a cliff with no ropes or handles to hold on to.

When I was hanging there, halfway up, holding on to a small crack in the rocks, I thought to myself that I would very likely fall down and die if my grip failed me at that point. It would be a shame to die after just a few hours in Brazil, so I was sure to hold on pretty tight.

My head was still dizzy from jet lag and the long overnight flight, so I struggled to keep my concentration. Despite that, I still acknowledged the photo opportunity and handed my camera to Hywel, who was a few steps ahead of me. I asked him to hurry up a bit before I fell down and suffered a beautiful death in the tropical valley beneath me.

We survived the climb and the rest of the way to the top was through the rain forest. I could hear monkeys all around us in the trees but I couldn't see any of them. My tired brain was convinced they were watching and following me, waiting for the right moment to strike and steal my shiny camera like their distant cousins stole the keys to my motorbike in Bali.

The view from the top was worth the struggle. I could see most of Rio de Janeiro from there with all the beaches, cliffs, mountain favelas, and skyscrapers. It was definitely one of the—if not the—naturally most beautiful cities I have ever seen.

Up until that point, all I had seen of Brazil had been the airport, the inside of a dark house, and a dense rain forest. Out of the blue, the whole place just opened up to me in all its glory. I looked down at it and thought about what it had to offer me; how my next two weeks there would unfold. The excitement was hard to keep inside.

I had finally made it to Brazil after so many years of thinking about it.

When we got back to the house, I had a chance to meet a few of the guys staying there. Some of them had already followed my blog and they were all really nice. It was a mix of mostly Americans and Europeans with a few Aussies thrown in.

Only half an hour after coming back from the climb, everyone was going to check out a Muay Thai project in a favela. I felt like I had been hit by a truck. The trip up and down the hill had taken many hours, and my legs were shaking. The one thing I wanted most in the world at that point was to lie down and relax. On the other hand, I didn't want to miss out on any experiences and opportunities to socialize with the rest of the house.

I met Dennis, an American black belt who had moved permanently to Brazil to train. He said that I was living his dream by traveling the world to train, but I am pretty sure, he was also living a lot of other people's dreams. He had set up Connection Rio, helping people from all over the world get to Rio de Janeiro to train Jiu Jitsu. The project had quickly expanded, and the two houses across the road from each other were busy with visitors most of the year round.

It was a short taxi ride to get there. We got out of the car and I was a little bit worried about being in a real favela, although I knew it was probably all just in my mind. Dennis was with us. He spoke Portuguese and knew people, which comforted me. We walked through the gate to a school. A group of young teenagers were standing there in the dark, looking at us. We were a big group of gringos who looked completely out of place. In my mind, I was somehow prepared for the thought of getting mugged in Brazil. All my friends had been in the past. I just didn't feel like getting mugged the first night so the thugs would have to wait a little bit.

Around the corner from the school building was a large fenced area with a basketball court. The fence was a good eight to ten meters high and held up a tin roof so the kids could use it in the rainy season as well. Only four lights—one in each corner—lit up the concrete floor. The court striping was long worn out, and I could only just make out the contour of where they had been.

At one end of the area, a large group of kids were doing Capoeira. At the other end was the Muay Thai training. There must have been around eighty kids from age ten and up. They were all standing in lines with bare feet on the hard floor. Some of them wore t-shirts with the name of the academy—"Tropa Muay Thai"—but most of them only had normal shorts and t-shirts on. They all had homemade hand wraps. No logos or shiny colors. It was just a piece of cloth tied around their hands.

A guy was standing in front of the class, giving the orders to the kids. He was in good shape, and his technique looked perfect as he demonstrated to everyone how to do them.

Left. Right. Lowkick.

The kids followed. Most of them were beginners, but there were a few in between that looked really impressive. They had fast combinations, crisp punches, and powerful kicks.

Dennis told me that Eduardo had been teaching the poor kids of that favela for free for over ten years. They don't have money to pay for training or equipment but what they do have is determination, showing up for every single class.

I sat down with my back against the fence and watched the class. My lower back and knee hurt from the long walk up the hill all day. They only had about ten pairs of boxing gloves and three pairs of focus mitts to share between the whole class.

A girl in her late teens started kicking the pads held by Rory, one of the guys from the house. The loud sound of her shin smashing into them made all of us turn around. Her technique was flawless and everyone was in awe of the amount of power coming out of that tiny girl. She rotated her hips perfectly into every punch, knee, elbow, and kick. It obviously didn't take a fancy training facility with all the right equipment to produce killer fighters.

As I sat there in the corner and looked around at the many kids training, I was overwhelmed with emotions. I was tired and probably a little easier touched than I would normally be, but at one point, I had to try and hold back my tears. The kids were impressive, and to see how much focus, energy, and enthusiasm they put into the training—even though, they had so little—touched me deeply. They were highly focused and passionate about learning. The small kids looked at the older ones with admiration and awe. They were kicking in the air and hitting each other's hands because they couldn't afford focus mitts.

When they were training, no matter if it was Jiu Jitsu, Muay Thai, and probably anything else, the world around them didn't exist. It didn't matter to them what they didn't have. The only thing present to them was the joy of training. None of them seemed to worry about living in absolute poverty with people being killed around them and little positive outlook for the future.

I looked in their eyes and I saw the kids I had trained with in Moldova. I saw the boys I was teaching back home, and I saw myself, walking back and forth on the wooden floor of my childhood Taekwondo gym, kicking and punching with a determination so strong that it would eventually lead my life to that very moment, sitting on the ground one humid June evening in Rio de Janeiro at the age of twenty nine.

Kids training martial arts were all the same anywhere in the world. They were one. There was the exact same glow in their eyes: The joy. The focus.

Tears were running down my face, and I dried them off with my shirt. I didn't want the others to see me cry, even though there was nothing to be ashamed of really.

I knew I had to help kids like these. Gis, gloves, and pads were in abundance in my part of the world, and here they had nothing. Through the blog, a lot of gis had already been shipped to Moldova and Dominican republic, but I needed to organize things better.

When training was over, we walked across the street to visit a Jiu Jitsu gym. It was down a side street that seemed a little dodgy. Walking up the stairs of what looked like an abandoned building was a tiny room with old, dirty puzzle mats. About fifteen guys were training there. It was exactly the experience I was looking for, and I was eager to come back and join in.

I had Dennis ask them if I could come and join the training there one day. The instructor seemed almost surprised that I wanted to train with them. He probably assumed that gringos only wanted to go to the big, fancy academies with the world champions. He said we were welcome any day. I couldn't wait to go there when I had recovered.

It was around midnight before I was back in my bunk bed. I had planned for a rest day but it had been anything but that.

I took a day off to rest my sore legs. Climbing up that hill hadn't done anything good for my tired body, and I told myself, there would be lots of time to train now I was finally in Brazil.

It didn't take long to get to know the guys in the house. They were mostly hard working white and blue belts who trained two to three times a day. I remembered my own enthusiasm about training as much as possible when I was at the same age and stage of my career as them. I wish I still had it in me but also know that my body cannot keep up with that pace anymore. I felt good about taking some time off to recover.

We were staying on the top floor of the house. There was a nice, big balcony with a beautiful view over the city. Monkeys came on a daily basis to see if we happened to have any bananas or nuts for them. It was a nice place to sit out and enjoy the sun, but it was mostly used for hanging gis out to dry. And by dry, I mean that they never dried, as it was just too humid.

I asked James, the guy in the bunk bed next to me, if he had been doing much other than training while in Rio. He had been there for three months, and all he had seen were the gym and a few times, the beach. He hadn't even been up the hill behind the house or seen the Christ statue. He wanted to make his money stretch as far as possible and get as much training out of his visit as he could.

I wouldn't mind training a lot, but being at the end of my trip—having done almost a hundred classes around the world—it had honestly become a little bit trivial to me. I enjoyed rolling for the fun of it but had no patience for drilling or listening to someone explaining techniques. Having experienced how powerful an engine Jiu Jitsu was for creating an amazing, adventurous life, full of experiences and friendships, being in a hurry to improve my skills seemed so infinitely unimportant. I just wanted to enjoy Brazil and throw in a few training experiences here and there. Dennis had already lined up a list of cool things I could do, places I could visit, and gyms I could train at. I had told him there was no rush. Everywhere else, I had stayed for just a few days, and in Brazil, I would be in for almost two weeks.

I still didn't feel super fresh when Hywel woke me up in the morning, telling me we could just make it to the sparring session at ten. I rolled up my gi in my belt, put on a pair of shorts and sandals, and dragged my feet down the road and around the corner to the gym. It was just a two minute walk from the house.

About twenty people were on the mat for the sparring class in the small gym. I counted at least ten black belts, amongst them Kyra Gracie. I also spotted Gordinho, with whom I had trained in Singapore for that lunch class where I was the lunch. I got changed and sat on the mat, trying to warm up. People looked serious, and there were a few hungry eyes on the skinny, blond guy with the brown belt; the new guy in class.

It was a strange feeling finally to be on the mat in Brazil. I had lost my nervousness about rolling with strangers on the trip, but that day, it came back. I was in the birthplace of the sport, and if there was one place I would have to prove myself and my belt color in, that would be it. Everywhere I had gone, people in the gyms had known me from my blog and travels. No one knew me in Brazil. I was a nobody. Just another gringo who was sitting on those gray mats, waiting for his turn to get his face cranked. Training there was going to be a completely different animal.

I felt like I was still sleeping and was in no mood for catching up with the hard sparring all the guys on the mat were doing. Then, I suddenly woke up in the bottom mount of a wide-shouldered, tattooed Brazilian guy with a jaw as square as a 1970s refrigerator from East Germany and a grinding face that made some strange noises as he wrenched my head to the side with his forearm.

All the muscles in my body hurt and it wasn't a particularly nice round of sparring, but at least it woke me up. No need for coffee, and my first training in Brazil was finally in the books. I had made it, and I had survived. So far, at least.

Then it hit me. Fever.

I felt a bit nauseous during the day but thought it was just dehydration. I woke up in the middle of the night with the bed and my sleeping bag completely soaked in sweat. It was like someone had thrown a bucket of water over me in my sleep. Every thirty minutes, I would wake up, either bathed in sweat or freezing like I had been lying outside in the snow.

I had been really lucky that I hadn't really been sick on the trip, apart from that food poisoning. When it finally happened, at least it was in a place where I was staying for two weeks.

I felt horrible. There was nothing left in me, and my body seemed like it was just a dead shell.

Dennis came by to hear what the status for the things I had planned was. I felt like absolute shit, so I would have to post-pone it all and probably skip a few things on the list.

All the things I wanted to do but couldn't were stressing me out. It didn't help me to get better, and the days went by with the fever not giving up. I was worried whether it could be Malaria. I looked at the little pills in my toiletry bag that I had brought from home. Malaria prevention pills cost a small fortune, so I had gotten the cheaper solution instead. The pills to cure it after it had infected me. The thoughts in my mind were constantly racing around in circles.

I had to visit more gyms. I had to go see stuff. I needed more experiences from that place to remember when I left.

I felt that I was missing out on so many things. I had expect-ed Brazil to be the most amazing and eventful destination of my trip, but I was just lying in a bed, sick and with no energy to do anything. The guys went to training and to the beach every day. I was depressed, but there was nothing to do but wait and stay hydrated. I couldn't even sit out in the sun.

It took days before I started to feel better. Eventually, I gathered the energy to go to the gym for an afternoon class that Dennis was teaching for the people living in the house. We were doing upside down guard drills, and my head didn't like it. I felt dizzy. Dennis told me to just go at my own pace.

I managed to roll two rounds, and it infused a bit of optimism in me.

I talked to Dennis and said I wanted to get going with some of the ideas we had. There was the little gym we had visited in the favela on the first day, and he knew several other interesting places to go.

I allowed myself one more day to rest, and then I would push the button and make things happen.

I convinced a few guys from the house to tag along for a training trip to the little gym in the favela. It was a different place than where we lived, for sure. The streets were full of people hanging out, shouting, and playing music. Being five white guys, we felt a bit out of place there, and many eyes seemed to be aimed at us as we walked down the little side street from the bus stop towards the gym. The rusty door in the heavy metal fence was unlocked so we could get in. It was some sort of a community building that hadn't seen much renovation for many years. An old, wooden table stood on the stone floor, and the walls were bare except for a moldy cork board with a few notes that seemed to have hung there forever.

The gym was upstairs. Several of the bare, concrete steps had lost their edges over the years, crumbled off without anyone noticing. The walls used to be white but were now predominantly gray, the color of the many holes in them. It looked more like an abandoned building someone might use for a paintball field rather than a place for a gym.

A small room upstairs had its floor covered with puzzle mats. They were different colors, laid out in no particular pattern, and didn't look like they were being washed often. Or ever. Another staircase led up to the third floor, but looking up, a big, dark emptiness and a small mountain of trash, convinced me that it wasn't being used for anything. Only half of the windows in the walls had glass in them, the other ones provided the authentic vibe of a genuine favela gym; the smell of a small sidewalk barbecue mixed with the sound of people shouting, motorbikes accelerating through narrow streets, and samba music.

The instructor was a small guy. And by small, I mean tiny. He was probably one of the smallest adults I have ever seen in my life. He was wearing a Gracie Barra gi and a black belt.

He concentrated on pronouncing his English as well as he could but only knew a few words. About fifteen other guys were on the mat, from white to brown belts. Some of them spoke English really well and translated for us. They seemed happy to have some guests at their training.

The class was great and everyone on the mat was tough. I still felt very low on energy after my fever adventure, but managed to go several rounds of sparring. It seemed like each of the high level guys had picked out a limp they were attempting to rip off me, and I had my hands full, trying to stay in one piece. Everyone was smiling and laughing after each round, though, like they were saying "I'll take that arm of yours next time!"

Back in the house, I texted Dennis. Being the ultimate connected Jiu Jitsu tour guide, he got back to me right away with a list of things he had arranged. He had set up a visit the next day to another favela gym where a guy was teaching kids for free.

My fever had been beaten. It was a tight victory on advantage points, but it was beaten none the less, and I had advanced to the next round. My time was running out in Rio, and I was ready for anything to happen.

Most of the time in the house was spent on couches with laptops. Everyone was training several times a day, and in between, they were too tired to do anything else. There was no TV and alcohol wasn't allowed due to recent episodes of madness before I had arrived. Facebook and cooking became the main source of entertainment during the day and evenings. Most guys were there to focus on training anyways, so it was the right environment for them.

For myself, I was a bit more interested in trying to do something else other than training and resting. I felt like I had lost a lot of valuable time in Rio already from being sore after the climb then lying in bed sick for days. After the fever, I had been able to make my way to the beach once and saw a lot of guys in the water on surfboards. I had set my eyes on trying to rent a board one day and get out there.

There were some real characters in the house. Darius, a German guy, had greatly improved his English during his extended stay there, and by greatly improved, I mean that it had gone from almost gibberish to "alright," including the heaviest possible German accent.

Like me, he had also been sick. Already, his genes hadn't gifted him with the most tanned skin, but coming out of the bedroom after half a week of fever, he still scared everyone on the sofas with his impression of the living dead. He found a bit of energy to tell everyone about his thunderous experiences with diarrhea over the several days where we hadn't seen anything of him.

"You know… ze one vere ze shit is like vater!" he explained vividly.

Nothing was happing that afternoon. I had convinced a few of the Irish guys to be offline for a few hours and join me for the next favela adventure. Dennis was coming along as well to translate.

After more than an hour of racing through one shady area after the other, the bus dropped us off on a busy street that was running past the neighborhood we were going into. It looked dark and quiet. The only people out were three guys pulling tires off a car in a small, outdoor mechanics workshop. Right next to it was a narrow alley that Dennis led us into. We walked in line—one behind the other—stepping over old bicycles and building debris. The houses were three or four floors high, and the smell of food came from little kitchen windows. The sound of a TV from a living room, meat frying on a pan, and someone showering ricocheted between the damp walls above us. We had to duck under people's laundry hanging out to dry and go through the back room of a closed restaurant before we got to the gym.

They lost their old place, so they had squatted in an abandoned class room instead, Dennis explained. There was still a blackboard on the wall but nothing had been written on it for a long time. Several different types of old mats were laid out on the floor and sitting up against the wall were about twenty kids in their old gis. There was only room for four or five pairs to roll at a time—everyone else would have to wait. I saw a glass cupboard filled with medals and trophies.

Dennis introduced me to the instructor, yet another small black belt. He was called "Drive In," because he used to work in a drive in. He didn't speak any English either, but Dennis had lived in Brazil for many years and was fluent in Portuguese.

Drive In proudly showed us the medals, and I counted many gold ones along with others from the World- and Brazilian Championships. Every month, the kids were handing in their attendance card from school to him. If they attended school and got good grades, they were allowed to continue training for free. If not, they would be kicked off the team.

Gary and I sat down by the wall and looked at the training. The kids must have been between six and twelve years old. Their faces were serious when they rolled. There was an obvious element of competition between them, and they went as hard as they could to beat each other. One little boy got tapped out in a triangle and pushed his opponent, shouting at him, when he got back up. Their temper was fierce. Some of them were stumbling under the pressure, sitting by the wall and crying after a round of humiliation by one of the six year old alpha males on the mat.

Drive In told me that since they didn't pay him for training, he didn't teach them any techniques. He just gave them a place to train and organized sparring every day. It was an interesting approach and a dog-eat-dog training environment. Putting one of my own kids from the gym at home in there, they would be eaten alive.

When the sparring was over, the kids were back to being kids again. They ran around on the mat, shouting, playing, and hanging around our legs, curious about who the guests were.

A few older kids around their mid-teens came in, and Drive In asked if we wanted to join in for some training. I smiled and told him that was what we had come for.

It was the same formula for his big kids. No techniques or drilling, just sparring.

They were super tough and strong, and I could see in their eyes how excited they were to have visitors from outside coming to train with them. A blue belt—who must have been around fifteen years old—had an almost impassable guard, and I had to turn up the pace to be able to hang with him. Drive In himself also proved to give me an interesting round as he was probably one of the most flexible guys I had ever rolled with. I felt comfortable in the side control top position, when suddenly, in some crazy way, he caught me in a crucifix and tapped me out. I was puzzled. This small guy could twist and turn his legs and body in a way I had never seen a high level Jiu Jitsu guy do before. It was way, way beyond rubber guard. More like rubber mount bottom.

I was impressed.

There was nothing hurting in my bad knee; my trip was almost over; I had been to fifty-six gyms; and—apart from slipping at the pool party and punching my self in the jaw—hadn't gotten a single injury. I couldn't believe my own luck, but on the other hand, my approach to—and confidence in—rolling with strangers probably had a lot to do with it. I never went full on with anyone, and always allowed people to play their game. I had done over a hundred training sessions around the world with a potentially bad knee injury hanging over my head, and the worst that had happened was a few sprained fingers from the competition in Los Angeles.

Drive In took us for a walk through the little shanty town to get some food. It was late evening and the streets looked pretty scary. If it was a movie, I couldn't imagine a better place for a scene where someone would get stabbed to death.

It was nice to have a local guy with us, and despite the danger of the place, I didn't feel insecure at all. Had we walked there alone, without Drive In, I would probably be in a hurry to find a way out.

It was great to feel that I was finally getting something out of my time in Brazil and not just wasting it in bed or on Facebook. The two visits to the favela gyms were exactly what I had been looking for. It was far from the usual Jiu Jitsu experiences that tourists get in Rio.

I didn't care about training with the best guys in the best gyms. My real interest lay in experiencing the world through Jiu Jitsu, to see how far it could take me. Going to the big, fancy gyms with lots of tourists was like traveling the easy way around the globe, only visiting places like New York, Tokyo, Paris, and never going down a side path. I wanted to see how deep into local societies I could get with the sport, and in the last two days, I had succeeded. Training in headquarter gyms in Copacabana and going to the beach, eating Acai, was all too easy and bored me.

I was excited taking things up a gear again and couldn't wait to see what else I could get out of the last half a week I had left.

Then, the next dose of bad luck hit me.

Wednesday and Thursday were national holidays, so everything was closed, and most people took Friday and the weekend off as well. Four days, where nothing happened. No training anywhere, everyone was on holiday. I had finally beaten the fever and was eager to make something out of my lasts days. I was leaving on Monday for Estonia, and it looked like I could do nothing but sit in the house and train with the guys there until then.

The days were slowing down. Nothing happened. The gym was closed, but I went there every day with the guys in the house to roll. It was fun, but most of the people staying in the house were beginners, who—apart from a few of them—couldn't provide me with the kind of challenge I had expected from training in Brazil. I loved to train with the guys, but there was something unsatisfying about coming all the way to Brazil and not rolling with any Brazilians.

We went to the beach during the day when the weather was good. The surf shop was closed for the holidays, so my plans of getting in the water had to be ditched.

I missed the people from my gym at home. The daily sparring with high level guys who knew my game inside and out was hard to find on the road. It was really some quality training I had there at home, and it was obvious to me when I was away from it that I needed to appreciate it more. I couldn't wait to get back on the mats with everyone.

They had been going to a few big competitions, and on the slow Internet connection in the house, I was watching all their matches every day. The kids were still doing awesome, and it looked like everything was just like I left it. The gym hadn't closed down, and people hadn't left the team as I had feared. I felt it was about time for me to come home and take over again, though.

My last days disappeared like sand between my fingers. Wherever I had gone, everyone had kept telling me that I should have stayed longer. In reality, in all those places I had stayed for two or three days, I had gotten more things done than I did in two weeks in Brazil.

Despite not doing anything, I felt very, very good. The weather was nice, and I spent a lot of time in the garden, just relaxing and enjoying the sun. A few guys from a Jiu Jitsu magazine came by to do an interview with me about the trip. Talking about it made me reflect on what I had achieved and how it had changed me. I hadn't done much in Brazil, but even so, being there had still put a lot of things into perspective for me.

I was sitting on the lawn after they had left. I pulled out some grass, squeezed it between my fingers, and put it to my nose. It smelled nice. The sun was burning the part of my legs that weren't covered by the worn out grappling shorts that I had carried with me all the way from home. It was in the afternoon, and the birds were singing around me. From the jungle on the hill behind the house, a humid heat slid down to the garden, accompanied by sounds of monkeys in the trees and eager cicadas.

I had been on the road for a really long time.

My couch. I tried to recall the feeling of my apartment at home. I couldn't.

It felt like I had never been home; like I had lived a lifetime of experiences since I got onto that very first plane to Paris.

I was free. Completely free.

My mind was vibrant, alert, and it was like all of my experiences and memories had come together as one. The feeling of my whole world being in a single city at home had been replaced with a feeling of the opposite. The entire globe and everything in it was my world. It was a playground; there was nothing I couldn't do. I felt the presence of everyone I had met along the way; every friendship, every personality, every interaction. They all melted together into a unity, a combined feeling of being one with everyone.

"We are all one," the text said on the back of one of my last, curled business cards I had made from home.

My appearance was simple. My clothes were dirty; my stubble beard and long hair dyed white by the sun, and the inside edges of my Bali cap were greasy from hair wax and sweat from my forehead. I was the most raw and honest version of myself possible. All the layers that society had wrapped around me through the years had been peeled off. I was me. Nothing else and no one else.

The person I used to be had been lost somewhere down the road, far behind me. He had hectically chased me for more than 70,000 kilometers around the globe until he finally couldn't catch up with me anymore. All the stuff that was usually in the back of my mind—the daily little worries, obligations, things to remember, bills to pay—I had left all of it with him. Every gram of those burdens I had carried on my shoulders were gone and I felt light as a feather.

I wondered how I could hold on to that feeling and keep it forever.

"The secret of Happiness is Freedom and the secret of Freedom: Courage," Thucydides, a Greek historian from 471 BC, had said.

I'd had the courage to be free, to break out of the life that was so easy to stay in at home. My reward was a powerful, deep, and warm feeling of happiness, stronger than I had ever experienced before.

It was the best I had ever felt in my life.

My last day in Brazil had come. My flight was leaving in the evening, so I had the day to relax. I was a little sad that I had been in Brazil for two weeks and managed to do so little training. Since I got the idea to go around the world, I had always imagined how I would end up in Brazil and train my ass off every day. It had been nothing like that. There was nothing to do but just accept it. So many places I had visited with no expectations and had some fantastic experiences. I'd had a lot of expectations for Brazil, and maybe that was what I had done wrong. When I look back, it is obvious that I had a great time there. I must have focused too much on how I thought it would be, so I was blind to how it really was.

There was a morning class that day, and I had set my alarm early so I could get up and join. It was my very last chance to get some training done in Brazil, and even though I had to get up at seven in the morning, I wouldn't miss it. I was flying east overnight in the evening and had to sleep in the plane, so it suited me fine to make sure I would be tired enough to fall asleep there.

I was the only one from the house at the class. About six locals had shown up, sitting around the mat. They were all black belts and didn't seem to speak any English, but were very nice and shook my hand.

The biggest guy of them all must have weighed way over a hundred kilos. His hair was blond, and he didn't look anything like a bad ass Jiu Jitsu fighter. He spent ten minutes teaching some technique. I wasn't accustomed to training that early in the morning and didn't pay much attention to what we were doing. I was on auto pilot and probably didn't really feel like training at that point, but did it anyways just to be able to "cross it off the list" of things I wanted to do.

While I sat there on the mat, tired as a dog, looking at the big guy showing the techniques, I wondered why I did things I didn't really want to do. I was in no rush with Jiu Jitsu and was fine with learning it at a slow pace. As long as I enjoyed every single training session, I couldn't care less if it would take me fifty years to reach black belt. The eagerness to progress quickly that I'd had when I was younger was gone. Now, I just wanted to enjoy the process of training, and I didn't really do that on that humid morning in Barra da Tijuca.

Sparring was like I expected it. They took turns trying to break the record of tapping out a gringo as many times in a minute as possible. Training my defense was fine with me.

After class, the big, blond guy asked me if I wanted to do some extra rounds. It was that situation again. I didn't really feel like it, but I was trying to live up to my own expectations of doing lots of training in Brazil. It was my very last chance to roll with a black belt there, and I couldn't say no.

He was a nice guy, but his game was brutal. He basically held me in knee-on-belly with all his weight on my sternum for a good half hour before he kindly released me back into the real world.

I woke up as I dragged my feet and worn out sandals along the small road back to the house.

That was it for the training in Brazil, I thought to myself, and didn't really know what to think about it. I could have done better for myself.

The house was empty as I packed my stuff, which seemed to be everywhere on, under, and around my bed. It was like someone had thrown a hand grenade into my bag, and all the contents had exploded all over the room. It was quiet. Everyone was at the gym for the first evening training after the holidays. I had to go to the airport and didn't have time to join.

I couldn't shake the feeling of disappointment—the lack of satisfaction. Brazil should have been more. Maybe it was just because I had set my expectations too high, or because I ended my trip there after all those other impressions? Maybe the same stay there would have felt completely different if it was in the beginning of my trip? Maybe it would have been different if I had more money left for it? Or hadn't been sick?

There was nothing to do about it now. It was too late.

The yellow taxi was waiting outside the house. I walked downstairs to the street, listening to the slightly bumping sound my socks made on the carpet-covered stairs. The smell of tomato ketchup was in the air and pieces of avocado left in the kitchen sink.

It was raining, and my backpack had already gotten a bit wet before I threw it in the trunk. It was a dark night. Rio had a certain feel to it that I had gotten used to over the two weeks I spent there. The streets had a special scent in the humid evenings, and there was a very specific way the little pebble stones on the asphalt road felt under my wet sandals in the rain. I heard the sound of a bus racing by a few blocks away. They were always in a hurry. The water ran down the concrete walls around the houses in a way that felt familiar. Little things that you notice in a place you spend a certain amount of time in. I was sad to leave.

I stopped by the gym around the corner to say goodbye. There wasn't much light on the mat, and something like thirty guys were sitting, listening to the instructor teaching the details of a half guard pass. I didn't want to interrupt him, and he didn't look like he was about to stop talking anytime soon. I had to leave. The stone floor on the little hallway of the gym was wet and slippery. I could see the taxi waiting outside in the rain.

That was it for my Brazilian adventure.

CHAPTER THIRTY-FIVE

Estonia

The airport in Tallinn was empty and quiet like the one in Helsinki. It felt like it was sleeping. There was no noise from passengers, no kids crying, no music in the hallways, and no buzz from the tax free shops. Occasionally, the footsteps of some staff member could be heard. They were probably longing to get off work and return home to relax.

I sat on a bench by the luggage belt. There was no one there. I was the only one waiting for a bag to arrive on a belt that didn't look anything like it was about to start moving. The remaining staff were closing off the airport for the night, and a few looked at me, probably wondering if I had planned to sleep there for the night.

Eventually, I gave up. The guys working at the luggage service counter looked like they were on their way to pack up and leave, so I thought it was about time to tell them I had lost my bag.

The guy behind the counter asked me for a phone number or an address of where I was staying. I had neither.

He gave me a receipt for the claim and told me I would have to call them when I knew where I was staying and they would deliver my bag there. I was planning on staying in a town hours away and didn't really believe what he said, but I had nothing else to hold on to if I wanted my bag back. In my mind, I had already lost it and everything in it. I had to accept it, no matter how horrible it would be to lose all my camera equipment and that last 500 euro bill which I had planned to fund my time in Estonia with.

No matter what, there was nothing I could do at that point but wait.

I had been in Tallinn the year before and remembered the name of the hostel we had stayed in. I knew it wasn't far away, and I could take a bus—maybe even walk there—but I was just too tired. It had been a long trip all the way from Brazil, so I decided to spend money on a taxi.

It was a nice little hostel, decorated in a very psychedelic way. There were big paintings on the walls, pillows all over the floor, and guitars to use for everyone. It felt a little like being in a hippie house in Goa. There were lots of travelers there who seemed friendly and social. Fortunately, they had a free bed for the night.

I was in bad need of sleep, but even more of my toothbrush that could be anywhere between Brazil and Estonia. I took a walk around town to see if I could find a convenience store or something that was open. I was so tired; it felt like I was inside a bubble. The world looked blurry, and the noise from all the people partying in the streets around me, faded away and sounded faint and deep. I couldn't find a toothbrush.

Back in the hostel, I emptied my small bag out on the bed to check the status of my possessions now I had lost my backpack: Wallet, credit card, earplugs, pocket camera, charger, iPad, two books, a pack of nuts, a handful of South American coins, and a big pile of receipts. No clothes, no food, and no toothbrush. I was lying down on my top bunk bed with all my clothes on. The stuff from the bag was spread all around me, and I was just staring at it without moving—face flat on the pillow, breathing through my half open mouth. I had no idea what to do. I was tired and dirty. My hair was messy and greasy. I hadn't shaved for weeks. The cap from Bali was dark from all the dirt and smog it had been through, and the t-shirt I was wearing really smelled from the armpits. The bracelet I got from Steven in Hawaii was dirty and looked more black than brown around my skinny wrist. I didn't even want to look at my socks—at that point, they were officially the only pair I owned.

Thoughts were piling up in my head about the lost bag, insurance, my photos on the camera, the money, and my clothes. Luckily, a sleepy feeling embraced them like a big heavy blanket, and before I knew it, I was knocked out.

I woke up to the sound of some Russians speaking loudly in the room. They seemed to keep going for hours as I was trying to hide my head under the pillow, looking for my earplugs that had rolled down onto the floor. Eventually, I just had to get up. I went to a supermarket to buy a toothbrush, soap, and clean socks. Brushing my teeth and taking a shower had rarely ever felt that good.

I had the reception call the airport. They said they would deliver my backpack a few days later, but I still didn't really believe in it.

It was a beautiful day, and the sun was shining from a clear, blue sky. I was rested, clean, and at that point, it was much easier to accept that I might have lost my backpack with everything in it. It was only that anyways: things.

A few backpackers were hanging out in the common room, looking at maps and planning where to go. I lay down on one of the big pillows and felt like I could stay there all day. There was no hurry to catch a bus and I was in a good mood. I played the guitar for half an hour before finally getting up and heading out the door.

The weather was beautiful and I didn't have much to carry, so I decided to walk to the bus station. I really enjoyed the feeling of not being in a hurry. If I didn't make the bus, I would just get on the next one.

Being back in Northern Europe was great. Even though Estonia is different from Denmark, it really felt like home compared to the many places I had been to prior to getting there. The wooden houses were beautiful, the weather was great, and people were smiling. My friends from the gym back home and Daniel, the Scottish guy from Taiwan, had already arrived in the town I was going to, and I couldn't wait to see them all again.

It was about an hour's stroll to get to the station. An old lady was working at the ticket counter. I guessed she was probably around sixty years old, and just being used to it, I assumed that she wouldn't speak a word of English. I was surprised when she told me about the ticket price and departure times with a near-perfect accent and a big smile.

The bus ride was beautiful. It was a hot summer's day, and we were driving through a long stretch of road through a forest of tall, slim trees, past golden and green fields with small farms scattered far between each other. A year earlier, I had been sitting in the same bus, looking out of the same window, going to the same city for the Jiu Jitsu summer camp. I had been thinking a lot about the around-the-world trip I was working so hard to plan, wondering where to go, what to do, and how to make it all happen. I loved nature and was craving to experience it without filter. The forest—quickly moving past the window—seemed to almost call to me. I wanted to get out there and touch the world.

Now, I was back on the same road and the trip was almost coming to an end. I had done it. It was hard to grasp that I had been around the world and only had one stop left. It almost didn't seem real.

The sun was high in the sky and there wasn't a single cloud to be seen as I sat on a bench by the bus station, waiting for Daniel to come by.

"Will be there in ten minutes, bro. Was just at the nude beach," he texted me.

When we were in Taiwan, I had told him about my summer trips to Estonia, and he had found a cheap ticket to go there and meet me for a week. It would be the third time during my trip that I would meet up with him.

I spotted him walking towards me in the sunshine from a hundred meters way with a big smile on his face. I didn't have any bag to carry around, and we weren't in a hurry, so we decided to start out by sitting in the sun and have a nice cold beer. It was a beautiful summer day and I was thrilled to be back. We were catching up a bit before walking to the hostel where my friends from the gym back home were staying.

They all got a big hug, and it was a special feeling to hang out with them again. The joy overwhelmed me. I was so close to being home and I couldn't wait to see the rest of the people there.

We had rented bicycles and drove them to the sports hall, where the camp was held. It had been growing steadily every year, and this time, there were more than a hundred people attending. Like me, a few Estonian guys had started teaching themselves MMA and BJJ from scratch with no instructors. Now, they had built up a serious community in the country with thriving gyms and athletes. They were also some of the best teachers I have ever come across in my Jiu Jitsu career.

I said hi to everyone. I had already told them beforehand that I wouldn't be training at the camp. A week later, I would be back in my own gym teaching and training, so I could really need a little break from it all before that. Estonia was a great place for a vacation and perfect to get my mind off training for a while.

It was a week of recharging my batteries. All the traveling had worn me out, especially after being sick in Brazil and flying such a long way to Estonia. I had hit rock bottom. There was nothing left in me. All I wanted to do was relax and enjoy the summer. And what a beautiful summer it was.

The days seemed endless. Sitting on the bed in our hostel room at eleven at night, the northern sun was still shining bright outside. There was no rush. We went to the beautiful beach late in the evening and it felt like it was in the middle of the day. During the day, I took my bicycle and slowly strolled through the quiet little streets. Big, European beech trees, full of light green leaves, were gently whispering the sound of summer above my head. Small, wooden houses in all colors decorated the streets, and friendly people seemed to be everywhere around us. One night, I slept on the grass in someone's garden and another night in a hammock. It was warm and smelled nice. Even during the night, the sky was blue. I loved it.

There was still no word from the airport about my backpack. I had to buy new clothes and toiletries. I knew the insurance would cover it, so I got myself a lot of new tank tops, shorts, sandals, and sunglasses: the proper summer attire for my little vacation.

After five days, I was more relaxed and revitalized than I had been on the whole trip. I was ready to go home, and I was excited about it.

The guys took different flights at different times, depending on when they had to be back at work. Daniel and I left a day later than everyone else. We had planned to take the bus to Tallinn the day before our flights, but looking at the time schedule at the bus station, I suddenly remembered something I'd wanted to do on the trip. Hitchhike.

We had all day to get there, so we were in no hurry. We sat on a bench outside a supermarket and tried to make a plan while sharing a big bottle of iced tea. The weather had been perfect the whole week, and that day was no exception. I walked to the office supply store and bought a big, red marker and a piece of white cardboard.

"Not serial killers," I wrote on one side and drew an axe with a cross over it.

We both agreed that we should try and find a place to start a little outside the city. Preferably by a field where we could relax and take our time, waiting for someone to pick us up.

We walked about an hour to the city limit. We were a bit hung over so we weren't that fast, but it didn't seem to matter. As we sat down, I held the sign, and Daniel raised his thumb to the cars that passed.

Just seven minutes later, a big car had stopped, and a blond guy jumped out. He went straight to the back of the car to open the trunk for our bags and told us with a heavy Russian accent that he was on his way to Tallinn as well and we could just get in the car.

His girlfriend was in the front seat. They were a young, friendly couple from Belarus who didn't speak much English but were very interested in talking to us. It was their first time ever picking up hitchhikers and our first time ever hitchhiking. Daniel's Scottish accent proved a little too much for them to understand, but I was a master of international travel-English, so we managed to keep a conversation going. They had a nice big car and it was much better and more interesting than taking the bus.

We spent the night back at the psychedelic hostel. I had no alarm clock but magically woke up on time. If I missed the flight home, it wouldn't be the end of the world anyways.

Two British guys were on a party trip and I ended up talking a little bit with them in the morning. They were eager to make new friends but I didn't have the energy to tell them the whole story of my trip again. It had just become too long at that point. I still hadn't heard anything from the airport, and considered my backpack lost. I crammed all my stuff into two plastic bags and changed into the least smelly t-shirt I had left, thinking that it would be best for the person who would be sitting next to me on the plane.

One of the guys was sitting on the bed with a big belly and a hangover, depressingly commenting on the deterioration of his own body when I took off my shirt, revealing a six pack from hell after rolling almost every day on the trip, burning off any fat that I had carried with me from home. He asked me if I did any sports or something like that.

"A little bit," I replied.

I needed to get home.

CHAPTER THIRTY-SIX

Denmark

Two of the instructors from the Estonian training camp, Martin and Priit, were in the airport as well on their way to Iceland via Denmark. So was my backpack. It had arrived the day before and smelled a little bit from the wet training clothes that had been in it for almost a week since I left Brazil.

Strangers were speaking Danish on the plane. It was the first time I had heard that in five months, and it was a really weird feeling. I was so close to home that I could almost smell it.

I was tired. My very own bed was suddenly within reach, less than an hour away. Home hadn't felt like home for so long, but now I ached to be there. I fell asleep on the airplane while I was trying to change music on my iPad. The bump of the plane landing woke me up. I was back in Denmark, and having just woken up, felt fairly confused.

Was the whole thing just a dream? Or was I still somewhere in South America, dreaming that the trip had ended?

I shook my head a little bit and looked out the window. It was true enough. The ground was flat, as far as the eye could see. Right next to the runway were small fields and houses. The trees looked familiar too.

"KØBENHAVN - COPENHAGEN," the sign on top of the airport building said.

I was home.

Walking out of the plane, I was freaked out by hearing my own language in the speakers. It felt so foreign, like a lost language I hadn't spoken since I was a child.

Martin and Priit welcomed me home and I raised my arms in a victory pose, laughing.

I updated the little statistics note I had kept on my cheap phone from Colombia that still had the coins from around the globe super glued onto it.

89,582 kilometers
140 days
35 flights
56 gyms
90 classes
43 cities
24 countries

It was in the middle of July and the airport was packed with people who were coming home from summer vacation. For the last time, I picked up my dirty backpack from the luggage belt. Getting it ready to put on my back had become second nature.

Open clip. Pull strap. Open knots. Release small clips. Tie up. Adjust straps. Lift and carry on right shoulder. Left arm through. Tighten straps around waist.

Ready to go.

My father and little brother were waiting for me at the arrivals hall. They worked together in their small two-man electrician company and always had time to come visit me in the gym during a lunch break. They had extended it a little bit that day to give me a lift home from the airport.

I gave them both a big hug. I was happy to have them in my life and it continued to fascinate me how similar our personalities were. The same level of passion I had for martial arts, my brother had for football. Just as I never stopped training, neither did he. Like myself, he had an extreme ability to never lose interest in a subject and is to this date the only person I know who has played Championship Manager continuously since 1993, when we had saved up to buy the very first game that came out. A good twenty years for one game.

Most people were on holidays and just a few cars went by on the street outside of my apartment. It was strange to sit on my couch again. Very quiet.

The silence was making too much noise inside of my head. Thoughts raced around. What now?

My girlfriend got home from work, and I was really happy to see her again. Strangely, it felt like we had only been away from each other for a few weeks. We went for a walk to the beach nearby. A handful of young boys were playing football in a school playground. I looked at them as we walked by and realized that one of them was a student from my kid's team in the gym. Before I had time to say anything, he saw me as well and sprinted towards me, giving me a big, jumping hug.

"Graugart! You are back!" he shouted.

All the kids on that team were like little brothers to me, and I was really happy to feel that I had been missed. I couldn't wait to get back on the mat and train with them all again.

I was sitting on the couch at home and tried to watch TV. It was the first time in five months that I had done it. For so long, I always had something to do, someone to talk to, and somewhere to go. There was never any need to sit and look into a screen feeding me with bullshit entertainment. It was nothing but a way to kill time while waiting to die. It didn't do anything good for my life. The newscast seemed strange to me. I had missed out on earthquakes, tsunamis, tornadoes, financial crises, wars, and political dramas. I had been in another world, where all those things didn't exist. Whether the place I had been was the real or the fake world was hard to tell, though. I think it was the real one. I turned the TV off. Whatever was on seemed so irrelevant.

I had been afraid to do it, but I knew I would have to check my bank account to investigate the damage. There was still a little bit left; just enough to get me through the rest of the month.

I had kept a very strict report on all my expenses during the trip, right until my phone got stolen in Colombia. Of course, I hadn't taken any backup of it. After that, I just checked my account balance now and then to get a rough estimate of how much money I could afford to spend.

It is difficult to say how much the entire trip cost me, but a rough estimate is around 90,000 kroner, which is equivalent to about 15,000 dollars in 2011 currency. It sounds like a lot, but with the money I had saved up, added to the little monthly salary I got from home while on the road, I pretty much broke even on the trip. The plan had succeeded.

Already, the next day, I was going to work in the gym. My business partner, Carsten, had done everything himself for five months, so he needed a hand badly. I spent the whole day cleaning up, fixing computers, answering emails, and doing administration work. Having a full time gym is more than just training. No more sitting on surfboards and driving around far away towns. I was back in the real world of work.

Late in the afternoon, people started to show up for training, and there were lots of hugs and handshakes.

"What's up with the beach boy?" one of my longest running training partners, Kári, said, as he entered the door and saw the most tanned version ever of me sitting on the couch.

I hung around for hours and just talked to people. Training was still on, just like it was when I had left. Nothing seemed to have changed, apart from the amount of people there. We had hit the six hundred member mark that month, and there were so many faces on the mats that I had never seen before.

Kári was teaching a no-gi class, and with nothing else to do, I decided to jump in. Even though I was too tired to do anything, it had become second nature for me to just jump on the mat and roll if there was an opportunity for it.

My cardio was epically bad, but I somehow managed to spar for a good 45 minutes. It was great to train with everyone again. Coming back to them, I had a clear measurement of how much my game had evolved on the trip. It was obvious to me that I had learned a lot and improved immensely.

I couldn't wait to pass everything on to people and tell them about all the stuff I had learned on the trip.

Driving home on my bicycle, it was a beautiful summer evening. Birds were singing, and there were green leaves on the trees. When I left, the place was covered in snow and the trees were bare and cold. Everything had been gray and depressing. It was a different world now, and it was a different me that came back to it.

I took the long road home, going through the city center. It was a joy to ride my bicycle again. It rolled smoothly through the little streets in the old part of town, taking me through all the places I knew so well. Every little corner, every smell, every sound was familiar. I drove through the street where my friend had jumped out of the window and stopped for a while at the spot where his life had ended so suddenly. The sun was shining, and the air was warm and heavy. A few young people walked by. They looked happy.

"I did it, Frank," I said with a subtle smile on my lips.

CHAPTER THIRTY-SEVEN

The Afterburn

It felt good to be home but also weird. I was thinking that I liked the place but also that it made no sense for me to stay. Just like I had passed through so many places on my trip, I also had to pass through this one at some point.

Change the scene. Live a different life. Seek adventure.

Staying and living in that one place for the rest of my life would be contradictory to everything I had learned on the trip. Life, friends and good experiences are everywhere in the world, just waiting to be discovered.

I started to get bored after three or four days at home in Copenhagen. I knew I would have to stay, but my brain was hardwired to think something else. It was still in travel-mode and ready to move on to the next place.

I panicked a little bit and began making plans for how to keep up my pace.

First thing was the training. I had learned so much from rolling with different people around the world that it would make zero sense to stop there and just roll with the guys in my gym again. I got in touch with people from gyms around town and arranged to train with them. I changed my regular Friday class to be a two and a half hour long open mat session, inviting everyone from any gym to come roll with us for free. Had I done the same a year earlier, I would probably have been a bit afraid that I would lose some team members who might become friends with people from other gyms. The thought didn't even cross my mind at that point, and the Friday sessions rapidly became a big success with 30-40 people from all over town on the mat every week.

I had renewed energy and inspiration to teach again, and every class I did, I tried to pass as many of my new experiences on to people as possible. I had the same passion for training as a beginner who just started and got hooked. In a way, I felt like I had re-discovered Jiu Jitsu for myself, stepping into a completely new era of my career on the mat.

Getting back into competition was the most natural thing for me to do. The confidence in my game was at an all-time high, and I knew that the best way to keep improving and inspiring those I was teaching would be to step on the mat and test myself again and again. To me, it was still just a feeling, like going to other gyms and rolling with people I didn't know.

I set up a team of guys for the tournaments that had filled the calendar hanging on the wall of my little office in the gym. It was a busy schedule, and I had ambitiously written down all the events I could find in Europe. I wanted to push myself as much as I could; to get out into the deep water and learn to swim.

We flew to Switzerland and competed in beautiful Geneva. The sunbathed Alps were right outside our doorstep, and I was eager to go for a walk on them, but the competition organizers were a bit slow so we ended up spending all our time in the sports hall instead. I lost the first match in my weight class but ended up taking gold in the open weight division.

In London, more than ten guys joined me for the IBJJF London Open. A loss to the sneaky inverted De La Riva game inspired me to study it in detail in order to fill the gap in my game.

Paris hosted the second European NAGA tournament, where I won the belt in the expert division, beating a black belt in my first match and then winning the finale by heel hook. It was a special city to me, since it was the first destination of my trip. Standing by the Eiffel tower, I remembered the rainy night I had been in the same spot, full of expectations and excitement for how my life would look six months later.

At the Scandinavian Open, I lost a close match to a tough Finish guy, and took home a swollen left testicle from a single leg attempt gone wrong.

Spending a week in Scotland, I drove mountain bikes around the highlands on the warmest day of the year, won two gold medals at the Glasgow Open, and taught a seminar at Daniel from Taiwan's gym in Edinburgh.

For my last trip of the year, I filled a bus with 45 people from my gym and drove five hours up in Sweden for the Swedish Open, one of Europe's biggest competitions. We took home seventeen medals and got the trophy for the best kid's team, finally beating that gym who had won it five years in a row.

My crazy burst of competitions had totaled 67 medals in two months for me and my students.

It was a fast paced autumn. All the short trips and many tournaments blurred together. I still didn't feel like I had arrived home. My mind was flowing in a state of traveling freedom. The pace of the many things happening were as hectic as the trip itself. People from all over the world came to visit, and it seemed like we had a new guy coming through the door every week. Fernando—one of the guys from Costa Rica—stayed for a few months, Jonathan from Kauai Kimonos had been on the road for a year when he came by Denmark, Eren from Turkey joined us for a bus trip to the competition in Sweden, and Mario—the passionate guy with the hammock from the Galapagos Islands—kept his promise and stayed with me for three weeks. I constantly had someone coming or leaving. If I couldn't get to the world, at least I would make it come to me for a while.

I might have returned home from my travels, but I had hit the ground running and it must have been strange for people around me to observe me in that period. I had changed on the inside and outside, as if it was a different person that had come home. I looked different, having lost a lot of weight on the trip, and was still without a haircut for half a year.

While I occasionally found myself sitting on my couch at home, having a break, thoughts and ideas in my head were constantly racing each other.

I saw a movie about a guy who took a pill and could suddenly use his entire brain to see the grand scheme of life and the world. The movie itself wasn't really that good, but while I certainly couldn't write a book in one night, I definitely identified with the feeling.

I could see the big picture. There was a mission with my life; not a second could go to waste.

I was chasing that feeling of ultimate freedom and being that raw version of myself. And exactly like during the trip, I found it in creating experiences for myself in a hectic pace. Anything I could do to get a small kick with the drug of life counted, and the more I could cram into a short period of time, the better.

Apart from traveling to basically every competition I could find around Europe, I was on the mats to train six days a week, got myself a surfboard and went surfing north of Copenhagen, skim boarded every sunny day on the beach, took long evening rides through the streets of my neighborhood on a longboard, stayed up late to write my book every night, bought a guitar and practiced playing every morning, coordinated gi-donations for poor kids around the world, worked on programming another website, took my mountain bike to the forest, started a business selling Jiu Jitsu t-shirts and went partying with my friends from the gym every single weekend the whole summer.

The rest of the world was functioning at a completely different and much slower, pace. Explaining my frantic pace and energetic state of mind to anyone was impossible. While I had been away for the experience of a lifetime, returning home with an afterburn that would make any space rocket engineer at NASA envious, everyone else had been living their usual slow-paced life of working five days a week, buying groceries, and feeding their cats. Most people around me seemed like strangers. We lived in parallel universes. I loved anyone to jump aboard my train and tag along, but I had no time to stop and try to pick them up.

I didn't seem to care about anything at all. All I could think was that my life could end the next day, and the world was still full of things to experience.

Pulling my bicycle out of the basement, unshaven, wearing my Jiggy-Jig hat, a colorful surfing t-shirt, and a skimboard under my arm, on my way to the beach in the morning with the sun in my eyes, made me so happy inside that nothing else could possibly matter.

Even though the weather guys on TV said it was the worst one in thirty years, I had the summer of my life. Like with Jiu Jitsu—where through years of training, I had opened a fat, wide, high-speed connection to my brain that analyzed and processed terabytes of chess-like information about positions and strategies in every split second of a match—I felt like I had similarly opened the hatch to life itself. Feelings, emotions and impressions were overwhelming me and my existence in the universe felt like it had more meaning than ever. I lived my life like a boss, thrusting forward at 100 mph, and enjoying every second of it. If I had come home to a 9-17 office job after the trip, it would have been pure hell for me.

Looking at the video interview from Brazil, I remembered the feeling of freedom I had, sitting in that garden in the sun. It was still inside of me. I was clinging on to it, at least for a bit longer.

When we finally got to January, the competition team had taken a big hit. Lots of injuries, financial problems, and cruel bosses not allowing time off work had cut us down to only seven people going to Portugal for the Europeans. It didn't matter—we were ready.

The competition streak in the fall had made me feel extremely confident in myself and my Jiu Jitsu. I was better than ever, and knew I stood a chance against anyone in my division. The fear of competing—the personality of someone who was never sure if he could perform at the high level or not—was long lost, dissolved by the many times I had pushed myself to step on the mat and just do it. I had become a competitor. One of those very guys I used to admire.

I looked at the matches going on around the mats. I could beat those people.

There were still no signs of a desire to win, but watching the other brown belts compete, they were doing nothing I hadn't been exposed to in the gyms around the world already.

Even more interesting, I realized that they didn't seem intimidating to me at all. A year earlier at the same competition, I had looked at the guys on the mats and in the warm up area. They all looked like they were some kind of super humans who possessed a secret knowledge or skill that I didn't. Observing them, I didn't see actual people, but rather dark, blurry silhouette shadows representing everything I feared about competing. I couldn't tell them apart; they were all the same. Like a uniformed army without individuals.

Now, they looked like normal people; like any of the hundreds and hundreds of guys I had met in gyms around the world. I could see how one of them was the funny guy who always joked around after class. Another one was the tough one, never giving young white belts a chance in sparring. There was the athletic talented guy, the one owning twenty different gis, and the geek who could entertain himself in details of an omo plata sweep for half a year. They were all there, and there were no super human aliens. Ok, maybe a few, but most were just regular guys like myself.

It became obvious to me that training with so many different people around the world, pushing myself through the fears of traveling, sparring, humiliation, and being a stranger in fifty-six gyms all over the world had paid off.

The outer layers of the opponents that my brain had created were peeled away, and as I looked around, I suddenly found myself in a sports hall in Portugal, together with 2,500 potential new friends. The year before, they had merely been mirrors, reflections of my own fear. There had never really been any other competition than myself. The enemy was the inner me, and stepping onto the mat for the first match of the brown belt division at the European Championships 2012 was a very different Christian to the one competing in 2011.

My skills had greatly improved; I had nothing to prove and no fear of either failing, or of what my opponent was capable of. It was an emotion-less cocktail that really proved to bring out the best in me when it was time to step up and perform at the highest level.

The referee signaled for the match to begin and I clapped hands with my opponent.

He looked around my size and probably hadn't cut any weight either. He was German and I had just witnessed him win his first match by a beautiful arm bar.

I felt like I was in pretty good shape and strong in all areas of my game, so I didn't really have a set game plan for the competition. However, the warm up hadn't been really thorough, so to start out nice and easy, I decided to pull guard on him right away.

As I had him in my open guard, my legs took over on autopilot and searched for holes, frames, blocks, and hooks. All I had to do was to mentally lean back and let the intuition of my guard—the sum of all its experiences, good and bad—take over. It felt like it was a living organism on its own.

A small hand placement mistake made by my opponent, too small for either of us to consciously notice, was immediately taken advantage of, and before I knew it, I had my legs wrapped around his arm and neck for a triangle choke. The rest of the work to close it in was on me. As he tried to pull out, I closed in an inverted triangle and waited for him to relax before I changed it to a regular one. My breathing was calm, and my mind was emotionless, concentrating on playing my moves right and not get excited or rushing anything. As he stood up to escape, I grabbed my shin and underhooked his leg, rotating around him to tighten the choke around his neck.

He tapped out.

I heard my team mates cheer and clap behind me. It had taken less than a minute, and I had moved on to the next round. It was the perfect warm up.

My opponent complimented my guard and said he would cheer for me as we shook hands and I thanked him for the match.

Next up was a Danish guy, from one of the other gyms in Copenhagen. I had known him for ten years and knew that he would be a very tough guy to beat. His style of passing fitted my guard really badly, and his closed guard looked like the gates of hell, so I didn't really have a clear plan for what position I would try and beat him in.

With no plan, he had the initiative and pulled me into his closed guard. His legs were powerful, and I had to use all my strength to keep my posture. He had cut a lot of weight for the tournament and was much stronger than me, I felt.

He tried everything but didn't manage to either sweep nor submit me. On the other hand, I didn't feel like I could pass his guard either and was only semi successful with one attempt. Eventually, I realized that my way to win would be to ride out the storm and hope for the referee's decision. I was on top and had a single guard pass attempt. If nothing else happened, I would probably get the win.

At one point, his closed guard was tightly wrapped around my arms, head, and one leg. I couldn't move an inch, and my muscles were stretched to their limit. All the defensive training I had done on my trip paid off as I managed to keep calm and wait for my opportunity to get out.

Time ran out. I did it.

The referee raised my hand, and I had moved on to the finale with the smallest possible margin for a win. At the highest level, even the smallest factor can determine the outcome of a match. It wasn't the most exciting win, but I played the game and made it through.

I hadn't had a chance to watch the guy I was meeting in the finale before the match. He was shorter than me and looked much stronger. With a five-month long shoulder injury, I hadn't been able to do any weight lifting since I got home from the trip and was still skinny and weak. My mind was sharp, though, and I was determined to try and beat that guy.

Unfortunately, he out-powered me. I threw everything at him, every single one of my best sweep attempts, but he was like a rock. He didn't move a bit. Whenever I went for something, he just flexed his muscles and stayed exactly where he was.

Eventually, he got a grip of my belt and ankle. There was no way I could break it and had to let him pass my guard.

He pinned me in side control like I had never been pinned before. He wouldn't give me an inch of space to move on. I kept my head calm, and at the right moment, escaped back to my guard. I ended up getting a deep half guard sweep on him and was just about to get up and jump for a guard pass when the time ran out.

I had lost the finale by points and gotten a silver medal at the European Championships.

It was the biggest result our little team had ever produced, but it didn't really do anything for me. As I stood on the podium, I felt the same as if I had lost my first match. I couldn't get myself to be bothered about it. All I was thinking about was what I needed to work on to beat that guy next time.

The ability I had developed as a child to close off emotions and focus on the task ahead of me had an interesting effect on my adult competition life. It was nice when I needed to perform without being affected by anger or fear, but when I finally achieved something, I missed a little bit of wild cheering and running around with my hands up.

After the Europeans—about half a year after I had gotten back home—things eventually started to slow down a bit. A shoulder injury combined with the cold, Scandinavian winter, put a dampener on all the activities I had done during the summer, and I could dedicate more of my mind to working on developing the gym. I was still being issued daily speeding tickets on my newly built superhighway of life, but the drug was beginning to lose its effect, and I probably started to seem more normal to people around me. I was getting into a regular rhythm of training and teaching and spent a lot of time writing my book. My promise to myself of trying to learn languages made me concentrate on getting better at Swedish, and when three deaf kids joined my Jiu Jitsu team, I started putting a lot of effort into learning sign language.

I hadn't thought the day would come but eventually, I got a little tired of traveling so much and so often. Just like the way tropical beaches had gotten less and less interesting over my period of discovering them, traveling in itself needed to be more extreme and less often for me to really enjoy it. I decided to have a more spacious calendar for the spring of 2012 and only settled on a few snowboard trips to Sweden and a handful of travels that I found too interesting to miss out on.

The guys from Chisinau in Moldova had really gotten started with Brazilian Jiu Jitsu and invited me back to do a seminar for almost a hundred people.

"I might use a few… dirty tricks on you," a hundred plus kilo Sambo guy there told me, sporting a Russian accent that any evil scientist would envy. His face looked like he had been working as a blacksmith since he was a baby.

I had no choice but to tap him with a body triangle cup fuck from back mount and a face crank after a minute and a half of him trying to drill his elbows into my rip cage.

It was in the coldest time of year and the coldest winter in ten years when I visited Moscow. It was cruel, but I loved the contrast. The city was dark. The silhouettes of tall, wide brick palaces and building cranes looked like evil robots watching over the city. Smoke from the chimney of a power plant filled half the sky and blocked out most of the sunlight during the day. Every building was the same color: Gray and dirty, like snow mixed with exhaust smoke from old cars. Abandoned warehouses and whole apartment blocks with no windows or walls were lit up by a rare ray of sunlight. Ice cold wind blew right through them, as if they were stadium-sized, concrete ventilation shafts from an apocalyptic future. Identical buildings lined up as far as the eye could see, holding apartments for tens of thousands of people, looked more like concrete prisons than someone's home.

It was far from warm and exotic, but extreme travel experiences like these were the only thing left that could satisfy my vampire-like lust for blood of adventure.

After the crazy competition race in the fall and the milestone performance at the Europeans, I started to reach a point in my training where I felt like everything was really coming together for me. My knee was feeling surprisingly fine, and I was able to train a lot.

My Jiu Jitsu had reached a level where I was observing my body performing it more than consciously doing it. I didn't think about how I had to move anymore. When I rolled, I would find a place of peace in my mind, sit back, relax, and just look at my physical body doing everything it needed to.

The best comparison I can think of would be tying shoe laces. It is something we probably all are black belts in. If we try to explain exactly how we tie the knots in our shoe laces, it is too difficult for us. It becomes even more obvious if we observe ourselves doing it. It is almost magic seeing the fingers work the laces in a complicated, expert fashion without consciously being able to tell what is going on.

That's when I knew it was about time. The black belt.

Already, when I was on the road, Kári had warned me that Robson was planning on getting me a black belt when I got home. I didn't want it at that time. The trip had matured me a lot, but I didn't feel like I was ready for that level just yet. My conditioning was terrible from all the traveling and lack of physical training, and also, I wanted to give the all time high confidence in my game a chance at competing with the brown belts, where I—as opposed to the black belt division—would stand an actual chance of winning something.

In the spring, things were different. I had somehow digested the many impressions, inputs, and experiences from around the world. The competition season was over, and I'd had some really good results all around Europe. Things were settling down in my head and body. I could see the big picture of life and Jiu Jitsu, and I felt like my game was at an all-time high.

Robson came by for training one day and made sure I knew he wanted me to come to the training camp and meet his trainer from Brazil. It was no secret what he meant. Robson was a first degree black belt and couldn't give out one himself yet.

I had always imagined that my black belt would come as a surprise out of the blue one day, but now I was somehow put in a situation where I could choose to go and get it or not. Of course, there were no guarantees. Edson would—without a doubt—thoroughly inspect my game, skills, and personality before deciding to go with Robson's recommendation or not.

I told him I would be there.

I wanted to just enjoy the training at the camp, but it was difficult to not think about the graduation. My thoughts were at war with themselves, one side wanting to finally achieve a black belt after 23 years of training; the other furiously denying taking on the pressure and responsibilities that came along with it. Was I even good enough to be a superhuman black belt? I just felt like a regular guy with no special talent for the sport other than an ability to stick with it. I was trying hard to ignore the battle inside of my head and focus on the training itself.

It was a long weekend of training, and my body felt like it had been hit by a truck by the end of it. About ten black belts were teaching for eight hours a day. I had made a big mistake of rolling hard for two hours the day before the camp, and I could feel it in every muscle.

Edson asked me to show a technique to everyone. In lack of instructors, I had been teaching Jiu Jitsu for thirteen years at that point. Since I was a white belt, teaching had been my way of learning the art myself. I felt completely at home trying to explain the basics of wrestling sweeps from the guard and was so indulged in getting the message across to the attendees that I almost forgot it wasn't me who was running the camp.

We lined up and Edson asked me and three other brown belts to come to the front. He gave a small speech about the importance of both skill level and personality for becoming a black belt, and asked Robson to give me mine. He tied it around my waist and gave me a big hug.

Everyone clapped for what seemed like an eternity. Some of the other guys with their new belts had tears in their eyes. Through my entire career in Jiu Jitsu, I had expected to be overwhelmed with emotions when I got my black belt, but I didn't feel much. Like in competitions, my mind was clear, and I was focused on the goal. There was no adrenaline, no emotions in the way.

All I could think about was the future. I was already planning the work needed to become the best possible athlete, teacher, and role model; thinking about what I needed to do to be able to compete at the highest level and how this final exam of my Jiu Jitsu education would open up an endless flow of new opportunities.

I had just gotten my ticket to the ultimate roller coaster of life and was standing first in line, getting ready to ride it.

The rest of the ceremony is blurry in my memory. Everyone congratulated me, but my thoughts were somewhere else. There was no time to cry or get excited. I had work to do.

I got ready for my first rounds of sparring with my new belt and told Robson I'd let him have the first dance. Over the years, I thought I had started to figure out his game a little bit and was able to handle myself against him pretty well. I had rolled with him numerous times in the gym and felt like I was catching up with the little, avid competitor. I was wrong.

To celebrate my new promotion, he turned up the pace to competition speed and ran over me like a steam train, flipping me upside down like a pancake, judo tossing me like a bag of potatoes, and submitting me left and right. I had nothing on the curly, smiling lightweight from the poor upbringing in Bahia's favelas. As the timer rang and I sat on the mat, trying to get myself together, I knew exactly what newly promoted black belts meant when they say they feel like white belts again. Competition was going to be tougher than ever, mentally and physically.

I was at the bottom of the food chain now, having to fight for my survival against primates that had already evolved many generations ahead of me. The effort, sweat, tears, and pain I had gone through to reach black belt seemed like nothing compared to what lay ahead of me. I stood at the gate of my new life—a completely new level of suffering and hard work.

There was no turning back.

On the train on the way home from Sweden, I took a photo of my new belt and sent it to my father. One of the things I remember most vividly from my childhood was my dream of one day becoming a black belt, just like him. I started the journey at the age of seven and somehow strayed away from it for some years along the way, but there I was, standing on the finish line. The quest had defined me.

My father was a young man in the early seventies when he stood in the reception of the first Karate school in the country and signed up for his very first class. No one had even considered my existence at that point, but the moment he wrote his name on that photocopied form in his beautiful handwriting, he instantly changed the course of my life forever, giving me opportunities and experiences he could never in his wildest dreams imagine.

My phone rang.

"I am very, very proud of you," he said.

CHAPTER THIRTY-EIGHT

There is No Difference

I would like to thank everyone who made my trip possible. I have met, hung out, partied, emailed, talked, and trained with hundreds and hundreds of people along the way, and each and every one of you has influenced me. The help, friendship, and hospitality I have experienced from you everywhere in the world has blown me away, and I cannot describe how much it means to me. I also had immense support from everyone at home, which has played a big role in realizing this project.

I'll advise anyone considering a trip like mine, or any trip really, to absolutely go for it. I totally believe that anyone can do what I did. You don't have to be a certain belt color or an Internet celebrity for people to be nice to you. The hospitality I enjoyed through the Jiu Jitsu community all over the world was so strong and overwhelming that I don't doubt for a second that anyone can do the same. Remember that white belts are real people too.

The most difficult thing for me was to make the decision and overcome the fears of leaving things and people behind; breaking out of the conformity of life at home; and the worries about jumping into deep water and having to find my way around the world with only the help of strangers.

It is like competing. Before the match, your stone-age brain will recognize the situation as dangerous for you and try to convince you not to do it, making it easy for you to regret and stay away instead. When you finally step on the mat, all that is forgotten and you just go. As soon as I had taken off with that first plane to Paris, everything was easy from there. It felt so natural to move around the world, and I was never in a situation where it was too difficult or I couldn't find people to train or stay with.

Sport is your key to experiencing the real world. I think any sport will do—whether you surf or play chess—but there is something special about the general culture in the world-wide Brazilian Jiu Jitsu community. Maybe it has something to do with the physical barrier quickly being broken down so fast. Within the first twenty minutes, you've gotten everyone's asses in your face. That'll break the ice.

Also, I think it is a matter of honesty. In this sport, there is no room for hiding. You have to prove yourself and confront your ego on the mat every single day. You cannot put on some belt and never have to prove that you deserve it. In other sports, you can maybe stay away from competitions, but if you train Jiu Jitsu, you will still have to spar in every class you attend. There is no way around it, and constantly confronting your ego like that, forcing you to be honest about yourself, is a very healthy thing.

I think that is why almost everyone I met in gyms around the world were cool people. They cannot pretend to be something they're not because as long as they train, there is nowhere to hide it. There is no need to act in a certain way because reality will be revealed on the mats anyways. There is simply no room for people who have a problem confronting their ego in our sport. It is about being the most honest version of you, and training Jiu Jitsu will help you with that.

This large collection of honest, secure, self-confident people are all yours to tap into for friendships, traveling, and experiences. I can't think of a better way to travel than to do it through the eyes and lives of locals. With Brazilian Jiu Jitsu, you will instantly have a network of local friends anywhere you go. It is your ticket to experiencing the real world behind the curtains of the tourist industry.

It's easy to do. No, trust me, it really is. Just find out where you want to go, look up a Jiu Jitsu gym there, and ask if you can come by. Everything else will fall in place for you, and you will have an amazing time. Don't believe me? Well, then you'll probably have to read this book again.

If you are wondering where to start, come by Denmark and visit my gym. You can train for free and I'll personally take care of you and make sure you have a great time here. And yes, that is a promise. I have a lot of hospitality to pay back in order to realign the karma balance of the universe, and I will be more than happy to do it.

So, as you can see, everything is already taken care of. All you need to do is to push the button. Start making long term plans today if you want to make things like this happen. I challenge you to do it, because I want you to do it. I hope someone will experience the same things as I did.

Personally, I don't really have an interest in Jiu Jitsu as in wanting to become the best, win something, or get to a certain belt level. To me, the sport is a means to live the life I want. It allows me to have a job I love, sleep as long as I want every day, meet amazing people who become my friends, be healthy, travel the world, and best of all, pass all these gifts on to others. With everything I can get out of it, winning some gold medal just seems so uninteresting to me.

Use Jiu Jitsu to live your life. You have all the tools right in front of you, and along the way, you will find out that you can also use them to do good and important things for other people.

Before I left, when people said that my trip would be a life-changing experience, I had a hard time believing them. I thought at times that it would just be a long journey that had the potential to be more stressful than enjoyable.

A year after I arrived home from being 140 days on the road, I am still amazed at how much it has changed my life… and how important a decision it was for me to go through with it. Somewhere out there in the big world, I met the rawest, purest version of myself, and I liked him. It's a cliché to say that someone is traveling to find themselves, but I actually did.

Traveling around the world and meeting all those fantastic people strongly reinforced what I believe in. In some way, I went out to confirm some things to myself, and I found what I was looking for. I feel vibrantly full of love from great friendships, belief in the good in people, and knowing that the world is definitely not a bad or dangerous place.

I am a better version of myself now, there is no doubt about it.

The trip might have ended long ago, but the effects of it will echo throughout my life—and maybe yours—for years and years to come.

So what is next for me? I don't know exactly, but things must keep happening.

I definitely intend to keep up with a high pace of life and have been ever since I returned home that summer in 2011. I am aware more than ever that the world is a wonderful place, and I only have one single chance to experience it. There is an expiration date on me, and I have no idea when it is, so not a day can go to waste. I could die tomorrow.

I have a vague master plan for my life. Whether it will happen or not, I don't know yet, but if there is one thing I have learned from that trip around the world, it is that I don't really need to plan or worry too much about details. As long as I keep enjoying training and am open towards anyone I come across being potential new friends, I completely trust that everything will work itself out for me and experiences will come.

The only thing I do know for sure is that traveling will continue to be a big part of my life. After all, it is the only thing in the world I can buy that will actually make me richer.

Somewhere in South America, as my journey was about to come to an end, I really started to feel deep inside of me how everyone I had met was the same. It is hard to describe the feeling of unity between every single person I have met, but it was very strong and powerful.

It makes no sense to say that we are different just because, we have been randomly born on one patch of land instead of another. In truth, there are no borders in this world. Any dividing and separation of people on this planet are manmade. It is not real. Friendships, love, adventure, experiences, and lives you can live are everywhere. No matter where I went, I met fantastic people. I have made more friends in five months than I could possibly do at home in a lifetime, and there seems to be no limitation to where these might be. Your next best friend or experience of a lifetime can be anywhere in the world, not just in your own little bubble.

We might seem different on the outside, coming from different countries, races, religions, beliefs, cultures, or even another Jiu Jitsu team. But when we are on the mat, clapping hands and ready to roll, it is so obvious that there *is* no difference.

We are, indeed, all one.

CHAPTER THIRTY-NINE

Ten years later

It's difficult to grasp that it's been almost a decade since I wrote that last chapter and closed the book, never to open it again until now. I remember spending an entire year sitting in my living room with earplugs, writing on an old laptop where I had killed the wifi card to avoid distractions.

The frustrations of the writing process were immense and I was close to giving up many times. As I started writing the book, I quickly realized that I had to tell everything or nothing. I couldn't just pick and choose a few things or filter my stories as I pleased. The book wouldn't be complete if I did that. I had to either put all of my thoughts there or none of them. I decided to write with complete honesty in the fullness of time, leaving everything out and never looking back.

In the process, I forgot why I was writing and what I was writing. It just came out of my fingers, like it was someone else controlling them. It started to have a strong, therapeutic effect on me. As I pressed along on the keyboard, it was like years of frustration, anger and sorrow came out through the words I put on the screen. Each difficult memory I managed to put in the chapters felt like a relief. When it was finally over, I closed the book and decided never to open it again. The purpose of writing it was fulfilled, and I had no desire to read it or even talk about it with anyone.

I can honestly say that in some strange way, it never crossed my mind that anyone would actually read this book. Of course, I had planned to publish it, and it wouldn't be a surprise if a few people bought it, but in a way, it felt like I was putting it down for the process of writing it and never for anyone else to read it.

I remember when the first person told me he had read it. It was the weirdest feeling and somehow a bit of a shock. Suddenly, I realized how personal and intimate those stories were and now some random stranger knew everything. Everything I had been keeping inside of my head for so many years is now out in the open. Then another one messaged me. And another one. Before I knew it, I had told my story to thousands of people.

It was bizarre for me and I can not say that I did not regret it just a little bit. Was this really what I wanted? To tell everything to the world?

Had I only known where the stories of that book would be taking me in the decade to come, I would never have thought twice about publishing it. I am forever grateful I took that leap of faith to travel and tell the world about it, as that project ended up shaping my entire life into something I could never even have dared to dream of.

In this final chapter, written ten years after the original book—once again on the couch with an old laptop and earplugs—I'll try to tell the story of what became of that young, curious BJJ Globetrotter. How one trip, one decision to leave, created ripples in the water that changed everything for years and years to come.

A lot has happened since then and I will try to keep it short—and honest.

CHAPTER FORTY

Tour Guide

At every single academy I visited around the world, I made sure to extend an open invitation to come visit me in Copenhagen. I even wrote it in this book as well. When my trip was over and I wasn't going out to see the world anymore, at least I could try to get the world to come to me. Anyone was welcome at any time and I promised to take good care of them. It was the least I could do after all the hospitality I had felt around the world.

It worked. And a little too well, in fact.

Hordes of people I had run into during my trip—as well as many readers of my book—took me up on the offer and came to Copenhagen. For the first few years, I don't think there was a single week where we didn't have a visitor on the mats for our Jiu-Jitsu classes. Some came by for a few days, some stayed for months and it was overwhelming to feel how many people wanted to come and train with me.

It was also exhausting. Every single week, I was making new friends, going sightseeing around Copenhagen, taking people out for dinners and going out to the bars at night. It felt very much like I had never stopped traveling and just continued doing all the same stuff at home instead. I loved every moment of it, but it was also wearing me out since it was pretty much constant. At one point, I realized I had been tour-guiding Copenhagen at least once a week for more than six months, non-stop.

That's when I had the idea to try to convince everyone to come in during the same week, so I could take care of my visitors in bulk instead of one at a time. It would be a much-needed rest period for me.

I managed to "re-book" around 25 friends—most of them whom I had met during my trip around the world—to show up during a cold week in November. I had timed it with an opportunity we had to host Royce Gracie for a one-day seminar, so there would already be a lot of people in the gym that week. I planned an overly ambitious schedule of training and social activities that I was really excited to email out to everyone. It was a small group, but we had an amazing time.

"We *have* to do that again" was the one thing that everyone could eagerly agree on once it was over and we were all completely burned out from overtraining and overdrinking.

I had no idea about it at the time, but that was the very birth of the BJJ Globetrotters camps.

We were trying to sign up for our annual trip to the European Championships in Portugal after I returned home. Apparently, there was another academy in the United States called "CSA", so we couldn't use that for our IBJJF registration. We had to come up with another name and someone suggested we use "BJJ Globetrotters", since I was the instructor and the blog of my recent trip had that name.

The idea came up that we should make patches or t-shirts for our little team of around twelve competitors that had just gotten a cool, new name. I sat one afternoon after training and sketched a patch with a bus and a sunset. Back then, almost all teams marketed themselves with pit bulls, gorillas or other in-your-face logos to claim their status as alpha tribes. I always found that a bit silly.

A designer friend of mine brushed it up for me and I posted it on my blog. It didn't take long before people from all over were messaging me, asking how they could get a patch and be part of this team. Many were also having a hard time signing up for the Europeans due to the complicated paperwork required by IBJJF and asked if I could help them out.

It had never really crossed my mind that "BJJ Globetrotters" would be anything but just a patch for the twelve of us going to Portugal that year. But there was clearly some sort of momentum from my trip that people wanted to be part of, and there also seemed to be a general desire for a simpler, more lightweight solution to competing with the IBJJF. The intricate system of signatures, hierarchy, perceived loyalty (both ways), and affiliations that often came with contracts and expectations were tiring people out.

The stories about Jiu-Jitsu politics I heard from people I met on the road haunted my mind for long after returning home. The feeling I had gotten from visiting all these academies around the world, finding friendships in each and every one of them made them painful to listen to. I had first-hand experience that nice people could be found in all academies, no matter what their so-called rivals perceived about them.

I grabbed the opportunity and decided to try and make a little team out of that patch. A straight-to-the-point alternative to the traditional way things worked. And now that we had gone through all the trouble of registering with IBJJF, I let anyone who wanted to, join in and compete alongside us for the European Championships.

Instantly, I realized that there was a real demand for this. I wasn't the only one who was tired of how things were being done.

Perhaps there was an opportunity there to do things differently, but it had to be done right. A new team like this could too easily fall into the trap of becoming just another closed group of people following a leader. And nobody would probably notice until it was too late to turn things around again. So the very first thing I did— from the outset of the idea of BJJ Globetrotters—was to write down a simple list of rules. I didn't think it was plausible, but looking at how so many other affiliations had ended up becoming unhealthy power structures, I wanted to make extra sure that this could never happen to me. In a sense, I was safeguarding myself from one day becoming a greedy tyrant who would abuse a position at the top of a hierarchy to control the people involved.

- *We don't pay each other any affiliation fees*
- *We wear any patches we like on our gis*
- *We are free to represent any (or no) team in the competition*
- *We encourage training with anyone regardless of affiliation*
- *We are willing to promote anyone who deserves it—members or not*

- *We arrange camps, seminars and visit each other for training and fun*
- *We believe everyone is equal both on and off the mats*
- *We strive to enjoy life, people and the world through Brazilian Jiu-Jitsu*

It was pretty much just a reverse list of all the things I didn't like about traditional affiliations. Methods of control, greed and close-mindedness that I had experienced and heard about too many times during my travels.

"If I ever make any changes to these values, please abandon the team immediately", I added.

I ordered a batch of 50 patches—which I felt was extremely ambitious—and posted on my blog that anyone interested could message me to join the team. The only requirement was that they agreed with the values listed.

More than anything, it was just sort of a provocative experiment against the establishment. Who was I to start a BJJ affiliation anyway? Nevertheless, more than a hundred emails poured in during the first week, and I suddenly found myself being very busy packing patches in envelopes and running to the post office to mail them around the world.

It was the point of no return.

The following summer, the 10th anniversary of our academy was coming up, and we wanted to host a big party. It was the perfect opportunity for us to organize another camp. The word had already spread and people were signing up from all over. As far as I remember, we ended up with almost one hundred people there; a staggering number for our small academy.

The party was one to remember. We had rented an old warehouse in Copenhagen and installed a full-sized cage, bar, barbecue and professional photo booth. We had put together a hilarious fight card that included—amongst actual professional and amateur matches—kids fighting adults and a grappling match in suits.

For the sake of entertaining the crowd, I decided to come out of retirement and fight MMA there as well. My friend and training partner, Christian—who you might remember as "Street Fighter Ken" from my very first Jeet Kune Do lesson described earlier in the book—was in on the challenge. None of us had done any real preparation for the match. I was mostly concerned about cutting weight to look in shape for the pictures. I remember eating a lot of roast pork from the party barbecue shortly before the fight. In retrospect, that probably wasn't the best idea, but the fight was a lot of fun. We had agreed on "seventy percent intensity", but I started out with a superman punch to his nose and then it was kind of on from there.

I lost the fight decisively and Christian and I proceeded straight to the bar for the first of many double Mojitos of the night.

At one point, I stood outside in the warm summer evening and talked to a group of people with a few drinks in my hands and a few bruises on my face. I suddenly realized that every single one of them was someone I had met during my trip around the world. The feeling of gathering friends like that from all over and having a fantastic time together was a real rush and I was eager to do that again.

More camps happened in Copenhagen. It was too much fun to not keep doing it as much as possible. The BJJ Globetrotters project was starting to gain a bit of momentum on the side and still wasn't much more than a patch when I got the idea to combine it with the camps. I believe it was our third or fourth camp when I suggested we used the BJJ Globetrotters name for it in an attempt to attract some of the people from that small, new community to join us. It worked.

I often timed the camps with celebrity seminars as it was very effective in attracting people to join. Keenan Cornelius, Clark Gracie and many others came through those years. But along the way, I realized that it didn't actually have that much value in the long term. Celebrity instructors on intense seminar tours are often socially desensitized and will rarely feel like taking part in anything outside of class. They have fans hanging around their legs all day, every day and mostly want to be left alone in their hotel rooms or hang out in small groups with people they feel equal to. It quickly became clear to me that this was not the way to build the camps. It did indeed have a big marketing value to have these people on the posters and it attracted many participants, but also left me feeling somewhat unsatisfied afterward.

The true value of the camps was how people were connecting with each other across all belt levels and backgrounds, just like I had done on my trip around the world. No matter where I had gone, any white belt hiding in the corner of the mat—a little shy about talking with the higher-ranked visitor—could very likely end up becoming a new friend for life. I had experienced that over and over again. Keeping an open mind towards every single person I met and treating them as a potential new best friend, had become the absolute key to how I wanted to live my life.

"We believe everyone is equal both on and off the mat" was one of the fundamental, unchangeable values I had written down for BJJ Globetrotters.

So why would I involve people as front figures of the event who didn't feel like they could participate equally with everyone there?

The culture is built from the top, so it is all-important to put the right people there. If they are excited to be there, everyone gets excited to be there. If they don't really have the energy to socialize or feel like they are somehow separate from the other participants, that'll set the tone and culture for everyone else as well.

The solution I found was ultimately simple: Involve those who are truly passionate about taking part—on and off the mats—and invite as many of them as possible.

And that's how the camps went from initially being celebrity seminars—with clearly defined "professors" and "students"—to become just holidays for a large group of friends. Often hundreds of friends. Some of them happened to be teaching the Jiu-Jitsu classes there, but only because they had trained for a bit longer than the others.

Everyone equal. On and off the mats.

CHAPTER FORTY-ONE

The Business of Belts

With the many people I met during my trip and a very successful book launch, I suddenly found myself to have become somewhat famous in the BJJ community. I was also a newly promoted black belt and granted the sudden supremacy to promote people, and with a growing BJJ Globetrotters community around me, a strange thing started to happen.

People from all over began to desire that I would be their instructor.

It didn't happen overnight and I didn't really notice it at first. But before I knew it, I was invited to teach seminars multiple times a month. I was happy to have an opportunity to keep traveling and I continued to meet fantastic people who I still consider friends.

I went all over Europe, to the Caribbean, Russia and even flew on a weekend trip to Hong Kong where a three-meter tall poster of me—holding all my medals—had been printed on the outside of the downtown Hayabusa gym. I started to be invited to several little training groups around Denmark and in nearby Sweden that I visited on a regular basis.

But there was something else.

An expectation of belt promotions.

It wasn't always explicitly being said, but it was in the air. Part of the deal of inviting an open-minded, black belt instructor like me to teach a seminar was that I didn't have any real expectations in return for promoting someone.

"We are willing to promote anyone who deserves it—members or not"

This was another fundamental value of BJJ Globetrotters, designed to avoid people having to build relationships they didn't want to be in, just to get a belt promotion. There should exist an alternative way of belt promotions for those who truly deserve it that does not require them to sign a business contract, carry a certain logo on their back, franchise their business or invite someone for seminars every year.

I didn't mind. I was happy to promote anyone who could live up to my standards. Our academy was highly competitive those years, so they were extremely high anyway.

But it still didn't feel right for me.

I was happy to travel and teach all my friends, but what kind of relationship was I really building with them? I would like to say it was only partly based on them wanting the validation of belt promotions from me. But if I honestly ask myself whether I believe they would pay to invite me for seminars like that if I had told them belt promotions wouldn't be considered, I think the answer would be no. I didn't get any invitations six months earlier when I was only a brown belt but my ability to teach was exactly the same. If I took my name and belt promotions out of the equation, the seminars wouldn't happen.

It took a while for me to realize where I was heading. I was setting myself up to run a business of me being someone's instructor. They would literally pay me to officially recognize their achievements in the sport, their increments up the ladder of the belt hierarchy. To validate their own training by putting my name on it, even though I had only the tiniest possible influence on their skills.

On the one hand, I had invested more than a decade in that black belt and this was a great opportunity to monetize it. I wasn't making much money at the gym and suddenly I had a decent income every other weekend. It was extremely tempting to go down that path.

On the other hand, nurturing these relationships where I was somehow "worth more" than my friends, was so contradictory to the feeling I had of meeting people around the world on equal footing.

More people were trying to book me for seminars. More people wanted to be "under me". But what would happen on the day where I couldn't promote them anymore? When they were all black belts themselves? And had become better athletes and teachers than me? What kind of friendship would we have then? Would I be forced to maintain my income through promoting black belt degrees? When too many people get to the top of the pyramid, you have to build another one on top of it to stay relevant.

"We are all one".

It was tattooed on the inside of my arm on my last day in Brazil, so that I never forget that this is what I believe.

And how could I believe that but also build a business based on me being different from everyone else? On my friends wanting something from me?

You only ever know the true character of someone when they don't need anything from you anymore. It was painstakingly true and it haunted me that I was setting myself up to build relationships based on people wanting something from me.

I had to get out before it was too late.

The camps in Copenhagen attracted a lot of people and the community was growing fast. I had my hands full trying to keep the little page on my blog manually updated with all the "affiliated" academies and individual members who messaged me to join.

"Hello from El Salvador!"

Another email dropped into my inbox that day and I initially didn't give it much thought. A guy called Luis had a house by the beach with mats in his garden and the idea of hosting Jiu-Jitsu camps there. With my confidence in hosting camps in Copenhagen, I was quick to jump on the idea and ten months later, I showed up at the airport in El Salvador. I had somehow managed to convince eighteen people from around the world to do the same.

I had no idea what I was doing but I just treated it as a holiday with friends and it seemed to work really well. We had a great time and many of the people at that camp continue to be my friends to this day and can still be found on the mats at our camps every year.

However, it was a giant logistical operation to run, as well as very expensive and risky. At our first ever attempt—where I had no idea if I could even sell a single ticket—eighteen participants just barely broke even. I believe there was a profit of around $1,000. It wouldn't have taken many fewer tickets sold before that would have become a very, very expensive holiday for me to El Salvador and I didn't really even have any money.

It was satisfying to have pulled off a camp outside of Denmark and even more to not have lost any money on it, but the risk of it also scared me off from doing more like that. I simply couldn't afford it if it didn't sell enough tickets.

CHAPTER FORTY-TWO

Cutting Weight

When I was on the road, I had masterfully managed to cut down the contents of my backpack to just 14 kilos. I had started out with more, but along the way found a rhythm of getting by with very few clothes and a single gi.

I enjoyed that. The feeling of being able to carry everything I needed on my back felt like an achievement and I craved to feel that sense of freedom again after I returned home. In Copenhagen, I had lots of things in my apartment and it didn't feel right. I started reading books on downsizing and simple living and it resonated strongly with me. I didn't own my things, they owned me.

The gym was starting to do quite well and it would have been so easy to fall into the trap of getting a nice car, a mortgage for a new home and for luxuries to become necessities. To start building a pretty, little, comfortable prison for myself.

Instead, I urged to free myself from possessions and anything that would wall me in.

I had always been able to afford what I wanted because I wanted what I could afford. I didn't want to change that, no matter how tempting it might be.

I was still together with the same girlfriend and we had just had a son. It was important to me that he would be able to experience the world, just like we had done ourselves. The only thing that mattered was the ability to keep living a life full of adventure for all of us and the flexibility to quickly act on any opportunities that might come along.

So I started selling and giving away as much as possible of my possessions as I could, to the point where I pretty much just owned a laptop, some clothes and a bit of furniture. My goal was optimal freedom so the method had to be letting go of anything that would keep me stuck in one place. To be able to carry my entire life on my back.

It felt fantastic but there was one big thing that seemed impossible to let go of. The elephant in the room that I knew I had to address at some point. The one thing that—if I was completely honest with myself—reduced my freedom of movement more than anything.

The gym.

That decision was very difficult. I had spent 15 years building that place up from scratch and I was nervously shaking when I finally one day proposed to my business partner that he could buy me out. Our personalities and views on how to run the place had grown widely apart over the years and business-wise, we had been in a standstill for a long time. So in a sense, I longed to get out but had been too afraid to do anything about it. We came to an agreement. I would still stay on board as a regular instructor and teach my classes as usual, albeit with more freedom to travel for seminars and camps as I wanted.

When I finally signed the contract, the relief was intense. Quitting my office job ten years earlier and selling off material possessions in my apartment had felt like a relief, but this was a different league. I had just let go of the biggest thing I had ever created and it felt incredibly good. My mind immediately felt lighter. So much stress, so many questions and decisions. In an instant, it was all gone. I was never going to log into that email account again. I felt bad for the employees. Like I had let them down. But I had to take care of myself and follow my principles.

My living expenses were cut down to a bare minimum and I had no desire to buy anything, so with a bit of savings and the money I got from selling the gym, I could keep myself going for a few years while figuring out what to do next.

It didn't take long.

With all my focus now on BJJ Globetrotters and nobody who had to agree on my ideas and decisions, I could go all in and do whatever I wanted. From a business perspective, that was incredibly refreshing and inspiring.

Hosting the camps was the most fun thing I knew of and the one thing that got me closest to the feeling of high intensity traveling around the world with an overflow of impressions and new friends. The only thing that made sense was to try and do as much of that as possible. El Salvador had been a financially scary mouthful and I had plenty on my hands at home with the gym, so I hadn't ventured outside of the safe camps in Copenhagen since. But with a newly found freedom to do anything I felt like, I was curious about experimenting with more international camps.

I got a message out of the blue from Valentin, an excited guy from Austria who was running a small training group in Linz and also happened to be a high-level snowboard instructor. I had been snowboarding a bit in Sweden with my little brother every winter and I loved it, so when Valentin invited me to visit him in the Alps, he quickly had my attention. With nothing holding me back and all the time in the world, it didn't take long before the ideas started rolling. Before we knew it, we were working on setting up a winter camp in the Alps. I already felt very confident in doing summer camps and there was a huge interest for them, so why not do something in the winter as well. A local on the ground was the key to make something happen far away from home.

"We did our homework man, just gotta show up tomorrow and enjoy the ride!"

I laughed hard today when I looked back through our email correspondence leading up to that camp. While we *believed* we had done our homework, the reality was much different. I'm pretty sure that the 66 participants had a great time, but behind the scenes, it was an absolute train wreck. And probably the only time in my life where I truly thought I was going to die from a stress-induced heart attack.

Many valuable lessons were learned that week which I still take with me today, more than sixty camps later.

Then things really took off. I made another trip to El Salvador shortly after the Winter Camp and apart from the annual camp in Copenhagen, I also managed to expand to Belgium and the U.S. that summer.

"I feel overwhelmed with joy in this moment", one of the guys at a camp in Copenhagen said as we walked down the street towards a music festival after a hard day of training. Sun in our eyes, neon green leaves on the trees.

I started to realize I was doing something right. If I could create such an experience for one person, what if I could do it for thousands?

Having lived in Copenhagen for almost 15 years at that point, I really started missing the forest where I grew up as a kid. I randomly saw some pictures from a kids' summer camp in the United States and got all nostalgic about it. I emailed and called probably every summer camp facility I could find on Google and got an especially excited reply from a guy called Mike who worked at one in New Hampshire. He was more than eager to help me set up something and I took the chance.

I hadn't even seen the place and before I knew it, one hundred people had signed up and expected an amazing experience, just like the big, successful camps from Copenhagen they had seen pictures of. But this was nothing like a camp in a pretty city where people would be staying in clean hotels and go sightseeing and eat ice cream in the afternoon after training. This was adults living in cabins in the woods, sleeping in bunk beds and showering with spiders.

It was what I had wanted for myself but would everyone else like it too? To say I was scared would be quite an understatement.

It was a long flight from Denmark and I arrived late in the evening the night before the first day of the camp, together with a few friends. It was in the middle of a thunderstorm and the rain was so heavy we couldn't see anything out the window of the car as we pulled into the campground. Mud was flooding down the little hills and thunder was roaring above our heads. Mike had told us to pick any cabin to sleep in and he would meet us in the morning. It was pitch black as we walked around in the mud, eventually finding the cabins down by the lake. They looked old and worn out; wooden built, decades ago. I opened the creaky door to one of them and the smell hit me.

Piss on mattresses. Homesick kids had been wetting those beds summer after summer.

The bunks were tiny and I had to curl up in a fetal position to fit in one of them. I tried to keep my cool and laugh a bit about it to the two friends that had come along for the early arrival, but inside of me, I was in shock.

What had I done?

The next morning, *one hundred* people would arrive and see this. They would all turn around on their heels and any trust that anyone ever had in my ability to host Jiu-Jitsu camps would be shattered. The rain was hammering away on the roof like it was trying to break in. I completely panicked and my mind was racing with thoughts on how I could stop it in time. Perhaps I could email everyone and tell them I had called the whole thing off before they would leave home? I would have to refund everyone's tickets and accept losing all the money I had paid upfront for facilities, food, staff and mat rental. I was more embarrassed than I had ever felt. All that work for nothing. Exhaustion from traveling eventually got the best of me and the next thing I knew was the sun hitting me in the face and birds singing outside the cabin.

Beaten and depressed, I stumbled out of the bed and opened the door.

The weather was perfect. The sun was rising over the crystal clear lake before me, and the rays hit my eyes. Birds were singing all around and I found myself in the middle of a stunning, green forest. The other cabins smelled fine, it was apparently just that one mattress.

"This place is amazing!!" a stocky guy I had never seen before said with excitement in his voice; as he walked up to me, hand reached out to shake mine.

He was the first camper to arrive and as I looked in between the trees from the terrace of the cabin, I could see more cars coming through the entrance.

That was the moment when I understood that everything was going to be just fine.

Mike came down the hill to welcome me and we walked together on the little trail towards the sports hall.

"How on earth did you convince one hundred people to come out here in the middle of nowhere?" I clearly remember he asked.

"I honestly have no idea", I replied.

Things really took off from there. I added more camps, friends and experiences to my yearly calendar than ever before. I was having a blast and I couldn't get enough of it. I traveled several times a month. If it wasn't for a camp, then I would be around Europe, scouting locations for future ones. Every second week, I would stand in the Copenhagen metro station early in the morning with bags under my eyes. The station was always full of people, except they were all going in the opposite direction than me. While they were all trying to squeeze into the train going towards the city, I would often be completely alone on the other side of the platform to get on the train towards the airport.

BJJ Globetrotters was rapidly expanding and started to make waves in the BJJ community. I suddenly found myself being the figurehead of what could, by all means, be defined as an actual Brazilian Jiu-Jitsu affiliation.

More and more people wanted me to be their instructor, to submit themselves to me being their "professor". Especially as the camps and community grew, I felt that people looked up to me differently. My best friend even told me it was weird to be around me in the bar at the camps because so many people wanted to be close to me and socialize.

I didn't feel like I had done anything to put myself on a pedestal but I somehow found myself sitting there anyway. I didn't like it and I realized that I had to actively do something to avoid going down that road. I wanted to stay on the same level as everyone else.

The first step was the decision to quit doing belt promotions. I would promote my own students at home, but I would no longer offer it as part of seminars or even at camps. Instead, anyone in the community who—for one reason or another—were up for a promotion and didn't have an instructor themselves, could be evaluated by all volunteering instructors at the camps. There would be a debate, a vote and the result would decide on a belt promotion or not. Myself, I would purposely stay out of it.

Next, I decided to start inviting as many black belt instructors as I could possibly fit in the schedule for each camp. That way, nobody would stand out as the one superstar, but instead, we would all sort of drown in the noise of the many black belts around. Myself included. It's hard to figure out who is supposed to be at the top of the hierarchy when too many are there to pick between.

It worked and I truly started feeling that I was just another participant of the camps, another friend on a holiday with friends. Nobody was trying to buy me lunch, hoping that I'll put a stripe on their belt at the end of the camp. As an instructor, I could teach a few classes at the camp, but apart from that, keep my profile in the background.

When my belt was washed enough times, the red bar started to fall off. I let it. No more stripes for me; a black belt is a black belt.

Perhaps it is me who is overly sensitive about these things and takes it to an unnecessary extreme. But my personal focus on building honest, equal, lasting relationships with people of all walks of life and creating quality memories for myself and others laid a clear foundation for how I wanted to build my own career as a black belt and ultimately for BJJ Globetrotters.

The absolute last thing I want is a "Team Graugart". And I truly believe that is a key factor in what has made BJJ Globetrotters such a big success.

CHAPTER FORTY-THREE

The Opportunity of a Lifetime

"Caribbean escape?" the subject line of the email read.

Pierre was part of a small training group in Saint Barthélemy, a small French island of just 9,000 people in the West Indies that I had never heard about before. He had just read my book and invited me to come teach for a few weeks since they didn't have any instructors on the island. Never turning down an adventure, it only took three months before I landed with the little propeller together with my girlfriend and our six months old son.

The place was like a dream. I had never seen anything like it.

I came back every winter to help out the little group and over the years, as BJJ Globetrotters started to catch momentum, that turned into a small camp.

I made many friends on the island and every time I visited, it felt more and more like coming home. I remember sitting in the airport café with a few of the locals from the gym, having a coffee and waiting for the check-in to open for my flight. I didn't want to leave.

In the spur of the moment, I told them that if they ever heard about an available apartment, they could let me know. While the dream sounded nice, I didn't for a moment believe that it would ever actually happen. Finding a place to live there was close to impossible and even though I had sold everything I owned at home—including the gym—I couldn't imagine actually moving out of Denmark.

It only took a week.

"We have a place for you. If you want it, you need to say yes now, or it's gone"

My heart dropped.

This was an opportunity of a lifetime. I aspired for adventure and there it was. I had worked so hard to set myself free, to be ready for any opportunities to present themselves. And here it was, right in front of me, demanding an immediate decision to completely change my life. Was I brave enough to actually do what I believed in? Would I put my money where my mouth was?

We couldn't not give it a shot.

It felt like an endless summer in Copenhagen when I left. The longest I can remember from living there all my life.

Some of the young boys from my old kids' class invited me out to eat and had bought me chocolates to say goodbye. I had poured my heart and soul into teaching those classes and they were all like little brothers to me. One thing was to sell my part of the gym; another was to actually leave after teaching there for such a long time. The average running time of memberships for students in my advanced class was eight years. It was difficult.

I started getting up at 6 AM to take my son for a walk in the stroller so he could sleep. There were only two days left in Denmark before we were leaving. It was pitch black outside. Only a few of the windows in the buildings had lit up. The leaves were struggling to hold onto the big old tree behind my house, and through them, I could see someone take their morning shower behind a foggy window. Everyone started their routine. Slowly, with yawns. It was strange to think that they would keep doing that when I'd left. As if nothing had changed at all. I had cleared out everything I owned and had no winter clothes left, so I was wearing two t-shirts and a pair of socks as gloves. A lonely kid was playing in the window of the next-door kindergarten, reminding me once again why I did not want a career job. Perhaps his parents had chosen so many luxuries that they had to give up all their time to earn enough money to pay for it. At the end of the day, the child ended up paying for their expenses—with his time. I didn't ever want my children to work hard for what I thought I needed of material possessions to be happy.

It was 3:30 in the morning when we were all sitting in the taxi on the way to the airport. Copenhagen was empty. It was raining. Eight degrees said a red light in front of a store. I felt a mix of happiness, excitement, nervousness and outright fear. Would the kids like it at all? Or did we just move for our own sake?

I had dreamed of this forever. Changing my life completely, trying to live somewhere else. Since that day when I departed for my trip around the world and saw Copenhagen from above out of the window in the plane, I hadn't been able to shake the thought. Why would I want to create my entire life on exactly that random little patch of land where I was born?

It wasn't pleasant to admit I was doing this for purely self-ish reasons and that it might not be a good experience for my kids. But we would give it a try. Maybe three months, maybe six. Maybe a year.

Fast forward a week and a half.

It was close to 10 PM and I had just finished teaching my first ever class on the island. It had been raining hard all night and we almost couldn't hear each other in the old metal building, constructed to sustain many hurricane seasons.

Bare-chested and with gi pants soaked in sweat, I sat on an old towel in my car with the windows down. A CD that probably had been stuck in there for years was playing a beautiful track I had never heard before. Maybe it sounded better because of where I was. Cicadas were singing in the hills around me. Warm air blew gently through the windows. The car had a scent from the former owner, a tanned woman in her 50s, living on a hill in a small house with a messy garden that reminded me of my time in Jamaica.

The lights from the stadium down the road lit up the heavy raindrops falling from the sky. It was the first quiet moment I had since we arrived on the island. I had been in a constant state of running around, trying to figure out how things worked, while at the same time having a one-month-old baby that kept us up at night.

Suddenly it was real.

"I actually live here. This is not a holiday", I thought to myself in awe.

During a visit to the island a few years earlier, I remember having driven down a narrow, winding road to a little fish-ermens' village; a sleepy corner of the island. A few people were sitting outside a small local shop and drinking coffee. Every building and road was crammed together to maximize the building space on the steep rocks and hills. Blue skies and not a sound to be heard. I remember wondering how it would be to live in a place like that. To live such a different existence than what I knew of.

And there, I suddenly found myself trying to start a new life in a small apartment, in that exact village with only a few hundred people.

A handful of days after we had arrived, I sat on the beach for the first time with my oldest son and looked at the sunset together. My heart and mind were racing. I was so nervous about whether I had made the right decision to take him out of his comfortable, safe life in Denmark around friends and family. He had been crying about it and said he wanted to go home. It gave me a knot in my stomach.

He eventually started in school and with no ways of communicating with the other kids—or the adults—it was a difficult time for him. He didn't really have many friends.

One afternoon, he sat alone in the sand—three years old—and played with a little plastic bucket and a shovel.

"Do you want to play with me", he stuttered in broken French as two slightly older kids raced past him. He didn't even get to finish the sentence before they laughed and made fun of him for not being able to say the words correctly, then ran off.

He looked sad. In Denmark, he had many friends that he played with every day. I tried my best to hide the tear rolling down my chin. It was so difficult to watch as a parent.

Should we just give up and move back to Denmark?

Luckily, things got easier for every week and every month that passed. It's been five years on the island now and I couldn't imagine anywhere else I would rather live at this point in my life. I have never found a place in the world that makes me happier than this.

At the age of five and eight, the boys already speak three languages fluently and have seen more countries than most adults will in a lifetime. They have been growing up on the beaches here and I can see clearly that they are genuinely happy. All my initial worries about moving away with them have completely vanished. Being able to give them a childhood like this is probably the one thing I am most proud of having achieved in my life.

I know they will want to see the world, to travel and seek out their own adventure at some point. They will leave, maybe even permanently, to settle somewhere far away. Adventure is in their blood and there's nothing I can do to stop it.

It scares me.

I understand that I did this to myself. I laid the foundation. I wrote this book—for them.

But thinking that my own sons will one day be taller than me and stand there at the airport with a backpack to say goodbye, gives me a lump in my throat. I feel it even now, writing this while I watch them play with their friends outside, unknowing of what life lies ahead of them.

My instincts want me to try and stop them. To protect them. But my quest for adventure has shaped me more than anything and I have to let them go one day to find their own. It will be the most difficult thing of my parenthood.

When you read this one day, I want you to know that whatever you choose to do or be in life, I will support it and I will cheer for you.

CHAPTER FORTY-FOUR

A Daring Adventure

When my friend and training partner Frank jumped out that window, it kickstarted a strong fear of missing out on life for me. Before that point, it had never even crossed my mind that I was going to die one day. That perhaps I too would not be able to experience all the things I had hoped to experience. I spent all of my days in the gym and was in no rush.

Our single most valuable resource in life is time. We are allocated a finite amount of it at birth and that's all we get. The tricky part is that nobody is told exactly how much that is. And even worse; there is no way to get more of it, once it's used up.

Going on that trip around the world was a desperate attempt at getting as much out of life as possible. Every single minute of it. I had set myself a high pace back then and I can honestly say that I haven't slowed down much in the 10 years that have passed. I was running away from ordinary life and I have been running ever since.

Who knows if I die in a car crash next week or get cancer in five years.

This fear of missing out is also pushing me to create experiences for myself.

I could sit around and wait for fun things to happen and for new friends to randomly enter my life. I would probably have to wait a long time for that. Then I could try to make some money and use that to buy experiences. To consume my way to memories. But it is simply too slow for me. I don't have time to wait for someone else to take charge of what will happen in my life.

The only alternative is that I create my own reality. So I make things happen—all the time.

When you think back to a certain time period, for instance, a year or a summer. What comes to mind? Do you remember it for certain days you went to work? How you spent your time buying groceries? Or do you define that period by the experiences that made you happy? A night out, a dinner with friends, a concert, meaningful conversations, a trip to the beach or a vacation.

Isn't it obvious that this is what life should be about?

To be as excited as possible. At the end of our days—on the deathbed—the only currencies that truly matter to have accumulated are friendships and experiences. Money will be worthless at that point.

I can honestly say that pretty much every single good memory I have and every single friend I have made in the last 20 years since I finished school has come out of something I have created myself. From the gym, academies, a trip around the world, parties, competitions, travels and camps. These things would not have happened if I hadn't somehow managed to convert them from an electric impulse in my brain to the physical reality. All those experiences and friendships would never even have existed in the universe. Someone who is my good friend now because of it—who I share passionate memories with—would be a complete stranger I passed on the street in another timeline. The same goes for all the friendships and memories other people have gotten from the things I have created.

I'm afraid that I'm missing out on things. But even more, I'm starting to become fearful of missing out on things that don't exist, but *could* have existed—ideas I haven't had yet. Projects I never followed up on. My trip around the world and so many other projects were created out of thin air, from merely a thought in my brain while sitting on the couch at home. They all strongly shaped my life and I couldn't imagine how things would be without them.

What other ideas did I skip at some point that could have had the same impact? Was there another project on the same level as my trip around the world that I ignored or which just never materialized?

It blows my mind to think about and pushes me to chase creations even more.

It's easy to lean back, get caught up in everyday life and forget that we are not going to be around forever. An office job can take years and years away that you will never get back. One thing that helps me a lot to see the big picture is to watch documentaries on the history and time of the universe. It is a good way for me to comprehend how unimaginably tiny and unimportant I am in the scope of the universe. My decisions and worries might seem important in the daily reality of myself and my life, but in terms of space-time, I am the tiniest of specks that have zero influence or meaning on a grand scale. Nobody will remember me in a few generations. Not a single thing I've done, thought or meant. In the history of the universe, my existence could simply not be less influential.

When I think about these things, I realize that there's one thing and one thing only that makes sense in life for me: Do whatever makes me happy and do as much of it as I possibly can.

Sometimes I definitely push this too hard, though. Doing things. There was one summer where I did three week-long camps back to back with a total of 600 participants. When I returned back home, my head was buzzing from stress and I had to lay on the couch for days without moving. Since I was a teenager—more precisely, exactly when my parents went through their divorce—I had always had some sort of light tics. Usually, I would have one for a few years before another replaced it. A sound, a habit or a movement that I couldn't get rid of. I've tried my best to hide it over the years.

It always got worse when I was tired or stressed and the many camps burned me out more than anything. I tried everything to get rid of it and eventually ended up laying on a mattress at a hypnotist, somewhere in Copenhagen.

I didn't really believe it and, to some extent, still doesn't. But in my mind, there is now a crystal clear memory of me going back to my childhood and having a conversation with myself. On a football field in the Canary Islands on a summer holiday with my grandmother. She took my brother and me traveling a lot when my mother was depressed from the divorce.

I found myself sitting there as an adult on a little wooden fence with a leather ball under my foot, next to a 13-year-old version of myself. He was lonely, scared and in despair. His mother was in very bad shape, his little brother caught in a difficult squeeze between parents and he had to be the man of the house, carrying more weight on his shoulders than any child of that age should. He looked skinny and his eyes were pale.

What he truly needed was a role model. A grown up man who could could give him a hug and assure him that things were going to be alright. That life would ultimately turn out just fine, even though things seemed to be going in a very bad direction at the time.

In an—admittedly—very, very strange way, I became that man that day on the football field in the Canary Islands or on the mattress in Copenhagen, depending on how you look at it. We had a long talk and the hypnotist had to check in with me a few times as he thought I had fallen asleep. I explained everything to my 13-year-old self about how his life would turn out. That his mother and brother would be just fine. That he would succeed in creating something meaningful for himself and for others. I was crying and crying; it felt so real.

The tics disappeared that day.

What's next for me?

As far as Jiu-Jitsu goes, I keep playing. It has been self-defense, MMA, sport Jiu-Jitsu and a job for me throughout the last 20 years. But now—at the age of almost 40—I practice it for fitness and social reasons. I still enjoy stepping on the mats at our small academy in Saint Barth and at the camps around the world, every single time. We have a strong little team here on the island and I get to roll with many hundreds of people at the camps every year. The young athletes I have taught and trained alongside since they were kids or teenagers have surpassed me a long time ago and I'm truly proud to be their friend and not their "professor".

BJJ Globetrotters has grown into an amazing community that really allows me to make some interesting things happen. I can not understate how important it has been for me to go out into the world and see it first hand. To make friends everywhere from all sorts of cultures and backgrounds. To see with my own eyes that there exist an infinite number of lives to be lived. On a bulletin board in a cheap hostel in Portugal, someone had posted a small handwritten note on a piece of paper that was torn from an old book. It was less than a year after returning from my big trip and I got goosebumps all over when I read it:

"The shortest way to yourself is around the world."

Going around the world was where I met myself. It was the most defining and important experience of my life and I was eager to share it with everyone. BJJ Globetrotters became a vehicle for that. In essence, it's a very organized version of attempting to re-create for others, the feeling I got from that trip. It's the least I can do to try and give something back.

At the point of writing, BJJ Globetrotters counts 831 affiliated academies and is by far the largest Jiu-Jitsu affiliation in the world by that metric. We have hosted 62 camps around the world with close to 10,000 unique participants. I always expect that there's a camp just around the corner that will be a little bit boring, but it just never happens. There hasn't been a single of those trips that has been anything less than 10 out of 10 for me and it still amazes me to think about.

Just like I pick who to involve by how excited they are, I also pick the camps by how excited they make me feel. When I think about a camp location, I must have butterflies in my stomach; otherwise, I know it is time to quit it, no matter how good a business is. I have stopped doing many successful camps because of this, even the classic ones in Belgium and El Salvador while they were at their peak. Many people were disappointed but I don't believe the camps will work if I am not extraordinarily excited about going to them. So usually after a few years, it is time to move on and find somewhere else to explore instead. Going back to the same place year after year would be kind of contradictory to the foundation of what we do and who we are.

It's called Globetrotters, after all.

Regarding myself, it very is clear to me what the defining moments of my life have been. When I quit my job. When I left to travel around the world. When I sold my business. When I moved to a different country.

Each of these were decisions to leave something that felt safe and familiar. To jump into the unknown, feet first. To quit.

It is human nature to do the opposite; to stay in your comfort zone. Don't leave your tribe and don't go see what is on the other side of the hill.

But adventure is on the other side of that hill. And that is where I have to go.

Sometimes the hill is a new career, sometimes it is a trip around the world and sometimes an entirely new life. The scarier it feels, the bigger the reward.

Many people will choose unhappiness over uncertainty, any day. To stay in a life they actually don't really enjoy, only because it feels safe. It's normal; that's how we're programmed.

I would like to believe that I have learned to live with uncertainty. I don't know what I will do in six months. I have no set plans for my business. I don't know where I will live in five years or where my kids will continue to grow up. I've put myself in that situation on purpose; to maximize the opportunities of changing up things. But the truth is, I am still deadly scared of quitting. I guess this will be a lifelong struggle.

I hope that my trip and this book can inspire even just a few people to do something similar. I truly believe that if we all traveled more and got to know each other better across countries and cultures, it would make the world a better place. Find friends in the most unlikely places; go see what is on the other side of your hill. Ambitiously chase healthy relationships and memories. Create things that make a difference and have a positive impact on other people.

As a clever person once wrote: "Life is either a daring adventure or nothing".

So what do you choose?

About the Author

Christian Graugart was born in 1982 in Copenhagen, Denmark.

In 2016, he moved to Saint Barthélemy in the French West Indies, where he is currently teaching and training Brazilian Jiu Jitsu.

He is the founder of BJJ Globetrotters, a world wide community of individuals and academies who share a non-political, open minded and positive approach to life and Jiu Jitsu.

His open invitation for anyone to come visit and train with him for free, still stands. Just go ahead and reach out directly to him by email:

GRAUGART@GMAIL.COM

BJJ Globetrotters is a world-wide community of travelers against Jiu Jitsu politics.

For more information, visit www.BJJglobetrotters.com

Special thanks to:

Bjørn A. Jørgensen
Daniel Reid
Dennis Gade Kofoed
Jes Hedegaard Knudsen
Maurizio Marotta

Made in United States
Orlando, FL
19 November 2024